新TOEIC®テスト
900点突破
20日間特訓
プログラム

トレーニングCD
3枚付

小山克明 著

アルク

TOEIC900点突破に必要なこととは？

　まず、右ページで自己チェックをしてみましょう。結果はいかがでしたか。実はこのリストには、900点突破のカギとなる項目が並んでいます。私が担当している**TOEICテスト900点突破対策コース**では、最初の授業の際、このリストで自己分析してもらいますが、すでに800点以上に到達していても、半分以上の項目に✓が入る人はまれです。つまり、**900点突破のために不可欠な実践**がなされていないため、思うようにスコアが上がらないのです。

　TOEICは決して難しいテストではありませんが、900点は生半可な勉強では獲得できません。**受験力プラス英語力の向上**が求められます。その突破口を開くためには、これまでの英語の学習習慣を根本的に変える大きな転換が必要です。

　では、英語力の飛躍的アップのコツとは何でしょうか。それは、**1) 英語の論理構造を知り、2) 語順に従ってチャンク（語のかたまり）で理解し、3) 発音の特徴を知った上でネイティブスピーカーのリズムやイントネーションをまねて音読する**、というメソッドの実践です。ネイティブスピーカーは英語特有の論理と発音をベースに、チャンクを単位として、英語の語順で話し、聞き、読み、書いているので、彼らの思考や論理、プロセス、スピードに近づき、身に付けるためにはこのような学習法が欠かせません。

　1) ～3) を踏まえた音読メソッドの実践で「リスニング力が向上し、内

TOEIC 対策自己チェックシート

自分でできていると思われる項目にチェック印を入れてみよう

- [ ] TOEICの特徴をよく知っている
- [ ] 各パートの問題パターンと攻略法をマスターしている
- [ ] TOEIC頻出語彙をマスターしている
- [ ] タイムマネジメント能力を身に付けている
- [ ] 集中力を養っている
- [ ] 自分の弱点・課題を知り、改善策を取り入れている
- [ ] 良質の実践問題で練習している
- [ ] 日々英語に接している
- [ ] 発音のルールを知っている
- [ ] 効果的な音読練習を取り入れている
- [ ] 英語学習のコツを知り、取り入れている
- [ ] 多読をしている
- [ ] 多聴をしている
- [ ] スコアアップ成功者の体験談を読み、motivationアップをしている

容をキャッチできるようになった」「リーディングスピードが速くなり、読解力がアップした」「アウトプット力が付いた」、などの効果を実感し、見事に900点を突破した受講生が数多くいます。

今、本当の英語力が問われる時代がやってきています。新しい学習習慣、正統派の学習法を体得し、着実にレベルアップしましょう。本書が皆さんのお役に立つことを、心から願っています。

2010年3月吉日

小山克明

Contents

はじめに………002
900点到達の最短ルートは「音読」トレーニング………006
本書の使い方………008
CD収録内容………010

1週目
音読トレーニングの準備運動とPart 3、Part 7の基礎学習を行う

- 1日目　音読を体験………012
- 2日目　**Part 3**　基礎トレーニング………032
- 3日目　**Part 3**　基本音読………046
- 4日目　**Part 7**　基礎トレーニング………058
- 5日目　**Part 7**　基本音読………076
- 6日目　**Review & Part 1**………094

2週目
Part 4、Part 6の基礎学習とともに、未体験のトレーニングに挑戦

- 7日目　**Part 4**　基礎トレーニング………108
- 8日目　**Part 4**　基本音読………122
- 9日目　**Part 6**　基礎トレーニング………135
- 10日目　**Part 6**　基本音読………150
- 11日目　チャレンジ**Reading!**………160
- 12日目　**Review & Part 2**………178

3週目
TOEIC問題よりも難易度の高い応用問題に挑戦。Part 3、4、6、7を仕上げる。

- 13日目 **Part 3　応用音読**………190
- 14日目 **Part 7　応用音読**………204
- 15日目 **Part 4　応用音読**………223
- 16日目 **Part 6　応用音読**………236
- 17日目 **チャレンジListening!**………252
- 18日目 **Review & Part 5**………266

4週目
これまでの学習の成果を確認するため、Part 3、4、6、7の模試に挑戦する

- 19日目 **TOEIC®テスト 難関パート　模擬試験**………279
- 20日目 **答えあわせと音読**………301

コラム

4カ国発音を攻略する！
　イギリス英語編………027
　オーストラリア英語編………148
　カナダ英語編………188

900点突破者たちの体験談………031、134、203、250

ハイスコアを目指すために………325

900点到達の最短ルートは「音読」トレーニング

　リスニングやリーディングで英語を速く正確に理解するためには、「耳で聞く音声」、「文字化されている語」、「意味」の3者を速やかに一体化させることが不可欠です。スピーチやトークを何度も聞くだけでは学習として不十分。本書では、実践が容易で、効果をすぐに実感できる音読メソッド・トレーニングを通し、TOEIC900点到達に必要な英語力を培います。

　ネイティブスピーカーにできるだけ近い形で、単語のかたまりごとに意味をとらえながら、発音、強勢（ストレス）、イントネーション、リズムをまねて、スピーディーに音読することで、英語を聞き分けたり、速読する力もアップします。脳研究の専門家である東北大学未来科学技術共同研究センター教授の川島隆太医学博士の研究によれば、目・口・耳を使う音読は多くの感覚を使用するため、ただ聞いたり、黙読したりするよりも記憶効率が高いそうです。

　では、最大限に効果的な音読はどのように行えばいいのでしょう。実践する際に重要なポイントを確認しましょう。

1) 英語の語順のまま理解する (Progressively)
　英語は通常、重要事項、結論が先に来て、その後に理由や例などさらに具体的な情報が付加され、最後に再び結論が述べられる論理構造になっています（「結承結」の構造）。この論理構造に基づいた、progressiveな理解の仕方を目指しましょう。

2) Chunk（語のかたまり）で情報を把握する (Chunking)
　chunk（チャンク）と呼ばれる「語のかたまり」「語の単位」ごとに理解するのが大切です。なぜならネイティブスピーカーは「音声」または「意味」のかたまりであるチャンクで聞き、話し、読み、書くので、chunkingでネイティブスピーカーの発想に近づくことができます。

3) 重要個所を強調して、リズミカルかつスピーディーに
   感情を込めて読む（Rhythmically with feeling）

　英語には音楽のような側面があります。発音、強勢、イントネーション、リズム、スピードが大切な要素なのです。どこにアクセントを置き、どの語を強調するかを意識しながら、リズミカルかつスピーディーに読むことで、自然とネイティブスピーカーの口と耳に近づいていきます。

　以上のポイントを踏まえて、TOEICテスト900点突破を目指し、本書の特訓プログラムをスタートしましょう。

音読の基本用語一覧

slash reading：意味の切れ目の個所にスラッシュ（/）を入れながら読むこと。

slash listening：スクリプトを見て、意味や音声の切れ目の個所にスラッシュを入れながら聞くこと。

repeating：文や語句を聞き終えた後に、聞いたとおりに繰り返すこと。

overlapping：スクリプトを見ながら、聞こえてくる音声と同じ速度で読むこと。

shadowing：聞こえてくる音声をやや遅れて、できる限り正確に繰り返すこと。

dictation：音声を聞いて、内容を書き取ること。

prosody：話し言葉に含まれる各種の音声要素のこと。発音、強勢（ストレス）、抑揚（イントネーション）、リズム、ポーズなど。

本書の使い方

本書の学習は、英語力・受験力を強化するため、音読を中心とするさまざまなトレーニングを行うTaskと、TOEICの本番形式の問題に挑戦するPracticeに分かれている。

● Task

本書の中心となるトレーニング。

パートや学習の段階ごとに内容が異なるので、指示文をしっかり読んで、理解してから取り組もう。

● Practice

TOEIC形式の問題に挑戦する。

リスニング問題はトラックの頭に設問を先読みするためのポーズが設けられていることが多い。CDを途中で止めずに、一気に受験しよう。

リーディング問題は、指示文末尾に解答時間が示されているので、必ず時間制限を守って解答しよう。

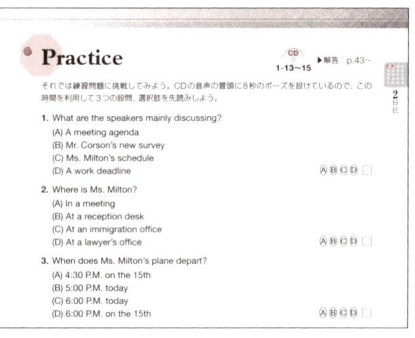

● 正解と解説

リスニング問題はスクリプトと訳、設問と選択肢の訳と各設問の解説が掲載されている。リーディング問題では、英文は再掲されていないので注意。

訳や解説を見て内容を理解してから、末尾に示されている正解を参照しよう。

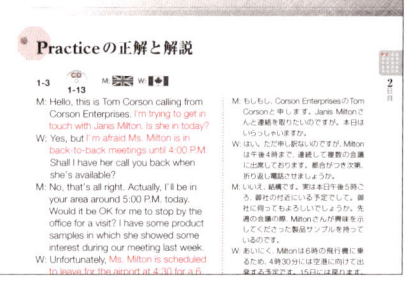

● 要注意フレーズ

音読する英文の中で、下線が引かれた、特に重視すべき語句を示す。

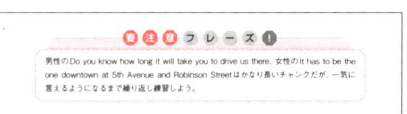

● 学習エネルギーをチャージする 今日の格言

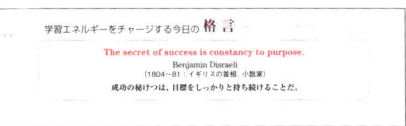

毎日の学習の最後に、モチベーションをアップする古今東西の格言を掲載した。こちらもぜひ音読しよう。

● 本書で使用されている記号

1-03~06：CD1のトラック3から6を聞く

W: 🇺🇸　M: 🇬🇧：女性はアメリカ人、男性はイギリス人の声を収録

/：短いチャンク専用のスラッシュ

/：長いチャンクを区切るスラッシュ

//：文末を区切るスラッシュ

本書のカリキュラム

	1週目	2週目	3週目	4週目
1日目	音読を体験	Part 4 基礎トレーニング	Part 3 応用音読	難関パート模擬試験
2日目	Part 3 基礎トレーニング	Part 4 基本音読	Part 7 応用音読	答えあわせと音読
3日目	Part 3 基本音読	Part 6 基礎トレーニング	Part 4 応用音読	
4日目	Part 7 基礎トレーニング	Part 6 基本音読	Part 6 応用音読	
5日目	Part 7 基本音読	チャレンジ Reading	チャレンジ Listening	
6日目	Review & Part 1	Review & Part 2	Review & Part 5	

リスニングセクションの学習

ハイスコア獲得の鍵となるPart 3、4、6、7については、

1. 基礎トレーニング
2. 基本音読
3. 応用音読　の3ステップで学習。

その他のパートについては、1~3週の各Reviewの日に、コンパクトに学習する。最終週には、Part 3、4、6、7のみの模試に挑戦。

CD収録内容

3枚の付属CDには、学習に必要な音声が収録されている。CDを使用する個所には、以下のようなマークが記されているので、必要なトラックを呼び出して学習しよう。

例： **1-8〜12** （CD1のトラック08〜12）

● **CD1**（収録時間：72分）

		トラック番号
タイトルコール		1
1日目	ニュース	2-3
	Task 9	4
	Task 10	5
	Task 11	6
	Task 13	7
	Task 14	8
	Task 15	9
	Task 19	10
	コラム	11
2日目	Task 1、2	12
	Practice	13-15
3日目	Practice	16-18
	Task 2	19-21
4日目	Task 1	22-24
	Task 4	25-27
5日目	Task 2	28-31
	Task 5	32-35
6日目	Task 3	36
	Task 4	37
	Task 6	38
	Task 7	39
7日目	Practice	40-42

● **CD2**（収録時間：73分）

		トラック番号
8日目	Practice	1-4
	Task 1	5-8
9日目	Task 1	9-10
	Task 4	11-12
	コラム	13
10日目	Task 1	14-15
	Task 4	16-17
11日目	Task 3	18-21
	Task 5	22-25
12日目	Practice	26
	Task 4	27-28
	Task 5	29
	コラム	30
13日目	Practice	31-33
	Task 1	34-36
14日目	Task 1	37-40
	Task 4	41-42

● **CD3**（収録時間：70分）

		トラック番号
(14日目)	(Task 4)	1-2
15日目	Practice	3-5
	Task 1	6-8
16日目	Task 1	9-11
	Task 4	12-14
17日目	Task 1	15-18
	Task 2	19
	Task 4	20
18日目	Task 4	21-23
19日目	Listening Section	24-33
20日目	Reading Section	34-44

※弊社制作の音声CDは、CDプレーヤーでの再生を保証する規格品です。

※パソコンでご使用になる場合、CD-ROMドライブとの相性により、ディスクを再生できない場合がございます。

※パソコンでタイトル・トラック情報を表示させたい場合は、iTunesをご利用ください。iTunesでは、Gracenote社のCDDB（データベース）からインターネットを介してトラック情報を取得することができます。

※CDとして正常に音声が再生できるディスクからパソコンやmp3プレーヤー等への取り込み時にトラブルが生じた際は、まず、そのアプリケーション（ソフト）、プレーヤーの製作元にご相談ください。

20日間 特訓プログラム

1週目 　1日目〜6日目
Part 3、Part 7の基礎音読学習

2週目 　7日目〜12日目
Part 4、Part 6の基礎音読学習

3週目 　13日目〜18日目
Part 3、4、6、7の応用音読学習

4週目 　19日目〜20日目
Part 3、4、6、7の模擬試験

さあ、トレーニングをスタートしよう

音読を体験

本書では、英語上級者を目指し、TOEICハイスコアを取得する手段として、効果的な音読トレーニングを行っていく。機械的に音読しても学習効果はあまり得られないので、本日のタスクを通して基本をしっかりと身に付けよう。

Task 1

1. CDに収録されているニュースを**1度**聞いて、重要なポイントを以下に英語で書こう。
2. 再度聞いて、内容を理解するためのキーワードと思われる語句を以下に書き出そう。

---

1. 重要ポイント

2. キーワード

書き終わったら右ページのScriptと訳を読んで、ニュースの要点を確認しよう。

Script

On a 9.6-hectare tract of land on the Texas coast south of Houston, a start-up company from Florida called Algenol, in partnership with the Dow Chemical company, plans to build more than 3,000 bioreactors, starting next year. The bioreactors will grow algae that can produce ethanol fuel through a special process that involves use of carbon dioxide from nearby coal-burning power plants to promote faster growth of the algae.

Algenol is already testing the process with 40 bioreactors in Florida, but the partnership with Dow and the U.S. Department of Energy on the Texas project is a major leap forward.

For Dow Chemical, the main focus will be producing material from algae that can be used to make plastics. The company currently uses natural gas for that purpose.

The Algenol bioreactors also produce oxygen as a byproduct and that can be fed into a power plant to burn coal more cleanly. Carbon dioxide produced by the power plant can be recycled back into the bioreactors to help promote more algae growth.（VOA News 02 September 2009）

訳

ヒューストンの南にあるテキサス州の海岸沿いの9.6ヘクタールにわたる土地で、Algenolというフロリダの新興企業が、Dow Chemical社と協力して3000超のバイオリアクターを来年から造る計画です。そのバイオリアクターは、特殊な工程を経ることでエタノール燃料を産出する藻を育てることになり、その工程には石炭を燃料とする近辺の火力発電所からの二酸化炭素の利用も含まれます。藻の成長を促進するためです。

Algenol社はすでにフロリダ州にある40のバイオリアクターで、その工程をテストしていますが、テキサス州でのプロジェクトでDow社やアメリカのエネルギー省の協力を得られるのは、大きな飛躍です。

Dow Chemical社にとっての主眼は、プラスチック生産に利用できる藻からの素材産出になるでしょう。この企業は現在、その目的のために天然ガスを使っています。

Algenol社のバイオリアクターはまた、副産物として酸素も産出します。そしてそれは、石炭をもっとクリーンに燃焼させるため、発電所に供給できます。発電所で排出される二酸化炭素はリサイクルしてバイオリアクターに戻し、藻のさらなる成長促進に役立てられるのです。(VOAニュース2009年9月2日)

Task 2

1-02

Scriptと訳を見て、話題、背景、キーワードを確認したら、もう一度音声を聞く。冒頭のコメントに特に注意し、キーワードを意識しながら内容をキャッチしてみよう。

Task 3

次に、チャンクで区切った英文を聞いてみよう。スラッシュ (/) のところのポーズで、英文の下に記されているチャンクごとの意味を確認しながら聞くこと。

On a 9.6-hectare tract of land on the Texas coast south of Houston, /
ヒューストンの南にあるテキサス州の海岸沿いの9.6ヘクタールにわたる土地で /

a start-up company from Florida called Algenol, in partnership with the Dow Chemical company, /
Algenolというフロリダの新興企業がDow Chemical社と協力して /

plans to build more than 3,000 bioreactors, starting next year. //
来年から3000超のバイオリアクターを造る計画です。//

The bioreactors will grow algae that can produce ethanol fuel through a special process /
そのバイオリアクターは、特殊な工程を経てエタノール燃料を産出する藻を育てます /

that involves use of carbon dioxide from nearby coal-burning power plants /
その工程には石炭を燃料とする近辺の火力発電所からの二酸化炭素の利用も含まれます /

to promote faster growth of the algae. //
藻の成長速度を促進するためです。//

Algenol is already testing the process with 40 bioreactors in Florida, /
Algenol社は フロリダ州にある40のバイオリアクターですでにその工程をテストしています /

but the partnership with Dow and the U.S. Department of Energy on the Texas project /
しかし、テキサス州でのプロジェクトにおいてDow社やアメリカのエネルギー省と協力するのは /

is a major leap forward. //
大きな飛躍です。//

For Dow Chemical, the main focus /
Dow Chemical社にとっての主眼は /

will be producing material from algae that can be used to make plastics. //
プラスチック生産に利用できる藻からの素材の産出になるでしょう。//

The company currently uses natural gas for that purpose. //
この企業は現在、その目的のために天然ガスを使っています。//

The Algenol bioreactors also produce oxygen as a byproduct /
Algenol社のバイオリアクターはまた、副産物として酸素も産出します /

and that can be fed into a power plant to burn coal more cleanly. //
そしてそれは石炭をもっとクリーンに燃焼させるために発電所に供給できます。//

Carbon dioxide produced by the power plant can be recycled back into the bioreactors to help promote more algae growth. //
発電所から排出される二酸化炭素は、リサイクルでバイオリアクターに戻され、藻のさらなる成長促進に役立てられます。//

Task 4

今度はポーズの後で、英文をリピートしてみよう。prosody(発音、強勢、抑揚、リズム、ポーズなど)を意識して聞きながら練習すること。

Task 5

以下のルールに従い、チャンクごとに意味をしっかり思い浮かべながら、音読してみよう。

音読の基本ルール

- [ ] 1. **内容語(content words)は強く、はっきりゆっくり発音**
   名詞・動詞・形容詞・副詞・疑問詞など実質的な意味内容を含んだ単語は、声の高さ(ピッチ：pitch)も高くする。
- [ ] 2. **機能語(function words)は弱く速くあいまいに発音**
   冠詞・前置詞・代名詞・接続詞・be動詞・助動詞など
- [ ] 3. チャンクは一気に、一息で読む
- [ ] 4. 前後の語句と一体化して発音が変わる語に注意(p.19〜26参照)
- [ ] 5. 子音だけの個所に余計な母音を入れない
- [ ] 6. Wh疑問文やHow疑問文の最後は、通常下げる

Task 6

では最後に、CDの音声に自分の声をオーバーラップさせて、リズミカルに英文を読んでみよう。

効果的な音読のチェックポイント

今後の本書での音読トレーニングは、以下のポイントを押さえながら行おう。

- [ ] 1. **言いたいこと（趣旨と目的）、話し手と聞き手、場所と状況をつかんでイメージし、**
最も大切なのは趣旨のキャッチ。誰が誰に向かって、何を、どんな目的で、どんな状況で伝えようとしているのか把握し、それを意識して音読する。

- [ ] 2. **流れを意識しながら（論理構造と論理展開を踏まえて）**
6ページのProgressivelyの項でもふれたように、英語の論理展開は結承結。それを意識すれば、次に何が来るかを予測しながら聞き、読むことが可能になり、理解も早くなる。

- [ ] 3. **英語の語順で後戻りせずに**
ネイティブの発想を身に付けるため、話され、書かれている語順で理解するよう努める。文の最後まで到達した後、文頭に戻る習慣をやめる。

- [ ] 4. **チャンクで区切って意味を把握しながら**
6ページのChunkingの項でもふれたように、チャンクごとに意味を把握し、英語の語順で意味を付加していく読み方、聞き方を心がける。聞く・話す・読む・書くスピードと正確さが向上し、情報把握力が飛躍的に伸びる。チャンク中のキーワードを意識するとさらに効果的。

- [ ] 5. **ネイティブの発音をよく聞いて**
prosodyに注意しながら聞き、音とリズムを音楽のように自分に染み込ませる。どの語が強調されているか、「その語本来の機能」と「文脈」の2つの視点で、強弱のリズムをチェックすること。

- [ ] 6. **重要なキーワードを強調して**
強調すべき語を強めに、ピッチを高くしてはっきり、ゆっくり発音すると、メッセージがわかりやすくなる。

- [ ] 7. **リズミカルかつスピーディーに**
7ページのRhythmically with feelingの項でふれたように、prosodyをまねながらリズミカルかつスピーディーに音読する。ニュースは1分あたり160〜165語で読まれるが、自分で読む際も160±20語程度のスピードを目安にし、1分あたりの語数の変化を記録しよう。

- [ ] 8. **登場人物になりきって感情を込めて生き生きと**
感情を伝えるには、リズムやイントネーションが重要。背景や状況を知り、メッセージの意味内容を把握することで、音読に感情を込めよう。

- [ ] 9. **人前でスピーチするレベルの大きな声で**
コミュニケーション力を付けるため、普段からニュースキャスターがテレビやラジオで話すくらいの大きさの声で音読練習するよう心がける。

Task 7

では仕上げに、14ページの英文を通して音読してみよう。
まずはトラック2の音声にオーバーラップさせて読み、全体の強弱のリズムをつかむこと。その後は、左のチェックポイントをクリアできるようになるまで繰り返し練習しよう。

Task 8

音読した英文の音声は、CDで繰り返し聞くようにしよう。集中して聞かなくても文頭から自然に全体の意味が取れるようになったら、その英文については「卒業」と考えていい。ほかの英文に挑戦しよう。

チャンクの区切り方のルール

Task 3で示したような「チャンクによる区切り」を自分で行うため、基本的なルールを身に付けよう。
チャンクの区切りは原則、句や節、慣用表現や、前後に息継ぎが入る部分になる。したがって、呼びかけ、列挙、挿入句など、カンマで区切られている場所は基本的に区切る。
それ以外のルールとして、以下のものが挙げられる。

1）主部が比較的長い場合、主部と述部の間を区切る。
A coworker of mine who attended the meeting yesterday / was so impressed.
（昨日の会議に出ていた同僚の一人は、大変感銘を受けていた）

2）主節と従節、従節と主節の間を区切る。
Could you give me a call / so we can reschedule the appointment?
（面会日時を再設定しますので、お電話いただけますか）

3）接続詞thatの前を区切る。
I was convinced / that I would be able to provide all the software they needed.
（私は、彼らが必要とするソフトはすべて提供できるようになると確信した）

4）関係代名詞・関係副詞と先行詞の間を区切る。
The devices are still available for the dates / that you have requested.
（その機器類はまだ、ご請求があった日付には利用可能です）

5）文頭の副詞（句）の後を区切る。
Initially / you undergo a five-day training period.
（初めに5日間の研修期間があります）

6）文中のhowever, for exampleの後を区切る。
Many of the shareholders, however, / requested higher dividends from the company.
（しかし株主の多くは、その会社により高い配当を求めた）

7）比較的長い目的語や補語の、前や後を区切る。
The nature center will be hosting / several educational programs for schoolchildren.
（その自然センターは学童向けの教育プログラムを主催する予定だ）

8）副詞句を導く前置詞の前を区切る。
We will have an informal tea party / on Wednesday afternoon.
（水曜日の午後に内輪のティーパーティーを開きます）

　最初はあまり神経質にならず、意味の固まりだと思われる個所にどんどん/（スラッシュ）を入れよう。/の位置は絶対的なものではないので、慣れるまでは細かく入れて構わない。慣れてきたら、区切るチャンクを長めにしていく。ネイティブスピーカーは一度に把握できる情報量が多いので、チャンクが長くなる傾向がある。

　チャンクによる理解にさらに慣れてきたら、実際には/を書かず、頭の中で/を入れながらチャンクで区切って読むようにする。初見のscriptや文書をこのように区切り、意味を把握しながらリズミカルかつスピーディーに音読できるようになれば、英語上級者の仲間入りは近いと言えるだろう。

Task 9

チャンクの区切りを意識しながら、Task 8の例文の音声をリピートしよう。

Task 10

以下の空所に冠詞aまたはanを入れてみよう。トラック5を聞いて解答を確認したら、ポーズの部分でリピートしよう。

1. It's ＿＿ apple.（それはリンゴです）
2. He's ＿＿ uncle.（彼は叔父です）
3. I need ＿＿ umbrella.（傘が必要です）
4. It's ＿＿ egg.（それは卵です）
5. I have ＿＿ idea.（アイデアがあります）
6. in ＿＿ hour（1時間で）
7. Mr. Wallace is ＿＿ heir.（Wallace氏は相続人です）
8. He is ＿＿ honest person.（彼は正直な人間です）
9. Mr. Brown is ＿＿ FBI agent.（Brown氏は連邦捜査局員です）
10. It's ＿＿ SOS.（それは遭難信号です）
11. He is ＿＿ MP.（彼は国会議員<MP=Member of Parliament>です）
12. in ＿＿ European country（ヨーロッパのある国で）
13. It's ＿＿ useful tool.（それは便利な道具です）
14. at ＿＿ university（大学で）

aになるか、anになるかは、スペルでなく発音で決まる。
単語の語頭の発音が母音ならan　例：an heir、an MP
単語の語頭の発音が母音でなければa　例：a university [jùːnəvə́rsəti]、a European [jùərəpíːən]

Task 11

▶解答：p.20

次は、知っているとリスニングが楽になる発音上のルールを学習する。CDの音声を聞いて、以下の英文の(1)～(4)の空所を埋めよう。

The Dow rebounded today after a poor showing last week. (1)(　　　　　) pharmaceutical companies apparently benefiting from the president's new health care proposals. Business leaders (2)(　　　　　　) the bottom of our spiraling economy and (3)(　　　　　　) next quarter. Investors are still wary of jumping in, however, and appear to believe (4)(　　　　　　　　　　) divested from the market and wait for a more solid recovery.

Task 11 の解答

(1) Top performers were   (2) and analysts say we may have reached
(3) are predicting big gains   (4) this is a good time to stay

訳

ダウ平均は今日、低調だった先週に対し反発した。その立役者となったのは、大統領の新しい医療政策案の益に浴したと思われる製薬会社だ。財界の首脳やアナリストによれば、経済の低迷は底を打ち、次の四半期には大規模な増益が予想される。投資家はしかし、まだ積極的姿勢には慎重で、市場と距離を置き、より堅調な回復を待つ好機ととらえているようだ。

脱落音（elision）のルール

ナチュラルスピードで話す際、あるべき音がほとんど、もしくはまったく発音されなくなる現象を脱落と呼ぶ。Task 11の(1)のTop performersのp、(2)のanalysts sayのsなどに見られるのがそれで、以下のような基本パターンがある。声を出しながら確認しよう。

1）同じ子音の連続による前の音の脱落

[d]+[d]、[f]+[f]、[g]+[g]、[k]+[k]、[l]+[l]、[m]+[m]、[p]+[p]、[s]+[s]、[t]+[t]、[dʒ]+[dʒ]、[ʃ]+[ʃ]、[ð]+[ð]など。big gainsなら、「ビッグ・ゲインズ」ではなく、「ビッ・ゲインズ」のように聞こえる。top performers「タッ・パフォーマーズ」も同様。

2）よく似た子音の連続による前の音の脱落

[b] +[p]、[d] +[t]、[g] +[k]、[k] +[g]、[p] +[b]、[t] +[d]などを指す。
analysts sayは「アナリス・セイ」、good timeは「グッ・タイム」。

3）文末の子音の脱落

[b]、[d]、[g]、[k]、[p]、[t]は、文末に来るとほとんど聞こえなくなる。
I have an appointment. では文末のappointmentの[t]はほとんど聞こえない。

Task 12

脱落音を意識しながら、CDの音声にオーバーラップしてTask 11の英文を読もう。

Task 13

CDの音声を聞いて、以下の英文の(1)〜(6)の空所を埋めよう。

(1)(   ) tonight to address (2)(
). I never expected to get this far in my research; (3)(   ),
I've been working on this issue for over 20 years. (4)(   ) to
find a cure for cancer, I had no idea (5) (   ). I'm happy to
report (6) (   ) we may be very near to
finding a cure.

Task 14

CDの音声を聞いて、以下の英文の(1)〜(5)の空所を埋めよう。

(1)(   ) around for a moment? (2)(
) the Expressionists' wing of the museum now and move into the
Modernists' wing, (3)(   ) a brief explanation of the Modernist school. The Modernists typically believed that traditional
forms of art were outdated in their newly industrialized world, and (4) (
) new styles of art to represent this shift. Now, (5)(
) into the next gallery?

Task 15

CDの音声を聞いて、以下の英文の(1)〜(4)の空所を埋めよう。

Hello Mr. Sherrod, this is Brian at Klinko's copies. (1)(
) of brochures and (2)(   )
as soon as this dangerous weather passes through. All the weather forecasts
predict that the hurricane will pass over us in the next 24 hours, (3)(
) any deliveries until after that. Thanks for your patience and
understanding, and if you have any questions (4)(   ).

Task 13の解答

(1) It's <u>an honor</u> to be here　(2) a group <u>such as</u> yours　(3) <u>after all</u>
(4) <u>When I</u> first <u>set out</u>　(5) how it would <u>turn out</u>　(6) that <u>there is</u> reason to believe

訳

今夜この場で、皆様のような方々に講演することができて光栄です。自分の研究をこれほど進められるとは思ってもいませんでした。何にせよ、この問題には20年余り取り組んできました。がんの治療法を見つけようとした当初は、どうなるのかまったく見当がつきませんでした。治療法の発見が近いだろうと根拠をもって考えられることを、喜んでご報告いたします。

連結音（liaison）のルール

　連結は、前の語の語尾の子音と、次の語の語頭の母音が一体化して1語のように発音される現象。聞き取りの際にネックとなりやすいので、次の基本パターンを頭に入れ、声に出して再現してみよう。

1）[n]の連結
前の語の語尾が[n]で、次の語の語頭が母音の場合。
an honorは「アナナー」、when Iは「ホウェナイ」、turn outは「ターナウ(ト)」。

2）[r]の連結
前の語の語尾が[r]で、次の語の語頭が母音の場合。
after allは「アフタロール」、there isは「ゼアリズ」。

3）[t]の連結
前の語の語尾が母音＋[t]で、次の語の語頭が母音の場合、[t]は日本語の「ラ」行の子音のように聞こえる。[t]の後の母音に応じて、「ラ」「リ」「ル」「レ」「ロ」のような音に変化する。
set outは「セラウト」、Not at all.なら「ナラロー」。

ほかにも、such as（サッチャズ）のように連結する音は多いので注意しよう。

Task 16

CD
1-07

連結音を意識しながら、CDの音声にオーバーラップしてTask 13の英文を読もう。

Task 14 の解答

(1) <u>Could you</u> all please gather　(2) We're <u>going to</u> leave
(3) but first I <u>want to</u> give you　(4) they <u>had to</u> develop
(5) <u>would you</u> all please follow me

訳

皆さん、ちょっとお集まりいただけますか。これから美術館の表現主義者のウイングを出て、モダニストのウイングに移動しますが、その前にモダニスト派について簡単にご説明します。典型的モダニストたちは、伝統的な芸術形式は、新たに産業化された自分たちの世界には時代遅れで、この変容を表現するための新しい芸術様式を生み出さなければならないと信じていました。では皆さん、次の展示室まで私についてきていただけますか。

同化音（assimilation）のルール

同化は、隣接した2つの音が影響しあって、別の音に変化する現象。1つの単語内や、隣り合っている単語間で見られる。代表的なパターンを取り上げよう。

1) 子音の後に[j]が続く場合
[d]+[j]が[dʒ]に変化: could you「クッヂュー」、would you「ウッヂュー」。
[t]+[j]が[tʃ]に変化: want you「ウォンチュー」。

2) 動詞/助動詞 + to
1語のように発音されることが多い。
going to(=gonna)「ガナ（ゴナ）」、want to(=wanna)「ワナ」、had to「ハドタ」のように聞こえる。ほかに、have to「ハフタ」、used to「ユースタ」、ought to「オータ」などにも注意しよう。

Task 17

1-08

同化音を意識しながら、CDの音声にオーバーラップしてTask 14の英文を読もう。

Task 15 の解答

(1) <u>I'm</u> calling to tell you that <u>we've</u> completed your order
(2) <u>they're</u> ready to be shipped (3) so <u>we've</u> decided to postpone
(4) <u>don't</u> hesitate to call

訳

もしもし、SherrodさんKlinko's copiesのBrianです。ご注文のパンフレットが仕上がり、この危険な天候が収まり次第、発送できるとお伝えするためお電話しています。天気予報はすべて、ハリケーンが24時間後にはこの付近を通り過ぎると予測していますので、それまでどの配達も見合わせることにしました。もうしばらくお待ちいただくことをご理解いただけますよう、お願いいたします。ご質問がありましたら、遠慮なくお電話ください。

短縮形（contraction）のルール

特に口語英語では、<u>短縮形</u>が多用される。不明瞭に聞こえがちなので、リスニングの弱点になることが多い。以下の6つのパターンを把握しよう。

1) 主語 + be動詞：I'm = I am、he's = he is、they're = they are

2) 主語 + 助動詞 will/would：it'll = it will、you'd = you would

3) 主語 + 助動詞 has/have/had：he's = he has、we've = we have、
they'd = they had

4) be動詞/助動詞 + not：wasn't = was not、don't = do not、haven't = have not、
mustn't = must not

5) 助動詞 + have：could've = could have、must've = must have

6) 疑問詞 + be動詞/助動詞：what's = what is/has、who's = who is/has

Task 18

短縮形を意識しながら、CDの音声にオーバーラップしてTask 15の英文を読もう。

Task 19

▶解答：p.26

脱落音、連結音、同化音、短縮形に注意しながらCDの音声を聞いて、以下の英文の(1)〜(10)の空所を埋めよう。

Feeling jaded? (1)(   )? Is your job leaving you too exhausted to enjoy your leisure? (2)(   )? A weekend city break! "(3)(   )," they say and after you've spent a weekend away with Out and About city tours (4)(   ).
Fly out on Friday and (5)(   ) in any one of 30 European city destinations. Out and About (6)(   ) on the canals of Amsterdam or Stockholm, or the famous waterways of Venice. Or (7)(   ) strolling in the Gothic quarter of Barcelona, the Latin Quarter of Paris, or the Jewish quarter of Prague. Then again you may prefer Out and About to fly you away to the new frontiers of the European Union, (8)(   ) the medieval quarter of Tallinn in Estonia, or beautiful Sofia in Bulgaria, or historic Riga in Latvia. (9)(   ) the 9 to 5 already. Spend a weekend Out and About and you'll come back home refreshed, re-energized and (10)(   ). Out and About city breaks: a memorable way to spend your weekends.

Task 19の解答

(1) <u>Fit to</u> drop（脱落音） (2) Know <u>what you</u> need（同化音）
(3) A <u>change is</u> as good <u>as a</u> rest（ともに連結音） (4) <u>you'll believe it</u>（短縮形と連結音）
(5) <u>sit down</u> to your evening meal（脱落音と連結音） (6) will <u>set you</u> afloat（同化音）
(7) maybe <u>you'd</u> prefer to <u>spend time</u>（短縮形と脱落音）
(8) to <u>have a look around</u>（ともに連結音） (9) I <u>bet you're</u> forgetting（同化音と短縮形）
(10) ready <u>for anything work can</u> throw <u>at you</u>（連結音、脱落音、同化音）

訳

うんざりしていますか？ 今にも倒れそう？ 仕事で疲れ過ぎて、余暇を楽しめない？ ご自分に何が必要かおわかりですか？ 週末に都心で過ごす休暇です！ 「変化は休息と同じくらいよいものだ」と言われますが、Out and Aboutのシティ・ツアーで週末をお過ごしになれば、信じるようになるでしょう。

金曜日に飛び立って、旅先となるヨーロッパ30都市のいずれかでご夕食の席に着きましょう。Out and Aboutは、アムステルダムやストックホルムの運河、あるいはベネチアの有名な運河へお連れいたします。それとも、バルセロナのゴシック地区やパリのカルチェ・ラタン、またはプラハのユダヤ人街を散策して過ごすほうがお好みかもしれませんね。はたまた、EUの新たな辺境の地まで、エストニアのタリンにある中世の市街地や、ブルガリアの美しいソフィア、ラトビアの歴史上重要なリガを見に、Out and Aboutで飛び去るのがお望みかもしれません。

すでに9時から5時のお勤めのことは忘れかけていますね。週末をOut and Aboutで出歩いて過ごせば、気分爽快に帰宅でき、再び元気いっぱいで、仕事でどんなことが振りかかろうと対応できますよ。Out and Aboutの都市での休暇は、思い出に残る週末の過ごし方です。

学習エネルギーをチャージする今日の 格言

Knowing is not enough; we must apply.
Willing is not enough; we must do.

Johann Wolfgang von Göthe
(1749～1832：ドイツの作家、詩人、哲学者、政治家。代表作『若きウェルテルの悩み』『ファウスト』等)

知るだけでは十分でない、使わなければ。やる気だけでは十分でない、実行しなければ。

4カ国発音を攻略する！

Vol. 1

イギリス英語編

　TOEICに登場するアメリカ以外の3カ国（イギリス、オーストラリアまたはニュージーランド、カナダ）の発音とアクセントは、聞き慣れないと違和感を覚えるかもしれない。しかし、特徴的な発音の違いを知り、頻出する語を中心に、各国のナレーターが話す言葉に耳を慣らしておけば、心配は無用である。

　本書のコラムでは、イギリス英語、オーストラリア英語、カナダ英語の特徴的な発音を順番に取り上げ、口に出しながら学んでいく。積極的に発音練習に取り組もう。

　まずはイギリス英語から挑戦してみよう。

❶ 語尾の /r/ は発音されないことが多い

米語（アメリカ英語）の /r/ が、イギリス英語では消失する。

	care	fare	more	repair
米	kèər	fèər	mɔ́:r	ripéər
英	kèə	fèə	mɔ́:	ripéə

＊ただし、すぐ後ろの単語が母音で始まるときは、次の単語の母音と結びついて、語尾のr がはっきり発音される。リエゾン（単語単体では聞こえない音が、その後に母音が来ると明確に聞こえる）を形成する。
ex. far away、a pair of

❷ /f/、/m/、/n/、/s/、/θ/ の前の母音が異なる

特に「子音＋a＋子音」の形の場合に、違いは顕著だ。
米語：/f/、/m/、/n/、/s/、/θ/ の前の母音は /æ/（アとエの中間の音）
イギリス英語：/ɑ:/（口を大きく開けて長めに伸ばしたアー音）

	ask	can't	forecast	last
米	ǽsk	kǽnt	fɔ́:(r)kæst	lǽst
英	ɑ́:sk	kɑ́:nt	fɔ́:(r)kɑ́:st	lɑ́:st

❸ 単母音 /ɑː/ の長さが異なる

米語の /ɑː/ が、イギリス英語では /ɔ/ となる（/ɑː/ は /ɑ/ とも表記される）。

	not	problem	stop
米	nάːt	prάːbləm	stάːp
英	nɔ́t	prɔ́bləm	stɔ́p

❹ 2重母音の音が異なる

米語の /ou/ が、イギリス英語では /əu/ の発音になる。

	know	home
米	nóu	hóum
英	nə́u	hə́um

❺ 米語の /iː/ が /ai/ になる

	either	neither
米	íːðər	níːðər
英	áiðə	náiðə

❻ 米語 /duː/ が /dʒuː/ になる

	due	duty	produce	reduce
米	dúː	dúːti	prədúːs	ridúːs
英	dʒúː	dʒúːti	prədʒúːs	ridʒúːs

❼ 子音 /j/ の音の変化

米語では /j/ 音が消失するが、イギリス英語では発音する。th、t、d、n の後ろに u、ew が位置する場合、つまり /j/ の直前に /t/ 音や /d/ 音がある場合は、子音が融合する。

	tuition	tune
米	tuːíʃən	túːn
英	tjuːíʃən	tjúːn

❽ 母音の間の子音 /t/、/d/ を明瞭に発音

米語では、母音で挟まれた /t/ や /d/ の音が日本語の「ラ行」子音に似た発音になるが、イギリス英語では明瞭に発音される。

	better	pity	rider	set up
米	bérər	píri	ráirər	sérʌ́p
英	bétə	píti	ráidə	sétʌ́p

❾ wh で始まる語の音が異なる

米語では /w/ の音の前にかすかに /h/ 音が入る。イギリス英語は /w/ 音から始まり /h/ 音は入らない。

	when	which
米	hwən	hwítʃ
英	wən	wítʃ

❿ そのほかの特徴的な語

	advertisement	leisure	often	schedule
米	ǽdvə(r)táizmənt	líːʒər	ɔ́ːfən	skédʒuːl
英	ədvə́ːtismənt	léʒə	ɔ́ːftən	ʃédjuːl

それでは以下の会話を CD で聞いた後、色文字の部分を意識しながら音読しよう。

▶訳：p.30

CD 1-11

M: It's a pity that Mr. Kent is resigning next month. It seems either Mr. Gonzales or Ms. Wallace is going to take over his duties. To be frank, I don't care who becomes boss.

W: Well, it does matter to me because I just can't get along with Mr. Gonzales. He is a capable manager, but I often find it difficult to work with him. He has too much confidence in himself.

M: John has exactly the same opinion as you. Anyway, I have to complete my project report quickly. The due date is Wednesday. Can you help me to review the contents?

M: Certainly. When will you be available? You should probably ask Jane to join us. She would be of great help, too.

4カ国発音を攻略する！ Vol.1 イギリス英語編

p.29の訳

M: Kentさんが来月辞めてしまうのは残念だな。GonzalesさんかWallaceさんが仕事を引き継ぐみたいだけど。正直言って、誰が上司になろうが構わないな。

W: う〜ん、私はGonzalesさんと折り合いが悪いから、気になるわね。有能な管理職だけど、一緒に働くのは難しいなとしょっちゅう思うわ。自信過剰なんだもの。

M: Johnも君とまったく同じ意見だよ。とにかく、僕はさっさと自分のプロジェクト報告書を完成させないと。締め切りが水曜日なんだ。内容を見直すのを手伝ってもらえる？

W: もちろんよ。いつがいい？　多分、Janeに加わってもらうよう頼むべきでしょうね。彼女も強力な助っ人になるわよ。

900点突破者たちの体験談(1)
弱点の補強でついに900点突破！

(T. K.さん 会社員 女性)

750点 → 905点

　今回ようやく900点ホルダーになることができた私は、学生時代には750点を取ったものの、社会人になって英語から遠ざかり、かなり力が落ちていました。外資系企業への転職には900点が関門でしたので、自分の弱点を冷静に見極め、補強を行うことにしました。

　まず着手したのは、TOEIC頻出単語を覚えることでした。以前は大学受験向けの単語集を使っていましたが、TOEIC頻出のビジネス・経済用語が苦手でしたので、TOEICに特化した単語集に思い切って切り替えました。『新TOEIC TEST英単語出るとこだけ!』(アルク)は、収録語数は多くありませんが、各パートで知っておくべき語彙がカバーされており、新しく登場した語がその後の例文で繰り返し使われます。覚えた単語が確実にTOEICに登場するので効果を実感できました。単語は目で見て、耳で発音を確認し、まねてリピートし、例文も聞いてから音読しました。

　リスニング対策は、まず戦略本で一通り各パートの有効な解き方やコツを身に付けた後、『TOEICテスト新公式問題集』(国際コミュニケーション協会)に挑戦しました。公式問題集は、内容、形式、ナレーターの声の質などが本番のテストに最も近いので、実践練習に最適だと思います。対策は特に難しいPart 3、4を中心に行いました。

　具体的な学習法ですが、毎日、起床後すぐにCDを聞きます。設問の先読みをしながら問題を解き、答え合わせをして、なぜ間違えたか分析します。その後チャンクでスクリプトを音読し、わからない個所の訳を確認します。次に1文ずつCDを止めてリピート。仕上げにスクリプトを見ながら全体をスムーズに音読し、内容がすぐ理解できるようになった後は、何も見ずにCDを何度も聞きます。聞き取れなかった個所は再度スクリプトを見て確認しました。このようにすると着実にリスニング力がアップします。設問、選択肢も意味を把握しながらすべて音読しました。

　リーディング対策ではタイムマネジメントを意識して、Part 7の設問を5問解くなら5分…というようにアラームを設定し、制限時間内に問題を解くようにしました。毎日最低1つの長文問題を解き、知らない単語や表現を辞書でチェックして、覚えるようにしました。Part 5、6は解答をチェックした後、正解を空所に入れた文を音読。こうすると、どこが理解できていないかが明確になります。Part 7も文書、設問、選択肢をチャンクで区切って音読し、すぐに意味を把握できるようにしました。これらはすべて、小山先生の講座を受講した際に勧められた勉強方法です。

　900点に到達するには、着実な勉強が必要です。私も何度か途中でやめようと思いましたが、勉強の仕方を変えて、最後には目標に到達できました。感無量です。

Part 3 基礎トレーニング

それでは早速、リスニングセクションの難関、Part 3から学習を始めよう。今日は基礎トレーニングとして、設問の速読練習を中心に行う。CDで解答時間を制限しているので、規定時間内で各Taskに取り組むようにしよう。

Part 3 解答のポイント

2人の人物の会話の後、その内容に関する3つの設問が読まれる。設問はテスト冊子に印刷されているので、会話が始まる前に先読みして、キーワードを把握することが大切だ。設問の順番とヒントが登場する順番は、同じであることが多い。

● 設問を先読みする

3つ目の設問が読まれてから、次の会話がスタートするまで8秒あるので、その間に次の3問を先読みする。頻出するタイプの設問は、3点攻略法でキーワードを素早くチェックする練習をすると先読みが楽になる。
要チェックなのは、通常、以下の①～③の3カ所（場合によっては④を加えた4カ所）。そこから会話で聞くべきポイントを絞り込もう。

What does the woman suggest?
①Wh疑問詞　②主語　③動詞

① **Wh疑問詞**：Whyならば、原因・理由を表す語句（due to、because of、owing to、as、since、in order to、caused byなど）に注意して聞く。
② **主語**：主語がwomanならば、womanの発言を特に注意して聞く。
③ **動詞**：動詞がsuggestならば、提案を示す表現（Why don't you ～?、How about ～?、Let's ～、You should ～）などに注意して聞く。
④ **その他**：動詞がdoで副詞がnextならば、未来表現（be going to do、be planning to do、I'll ～）などに注意して聞く。

設問によっては、右記のtomorrowのような時に関する副詞（句）、または動詞の目的語などが第4のキーワードになる（4点攻略法）。第4のキーワードは、会話の中にそのまま登場することが多く、聞くべき個所をフォーカスしやすいので、非常に重要だ。

What will the man do tomorrow?
　①　　　　②　③　④（時に関する副詞句）
Why did the woman call Mr. Kent?
　①　　　　　②　　③　④（動詞の目的語）

● 問題タイプを見分ける

● 全体情報タイプ

「話題」「会話の場所」「職業」を問う問題で、1番目の設問に多い。通常、会話全体にヒントが複数回登場するので、解答の順番としては次記の個別情報タイプを優先する。

例 話題：What are the speakers discussing?
　　　会話の場所：Where does this conversation probably take place?
　　　職業：Who most likely are the speakers?

● 個別情報タイプ

「時」「手段」「理由」「次の行動」「問題点」「提案の内容」「示唆の内容」などを問う問題で、ヒントは1回しか登場しない。

例 理由：Why are the speakers going to London?
　　　次の行動：What will the woman probably do next?
　　　問題点：What problem does the woman have?
　　　示唆の内容：What is suggested about the new office?

Part 3　解答のポイント

●**選択肢の先読みと縦読みを使い分ける**

●**短い選択肢は先読みする**
時刻、曜日、場所、職業など短い名詞（句）が並ぶ選択肢には、設問チェック時に目を通しておく。

●**長い選択肢は縦読みする**（p.37、112参照）
キーワードのみチェックして要点を把握する。事前にすべての選択肢を細かく読む必要はない。

●**マークシートは塗らない**
リスニングに集中し、先読みの時間を確保するため、マークシートは軽く印を付ける程度にする。Part 4までのリスニングセクションがすべて終わってから、リーディングセクションに取り組む前に、1、2分でさっと塗るようにしよう。

　例：Ⓐ Ⓑ Ⓒ Ⓓ

Task 1

▶解答：p.38〜

CDには、**問題番号**⇨**ポーズ1**（8秒）⇨**合図音**⇨**ポーズ2**（20秒）が収録されている。
ポーズ1で**3つの設問**を読み、**ポーズ2**で各設問のキーワードを参考に、【　】の中に「設問で問われている内容」を簡潔に記入しよう（日本語でも英語でも可）。(A)〜(D) の選択肢はTask 2で使うので、ここでは気にしなくていい。

1. Where does this conversation probably take place?
    (A) In a drug store
    (B) At an airport
    (C) In an office
    (D) At a hospital

2. What does the man want to do this afternoon?
    (A) Make an appointment
    (B) Visit a warehouse
    (C) Speak with a manager
    (D) Get a prescription

3. Who will the woman meet with tomorrow morning?
    (A) A journalist
    (B) A physician
    (C) A factory manager
    (D) A travel agent

【1.　　　　　　　　2.　　　　　　　　　　　3.　　　　　　　　　】

GO ON TO THE NEXT PAGE

4. What is the conversation mainly about?
   (A) An office location
   (B) A colleague's transfer
   (C) A recruiting procedure
   (D) A business alliance

5. What department does Mr. Barton work in?
   (A) Marketing
   (B) Public relations
   (C) Accounting
   (D) Administration

6. What does the woman offer to do?
   (A) Send some information
   (B) Arrange a farewell party
   (C) Work with an ad agency
   (D) Look over the contract

[4.   5.   6.   ]

7. Who is Ms. Rossi?
   (A) A novelist
   (B) A bookseller
   (C) A broadcaster
   (D) A librarian

8. Where did Ms. Rossi go?
   (A) To a book fair
   (B) To a publishing firm
   (C) To an industry conference
   (D) To a public debate

9. Why is the man looking for Ms. Rossi?
   (A) To discuss sales results
   (B) To decide an agenda
   (C) To place an order
   (D) To make an inquiry

[7.   8.   9.   ]

選択肢のチェックポイント1

設問の4つの選択肢を素早く読むには、いくつかのコツがある。2回に分けて、それを伝授しよう（続きはp.112参照）。

1. 共通個所は読まずにキーワードを縦読みする

What does the woman say about yesterday?

(A) She completed the sales report.
(B) She booked a flight.
(C) She made plans for the presentation.
(D) She met her client.

Sheは共通なので読まずに、キーワードとなる動詞部分のみをまず縦読みしてポイントを把握する。「完成した」、「予約した」、「計画した」、「会った」と意味がまったく異なるので、全文を読まなくても違いが明確になり、正解を選ぶための絞り込みが短時間でできる。

2. 行動が問われている設問は、動詞⇒目的語を縦読みする

What will the woman probably do tomorrow?

(A) Call her client
(B) Attend a conference
(C) Get in touch with her supervisor
(D) Speak to her coworker

行動を問う設問では、選択肢の動詞部分をざっと縦読みして違いを把握する。上記のように動詞の意味が似ている場合は、動詞の目的語（下線部）が重要なので、これも素早く縦読みする。

Task 2

▶解答：p.38

Task 1と同じ設問を使って、選択肢を早読みする練習をしよう。Task 1と同じ音声を使い、**ポーズ1**で3つの設問の選択肢を読み、**ポーズ2**でポイントを示すキーワード語句に下線を引こう。

Task 1 & 2 の正解と解説

1. Where does this conversation probably take place?
(A) In a drug store
(B) At an airport
(C) In an office
(D) At a hospital

この会話はどこで行われている可能性が高いか。
(A) ドラッグストアで
(B) 空港で
(C) オフィスで
(D) 病院で

Task 1： 解答例 場所　会話を聞く際は特に前半に注意。
Task 2：解答は赤色の下線部参照（以下同）。選択肢に共通するIn a、At anなどは読まない。

---

2. What does the man want to do this afternoon?
(A) Make an appointment
(B) Visit a warehouse
(C) Speak with a manager
(D) Get a prescription

男性は今日の午後に何をしたがっているか。
(A) 面会の約束をする
(B) 倉庫を訪れる
(C) 部長と話す
(D) 処方せんを入手する

Task 1： 解答例 男性の行動　男性がヒントを言うはず。また、this afternoonやその言い換え表現が登場すると予測できる。
Task 2：doの設問なので、動詞部分をまず縦読みする。make、getは目的語なしでは要点がわからないので、目的語に視点を移し、縦読みする。

---

3. Who will the woman meet with tomorrow morning?
(A) A journalist
(B) A physician
(C) A factory manager
(D) A travel agent

女性は明朝、誰と会うか。
(A) ジャーナリスト
(B) 医者
(C) 工場長
(D) 旅行代理店の社員

Task 1： 解答例 女性が会う相手　女性がヒントを言うはず。tomorrow morningか、その言い換え表現を待つ。
Task 2：選択肢共通のAは読まない。

4. What is the conversation mainly about?
   (A) An office location
   (B) A colleague's transfer
   (C) A recruiting procedure
   (D) A business alliance

会話は主に何についてか。
(A) オフィスの所在地
(B) 同僚の異動
(C) 新規採用の手続き
(D) 業務提携

Task 1： 解答例 話題　会話冒頭の2人のコメントに注意する。
Task 2： location、transfer、procedure、allianceと最後の1語を縦読みすれば、短時間である程度違いが明確になる。

----

5. What department does Mr. Barton work in?
   (A) Marketing
   (B) Public relations
   (C) Accounting
   (D) Administration

Barton氏は何の部署で働いているか。
(A) マーケティング
(B) 広報
(C) 経理
(D) 総務

Task 1： 解答例 Bartonの部署　Bartonという語が、会話に登場するのを待つ。

----

6. What does the woman offer to do?
   (A) Send some information
   (B) Arrange a farewell party
   (C) Work with an ad agency
   (D) Look over the contract

女性は何をすると申し出ているか。
(A) 情報を送る
(B) 送別会を設定する
(C) 広告代理店と仕事をする
(D) 契約書に目を通す

Task 1： 解答例 女性の申し出　女性がヒントを言うはず。
Task 2： offer to doと、doの部分が問われているので、動詞を縦読みすれば違いはわかる。会話を聞きながら目的語も縦読みし、正解を絞り込む。

7. Who is Ms. Rossi?
 (A) A novelist
 (B) A bookseller
 (C) A broadcaster
 (D) A librarian

Rossiさんとは誰か。
(A) 小説家
(B) 書籍販売業者
(C) アナウンサー
(D) 図書館員

Task 1：　解答例　Rossiの職業　職業を示すコメントを待つ。

---

8. Where did Ms. Rossi go?
 (A) To a book fair
 (B) To a publishing firm
 (C) To an industry conference
 (D) To a public debate

Rossiさんはどこに行ったか。
(A) ブックフェアへ
(B) 出版社へ
(C) 業界の会議へ
(D) 公開討論へ

Task 1：　解答例　Rossiが訪問した場所　訪問に関するコメントを待つ。
Task 2：最後の1語を縦読みするのが有効。

---

9. Why is the man looking for Ms. Rossi?
 (A) To discuss sales results
 (B) To decide an agenda
 (C) To place an order
 (D) To make an inquiry

男性はなぜRossiさんを探しているか。
(A) 営業成績について話し合うため
(B) 議題を決めるため
(C) 注文をするため
(D) 問い合わせをするため

Task 1：　解答例　Rossiを探す理由　理由を示す表現を待つ。
Task 2：動詞を縦読みすると、discussとdecideの違いが不明確。placeとmakeも単独では要点が不明なので、すべての目的語を縦読みする。

勘ボックスを活用しよう！

本書のPracticeでは、解答欄のABCDまたはABCのマークの横に □ が付いている。これは「勘ボックス」で、正しいかどうか自信がなく、勘で解答した場合はここにチェックを入れる。チェックを入れた問題は、たとえ正解していても攻略できたとは言えないので、弱点と考えて後でしっかりと復習すること。

Practice

CD 1-13〜15　▶解答：p.43〜

それでは練習問題に挑戦してみよう。CDの音声の冒頭に8秒のポーズを設けているので、この時間を利用して3つの設問、選択肢を先読みしよう。

1. What are the speakers mainly discussing?
    (A) A meeting agenda
    (B) Mr. Corson's new survey
    (C) Ms. Milton's schedule
    (D) A work deadline　　　Ⓐ Ⓑ Ⓒ Ⓓ ☐

2. Where is Ms. Milton?
    (A) In a meeting
    (B) At a reception desk
    (C) At an immigration office
    (D) At a lawyer's office　　　Ⓐ Ⓑ Ⓒ Ⓓ ☐

3. When does Ms. Milton's plane depart?
    (A) 4:30 P.M. on the 15th
    (B) 5:00 P.M. today
    (C) 6:00 P.M. today
    (D) 6:00 P.M. on the 15th　　　Ⓐ Ⓑ Ⓒ Ⓓ ☐

4. Where does the woman most likely work?
    (A) A shipping company
    (B) An automobile repair shop
    (C) A customer service center
    (D) A computer assembly plant　　　Ⓐ Ⓑ Ⓒ Ⓓ ☐

5. What has the man done?
    (A) Customized a computer
    (B) Bought an electronic device
    (C) Received a defective product
    (D) Indicated an alternate route　　　Ⓐ Ⓑ Ⓒ Ⓓ ☐

6. What will the man most likely do?
    (A) Wait for the delivery
    (B) Call the distribution center
    (C) Inquire about a warranty
    (D) Get a refund　　　Ⓐ Ⓑ Ⓒ Ⓓ ☐

GO ON TO THE NEXT PAGE

7. At what kind of business does the conversation take place?
 (A) A clothing store
 (B) A dry cleaner's
 (C) A textile plant
 (D) A grocery store

8. What do we know about the woman?
 (A) She wants to have her garment repaired.
 (B) She has been informed of the renovation plan.
 (C) She will be giving a presentation.
 (D) She has a leather garment.

9. What is inferred about the service?
 (A) It requires a six-day examination.
 (B) She will designate the place for delivery.
 (C) It will be completed within a week.
 (D) An extra fee will be added.

Practiceの正解と解説

1-3 CD 1-13 M: 🇬🇧 W: 🇨🇦

M: Hello, this is Tom Corson calling from Corson Enterprises. I'm trying to get in touch with Janis Milton. Is she in today?
W: Yes, but I'm afraid Ms. Milton is in back-to-back meetings until 4:00 P.M. Shall I have her call you back when she's available?
M: No, that's all right. Actually, I'll be in your area around 5:00 P.M. today. Would it be OK for me to stop by the office for a visit? I have some product samples in which she showed some interest during our meeting last week.
W: Unfortunately, Ms. Milton is scheduled to leave for the airport at 4:30 for a 6 o'clock flight. She will be back on the 15th. Would you like to leave her a message?

M: もしもし、Corson EnterprisesのTom Corsonと申します。Janis Miltonさんと連絡を取りたいのですが、本日はいらっしゃいますか。
W: はい。ただ申し訳ないのですが、Miltonは午後4時まで、連続して複数の会議に出席しております。都合がつき次第、折り返し電話させましょうか。
M: いいえ、結構です。実は本日午後5時ごろ、御社の付近にいる予定でして。御社に伺ってもよろしいでしょうか。先週の会議の際、Miltonさんが興味を示してくださった製品サンプルを持っているのです。
W: あいにく、Miltonは6時の飛行機に乗るため、4時30分には空港に向けて出発する予定です。15日には戻ります。何かご伝言はございますか。

1. 話者は主に何について話し合っているか。
  (A) 会議の議題
  (B) Corson氏の新たな調査
  (C) Miltonさんのスケジュール
  (D) 仕事の締め切り

解説 設問のキーワードはWhat、speakers、discussing。「話題」を問う設問で、会話全体に複数のヒントが登場する。通常冒頭に出てくることが多く、ここでも最初のやりとりが大きなヒントとなる。
解答 (C)

2. Miltonさんはどこにいるか。
  (A) 会議中
  (B) 受付カウンターに
  (C) 入国管理所に
  (D) 弁護士事務所に

解説 キーワードはWhere、is、Milton。「Miltonさんの居場所」を問う個別情報タイプ。女性のMs. Milton is in back-to-back meetings until 4:00 P.M.がヒントとなる。 **解答** (A)

3. Miltonさんの飛行機はいつ出発するか。
  (A) 15日の午後4時30分
  (B) 今日の午後5時
  (C) 今日の午後6時
  (D) 15日の午後6時

解説 キーワードはWhen、Milton's plane、depart。「飛行機の出発時間」を問う個別情報タイプ。会話には複数の時間が登場するはず。女性の後半のコメント a 6 o'clock flightから正解がわかる。 **解答** (C)

4-6　CD 1-14　W: 🇨🇦　M: 🇺🇸

W: **This is the Central Computer Company Helpline.** Thank you for calling. How may I help you?
M: Hello. I've purchased a computer from your online store. It was delivered today, and that's no problem. But **I also ordered some stereo speakers with it**, and they haven't arrived. I'm wondering whether there's been a mistake with the order.
W: Thank you for your order, sir. And we're sorry for any inconvenience. All equipment other than the computer itself are shipped to you from separate suppliers. Those separate shipments typically take one to two additional working days to arrive.
M: I see. It's Wednesday today, so **I'll wait a little more**, and if the speakers don't arrive by Friday, I'll call you again. Thanks.

W: こちらはCentral Computer社の電話相談サービスです。お電話ありがとうございます。どうなさいましたか。
M: もしもし。そちらのオンラインストアでコンピューターを買ったんです。今日着いて、何の問題もありませんでした。ただ、一緒にステレオスピーカーを注文したのに、まだ届かないんです。注文に何か間違いがあったのかと思いまして。
W: ご注文いただき、誠にありがとうございます。ご迷惑をおかけしたことをおわび申し上げます。コンピューター本体以外の機器はすべて、別の納入業者から発送されます。別便でお送りする荷物は、通常、到着まで1、2営業日余分にかかります。
M: わかりました。今日は水曜ですから、もう少し待ってみます。金曜までにスピーカーが到着しなかったら、またお電話します。ありがとう。

4. 女性はどこで働いていると思われるか。
(A) 運送会社
(B) 自動車修理店
(C) 顧客サービスセンター
(D) コンピューター組立工場

解説 設問のキーワードはWhere、woman、work。女性の「職業」を問う全体情報タイプだ。冒頭のThis is the …から正解は明らか。
解答 (C)

5. 男性はすでに何をしたか。
(A) コンピューターをカスタマイズした
(B) 電子機器を購入した
(C) 欠陥品を受け取った
(D) 別の経路を指摘した

解説 キーワードはWhat、man、done。男性の過去の行動を問う個別情報タイプで、男性の発言に注意する。選択肢のelectronic deviceはstereo speakersの言い換え。**解答** (B)

6. 男性は何をすると思われるか。
(A) 配達物を待つ
(B) 流通センターに電話する
(C) 保証について尋ねる
(D) 払い戻しを受ける

解説 キーワードはWhat、man、do。男性の次の行動を問う個別情報タイプで、男性がヒントを言うはず。女性のThose separate shipments … to arrive.の発言に、I'll wait a little more、と答えている。**解答** (A)

7-9

W: 🇦🇺 M: 🇺🇸

W: Hello. I've got a few items here that I need to have washed.
M: No problem at all. Let's see here ... I think these shirts can be laundered and pressed. And this leather overcoat is going to require some special treatment. I'll have to send it out to a specialist for cleaning and conditioning.
W: Will that take more time than the rest of the items? I'd like to have it back in a week.
M: It will take one extra day, but I can still have it back for you in six days.

W: こんにちは。いくつか洗っていただきたいものがあるんですけど。
M: かしこまりました。なるほど……こちらのシャツ類は、洗濯とアイロンがけができます。それから、こちらの革のコートは特別な処理が必要ですね。クリーニングとコンディショニングの専門家に送る必要があるでしょう。
W: そうすると、ほかの物より時間がかかりますか。1週間後には受け取りたいんです。
M: 1日余分にかかりますが、6日後にお渡しできますよ。

7. この会話はどんな仕事の場で行われているか。
 (A) 衣料品店
 (B) ドライクリーニング店
 (C) 織物工場
 (D) 食料雑貨店

解説 キーワードはwhat、business、take place。「場所」を問う全体情報タイプ。need to have washed、these shirts can be laundered and pressed、this leather overcoatなど、会話中の複数のヒントを拾う。**解答** (B)

8. 女性についてどんなことがわかるか。
 (A) 彼女は衣類を繕ってもらいたい。
 (B) 彼女は改修計画を告知されている。
 (C) 彼女はこれからプレゼンを行う。
 (D) 彼女は革の衣類を持っている。

解説 設問のキーワードはWhat、we、know、woman。女性に関する個別情報タイプ。通常は女性がヒントを言うが、ここでは男性がthis leather overcoat ...と、ヒントを述べていることに注意しよう。**解答** (D)

9. サービスについて何が示唆されているか。
 (A) 6日間のテストが必要だ。
 (B) 彼女が配達場所を指定する。
 (C) 1週間以内に完了する。
 (D) 追加料金が上乗せされる。

解説 キーワードはWhat、inferred、service。サービス内容を問う個別情報タイプ。設問が漠然としているので、選択肢の早読みでチェックすべきポイントをあらかじめ予測しよう。**解答** (C)

学習エネルギーをチャージする今日の **格言**

The secret of success is constancy to purpose.
Benjamin Disraeli
（1804〜81：イギリスの首相、小説家）
成功の秘けつは、目標をしっかりと持ち続けることだ。

Part 3 基本音読

3日目 / 20

今日からは本書の学習の中核である「音読」に挑戦する。ただ声を出すのではなく、15ページの基本ルールを確認しながら取り組もう。まずは昨日の復習からスタート。

Task 1

CD 1-12　▶解答：p.48

CDには、**問題番号**⇨**ポーズ1**(8秒)⇨**合図音**⇨**ポーズ2**(20秒)が収録されている。

1) **ポーズ1**で、キーワードに注意しながら**3つの設問**を読み、**ポーズ2**で、キーワードを参考に、【　】の中に各設問の要点を日本語または英語で書こう。
2) 同じ音声を使い、**ポーズ1**で**3つの設問の選択肢**を読み、**ポーズ2**で各選択肢のキーワードに下線を引こう。

1. Where most likely are the speakers?
   (A) At a hotel reception desk
   (B) At a train station
   (C) At a convention center
   (D) At a box office

2. What will Ms. Walsh receive?
   (A) A breakfast voucher
   (B) An information package
   (C) A performance schedule
   (D) An itinerary

3. What does Ms. Walsh ask about?
   (A) The time of an event
   (B) A place to eat
   (C) The capacity of the hall
   (D) The person in charge

【1.　　　　　　　2.　　　　　　　3.　　　　　　　】

4. Who is the man talking to?

(A) An executive secretary
(B) An architect
(C) A personnel director
(D) An interior designer

5. What will the man do at 2 o'clock tomorrow?

(A) Demonstrate some designs
(B) Return to his office
(C) Speak with a manager
(D) Hold a conference

6. What does the woman suggest?

(A) Making a reservation
(B) Rescheduling a meeting
(C) Returning the call
(D) Getting an application form

【4.　　　　　　5.　　　　　　6.　　　　　　】

7. What are the speakers discussing?

(A) A sales figure
(B) A meeting agenda
(C) A computer system
(D) A draft contract

8. Why might the man make a phone call?

(A) To confirm the schedule
(B) To postpone the conference
(C) To provide technical assistance
(D) To place an order

9. Whom does the man say he contacted earlier?

(A) His supervisor
(B) His client
(C) A repair person
(D) An advertising agency

【7.　　　　　　8.　　　　　　9.　　　　　　】

Task 1の正解と解説

1. 話者はどこにいる可能性が高いか。
   (A) ホテルのフロントに
   (B) 列車の駅に
   (C) コンベンション・センターに
   (D) チケット売り場に

2. Walshさんは何を受け取るか。
   (A) 朝食券
   (B) 資料ファイル
   (C) 公演日程
   (D) 旅程

3. Walshさんは何について尋ねるか。
   (A) イベントの時間
   (B) 食事する場所
   (C) ホールの収容人員
   (D) 責任者

解答例 設問の要点：1. 場所　2. Walshの受け取る物　3. Walshの質問
選択肢のキーワード：1. At a 以降の語句　2. 冠詞以降の語句　3. time、place、capacity、person と縦読みする。

---

4. 男性は誰に話しているか。
   (A) 重役秘書
   (B) 建築家
   (C) 人事部長
   (D) インテリア・デザイナー

5. 男性は明日2時に何をするか。
   (A) いくつかのデザインを示す
   (B) オフィスに戻る
   (C) 部長と話す
   (D) 会議を開く

6. 女性は何を示唆しているか。
   (A) 予約をする
   (B) 会議を再設定する
   (C) 折り返し電話する
   (D) 応募用紙を入手する

解答例 設問の要点：4. 男性の話し相手　5. 男性の行動　6. 女性の示唆
選択肢のキーワード：4. 冠詞以降の語句　5. 最初に動詞を縦読みし、ReturnやHoldのポイントが不明確なのでdesigns、his office、manager、conferenceにも目を通す。6. まず動詞を縦読みし、Making、Returning、Gettingのポイントが不明瞭なので、reservation、call、application formも読む。

---

7. 話者は何について話し合っているか。
   (A) 営業成績
   (B) 会議の議題
   (C) コンピューター・システム
   (D) 契約案

8. 男性はなぜ電話をするかもしれないのか。
   (A) 日程を確認するため
   (B) 会議を延期するため
   (C) 技術的な援助を提供するため
   (D) 注文をするため

9. 男性は自分が以前誰に連絡したと言っているか。
   (A) 自分の上司
   (B) 自分の顧客
   (C) 修理担当者
   (D) 広告代理店の社員

解答例 設問の要点：7. 話題　8. 男性の電話の理由　9. 男性が連絡した相手
選択肢のキーワード：7. 冠詞以降の語句　8. 先読みでは、動詞を縦読みすれば十分。会話を聞きながらschedule、conference、technical assistance、orderも縦読みする。9. Hisや冠詞以降の語句。

48

Practice

1-16〜18 ▶解答：p.51〜

それでは練習問題で、実際に問題を解いてみよう。CDの音声の冒頭に8秒のポーズを設けているので、この時間を利用して設問・選択肢を先読みしよう。

1. When did the woman return?
   (A) A couple of days ago
   (B) Three days ago
   (C) Seven days ago
   (D) Ten days ago

2. What is the man explaining?
   (A) A travel itinerary for the woman
   (B) How to file an expense report
   (C) A colleague's transfer
   (D) Details on the loss of an article

3. What should the woman do first?
   (A) Register her identification number
   (B) Complete the project report
   (C) Organize her receipts
   (D) Go to the accounting department

4. What is the woman most likely doing?
   (A) Searching for the instruction manual
   (B) Driving a vehicle
   (C) Guiding a tour
   (D) Managing a convention

5. What is the man uncertain about?
   (A) Local currency
   (B) The itinerary
   (C) The address of the insurance company
   (D) The location of his destination

6. What does the man imply?
   (A) Enroll in a workshop
   (B) Hold a seminar
   (C) Participate in a conference
   (D) Get a hotel voucher

GO ON TO THE NEXT PAGE

7. Where does the conversation most likely take place?

(A) In the accounting department
(B) At an architect's office
(C) In a board meeting
(D) In a company mailroom

Ⓐ Ⓑ Ⓒ Ⓓ ☐

8. What is the woman doing?

(A) Interviewing an applicant
(B) Giving instructions to the man
(C) Checking the inventory
(D) Filling out forms

Ⓐ Ⓑ Ⓒ Ⓓ ☐

9. What will the man most likely do next?

(A) Distribute the letters
(B) Call his immediate supervisor
(C) Submit the documents
(D) Confirm the delivery schedule

Ⓐ Ⓑ Ⓒ Ⓓ ☐

解答行動分析リスト

Practiceで正解できなかった設問について、原因を探ろう。以下から当てはまる項目を選び、次ページからの解答の横の[　]に番号を記入すること。

❶ 設問の先読みができなかった
❷ 設問のポイントがすぐにわからなかった
❸ 設問の意味を誤解した
❹ 短い選択肢の先読みをしなかった
❺ 選択肢の縦読みをしなかった
❻ 選択肢の内容を誤解した
❼ 長い選択肢を読みきれなかった
❽ 選択肢に知らない語彙があった
❾ 会話の冒頭で状況を把握し損ねた
❿ 会話の状況が理解できなかった
⓫ 会話の中の知らない語彙に気を取られた
⓬ 会話の内容を誤解した
⓭ 会話のスピードが速くて把握しきれなかった
⓮ 音の崩れなどがよく聞き取れなかった
⓯ 漠然と聞いてしまった
⓰ 設問の主語に注意して会話を聞かなかった
⓱ 時の副詞句や、理由・依頼を示す表現など、設問にかかわるキーワードに注意しなかった
⓲ 個別情報タイプを優先的に解かなかった
⓳ 1問に時間をかけすぎた
⓴ 言い換えに気づかなかった
㉑ マークに印を付けている間にヒントを聞き逃した
㉒ マークに印を付け間違えた
㉓ 前の問題をひきずって切り替えができなかった
㉔ 正解を絞りきれず迷った
㉕ 思い込みがあった
㉖ 集中力が欠如していた
㉗ パニックに陥った

Practiceの正解と解説

1-3 **CD 1-16** W: 🇦🇺 M: 🇺🇸

W: Hi, I returned from a business trip to Chicago about a week ago. And I haven't reported my expenses yet. Can you tell me how to go about it?
M: Sure. The first thing you need to do is gather up all the receipts. We can only reimburse you for expenses for which you've kept receipts. And, it's better to turn in your document within a couple of days since the closing day is approaching.
W: Thank you for reminding me. I may have paid cash for a meal or two without getting a receipt. But it's nothing major.
M: Good. Fill out this form, and follow the instructions, then bring it back to me. We'll be able to get things done within about three days.

W: どうも。1週間ほど前に、シカゴへの出張から戻りました。それでまだ、経費の報告をしていません。どうしたらいいのか、教えてもらえますか。
M: いいですよ。まずは領収書を全部集めてください。領収書がある分しか、払い戻しはできません。それから、2、3日以内に書類を提出したほうがいいですよ。締切日が迫っていますから。
W: 思い出させてくれてありがとう。食事の際に1、2回、現金で支払って領収書を受け取らなかったかもしれません。でもまあ、たいした金額ではありません。
M: それはよかった。こちらの用紙に記入して、指示に従い、その後で私に提出してください。3日ほどで処理が済むはずです。

1. 女性はいつ戻ったか。
(A) 2日前
(B) 3日前
(C) 7日前
(D) 10日前

解説 設問のキーワードはWhen、did、woman、returnで、「時間」を問う個別情報タイプ。設問の主語である女性が冒頭でreturned ... about a week agoと述べている。a weekとseven daysの言い換えに注意。
解答 (C) 解答行動の分析 [　　　]

2. 男性は何を説明しているか。
(A) 女性の旅行日程
(B) 経費報告書の提出方法
(C) 同僚の転勤
(D) 物品紛失の詳細

解説 キーワードはWhat、man、explainingで、「主題」を問う全体情報タイプ。女性がhaven't reported my expenses、how to go about it?と尋ねたのに対し、gather up all the receiptsなどと答えている。
解答 (B) 解答行動の分析 [　　　]

3. 女性はまず何をすべきか。
   (A) 自分のID番号を登録する
   (B) プロジェクト報告書を完成させる
   (C) 自分の領収書をまとめる
   (D) 経理部へ行く

解説 キーワードはWhat、woman、do、firstで、「女性がすべき行動」を問う個別情報タイプ。ただし男性の指示がヒントになっているので注意。The first thing you need to do is ...から解答がわかる。

解答 (C) 解答行動の分析 [　　　]

4-6 CD 1-17 M: 🇬🇧 W: 🇦🇺

M: Hi. We need to go to the Gracewood Hotel. Do you know how long it will take you to drive us there, and about how much it'll cost?

W: Can you tell me which Gracewood location you mean? There are at least three Gracewood hotels within driving distance.

M: I'm afraid I've misplaced the instructions we were supposed to bring with us. But we're here to attend the Insurance Industry Expo, it's a business convention that opens tomorrow at the hotel.

W: OK. In that case, it has to be the one downtown at 5th Avenue and Robinson Street. That's the only one with a convention center. The fare is about $11 from here. Shall I take you there?

M: すみません。Gracewoodホテルに行きたいのですが。そこまで乗せてもらうのにかかる時間と料金は大体わかりますか。

W: どこにあるGracewoodのことか教えていただけますか。車で行ける範囲内に、少なくとも3軒Gracewoodホテルがあるんですよ。

M: 持参するはずだった案内を忘れてきてしまって。でもここにはInsurance Industry Expoに参加するために来ました。これは業界の大会で、明日ホテルで開催されるんです。

W: なるほど。それならきっと中心街の5th AvenueとRobinson Streetのところにあるホテルでしょう。コンベンション・センターがあるのは、そこだけですから。ここからの料金は11ドル程度です。そちらまでお連れしましょうか。

4. 女性は何をしていると思われるか。
   (A) 取扱説明書を探している
   (B) 車を運転している
   (C) ツアーの案内をしている
   (D) 大会の運営をしている

解説 キーワードは What、woman、doingで「女性の行動」を問う全体情報タイプ。男性のDo you know ...?という問いと、女性のCan you tell me...?、Shall I take you there?などの発言からタクシーの運転手だとわかる。

解答 (B) 解答行動の分析 [　　　]

5. 男性は何がわからないのか。
   (A) 現地通貨
   (B) 旅行日程
   (C) 保険会社の住所
   (D) 自分の目的地の場所

解説 キーワードはWhat、man、uncertain aboutで、個別情報タイプだがかなり漠然とした設問。男性の発言に注意すると、I'm afraid I've misplaced...と、質問に答えられない理由を述べているのがわかる。

解答 (D) 解答行動の分析 [　　　]

6. 男性は何を示唆しているか。
   (A) 研修会に参加する
   (B) セミナーを開く
   (C) 会議に出席する
   (D) ホテル宿泊券を入手する

解説 キーワードはWhat、man、implyで、「男性の行動」を問う個別情報タイプの設問。主語である男性のwe're here to attend ...という発言から答えがわかる。

解答 (C) 解答行動の分析 [   ]

7-9 CD 1-18 W: 🇨🇦 M: 🇬🇧

W: Now that we're finished sorting and bundling the mail, our next job is going to be to deliver each bundle to the appropriate department within the company.
M: All right. I think I can handle this. I've become pretty familiar with the layout of the building since I started training.
W: Great. Why don't you handle the delivery run on your own? I'll just come along in case you need help.
M: Certainly. The accounting department is closest, so I'll drop off their mail first.

W: これで、郵便物を仕分けして束ね終えたので、次の仕事はそれぞれの束を社内のしかるべき部署に届けることです。
M: わかりました。できると思います。研修開始以来、このビルのつくりには随分慣れたので。
W: 素晴らしい。配達作業はあなた1人でやってみてはどうですか？ 私はただ、助けが必要な場合に備えて、一緒に行きます。
M: はい。経理部が一番近いので、そこへの郵便物を最初に持っていきます。

7. この会話はどこで行われている可能性が高いか。
   (A) 経理部で
   (B) 設計事務所で
   (C) 役員会議で
   (D) 会社の郵便仕分け室で

解説 キーワードはWhere、conversation、take placeで、「場所」を問う全体情報タイプ。ヒントは会話全体に登場するが、女性の第一声と、男性の最後の言葉が最も重要だ。

解答 (D) 解答行動の分析 [   ]

8. 女性は何をしているか。
   (A) 志願者の面接をしている
   (B) 男性に指示を与えている
   (C) 在庫をチェックしている
   (D) 用紙に記入している

解説 キーワードはWhat、woman、doingで、「女性の行動」を問う個別情報タイプ。設問の主語である女性のWhy don't you handle ...?から正解がわかる。

解答 (B) 解答行動の分析 [   ]

9. 男性は次に何をすると思われるか。
   (A) 手紙を配達する
   (B) 直属の上司に電話する
   (C) 書類を提出する
   (D) 配達予定を確認する

解説 キーワードはWhat、man、do nextで、「未来の行動」を問う個別情報タイプ。女性のWhy don't you ...?という提案に、Certainly.、I'll drop off their mail first.と答えているので正解は明らか。

解答 (A) 解答行動の分析 [   ]

いよいよ音読を開始しよう！

Task 2

いよいよ音読だ。まず、**1)** すべての区切り（**/** と / と //）で区切って音読しよう（**短いチャンク**）。意味をつかみながら読めるようになったら、今度は**/**のところはつなげて**長いチャンク**に挑戦。**2)** 会話のみ、トラック19～21のポーズの部分でリズミカルにリピートしよう。**3)** きちんとリピートできるようになったら、仕上げに設問・選択肢と会話を長いチャンクで音読しよう。

1. When did the woman return? //
   (A) A couple of days ago //   (B) Three days ago //
   (C) Seven days ago //   (D) Ten days ago //
2. What is the man explaining? //
   (A) A travel itinerary / for the woman //   (B) How to file an expense report //
   (C) A colleague's transfer //   (D) Details on the loss of an article //
3. What should the woman do first?
   (A) Register her identification number //   (B) Complete the project report //
   (C) Organize her receipts //   (D) Go to the accounting department //

CD 1-19

W: Hi, / I returned from a business trip / to Chicago about a week ago. //
   And I haven't reported my expenses yet. //
   Can you tell me / how to go about it? //
M: Sure. // The first thing you need to do / is gather up all the receipts. //
   We can only reimburse you / for expenses / for which you've kept receipts. //
   And, it's better to turn in your document / within a couple of days /
   since the closing day is approaching. //
W: Thank you for reminding me. //
   I may have paid cash / for a meal or two / without getting a receipt. //
   But it's nothing major. //
M: Good. //
   Fill out this form, / and follow the instructions, / then bring it back to me. //
   We'll be able to get things done / within about three days. //

要注意フレーズ！

選択肢の音読もしっかりとこなそう。下線部のフレーズは会話やトークの中にも頻出するので、口に出して体にしみ込ませること。この会話のように長い文は、きちんとチャンクごとの意味を確認しながら音読しよう。

4. What is the woman / most likely doing? //
   (A) Searching for the instruction manual //   (B) Driving a vehicle //
   (C) Guiding a tour //   (D) Managing a convention //
5. What is the man uncertain about? //
   (A) Local currency //   (B) The itinerary //
   (C) The address of the insurance company //   (D) The location of his destination //
6. What does the man imply? //
   (A) Enroll in a workshop //   (B) Hold a seminar //
   (C) Participate in a conference //   (D) Get a hotel voucher //

CD 1-20

M: Hi. // We need to go to the Gracewood Hotel. //
   Do you know how long it will take you / to drive us there, /
   and about how much it'll cost? //
W: Can you tell me / which Gracewood location you mean? //
   There are at least three Gracewood hotels / within driving distance.
M: I'm afraid I've misplaced the instructions /
   we were supposed to bring with us. //
   But we're here / to attend the Insurance Industry Expo, /
   it's a business convention / that opens tomorrow at the hotel. //
W: OK. // In that case, /
   it has to be the one downtown / at 5th Avenue and Robinson Street. //
   That's the only one / with a convention center. //
   The fare is about $11 from here. // Shall I take you there? //

要注意フレーズ！

男性のDo you know how long it will take you to drive us there、女性のit has to be the one downtown at 5th Avenue and Robinson Streetはかなり長いチャンクだが、一気に言えるようになるまで繰り返し練習しよう。

7. Where does the conversation / most likely take place? //
   (A) In the accounting department //
   (B) At an architect's office //
   (C) In a board meeting //
   (D) In a company mailroom

8. What is the woman doing? //
   (A) Interviewing an applicant //
   (B) Giving instructions to the man //
   (C) Checking the inventory //
   (D) Filling out forms

9. What will the man / most likely do next? //
   (A) Distribute the letters //
   (B) Call his immediate supervisor //
   (C) Submit the documents //
   (D) Confirm the delivery schedule //

CD 1-21

W: Now that we're finished sorting / and bundling the mail, /
our next job is going to be to deliver /
each bundle to the appropriate department / within the company. //

M: All right. // I think I can handle this. //
I've become pretty familiar / with the layout of the building /
since I started training. //

W: Great. // Why don't you handle the delivery run / on your own? //
I'll just come along / in case you need help. //

M: Certainly. //
The accounting department is closest, / so I'll drop off their mail first. //

要注意フレーズ！

7と9の設問は頻出なのでしっかり音読しよう。9の選択肢も重要フレーズの宝庫だ。会話の中では、頻出表現2つをピックアップしたので、丸ごと覚えるつもりで音読しよう。

Task 3

CD 1-19〜21

CDの音声を聞いて、ポーズの部分で**各チャンクの意味を頭に浮かべよう**（同時通訳の要領で声に出しても可）。すべての会話を聞いて、ポーズのときに意味が出てこない個所があれば、51〜53ページの訳をチェックしよう。

Task 4

CD 1-19〜21

CDを聞いて、**スクリプトを見ないで**ポーズの部分でリズミカルにリピートしよう。

Task 5

CD 1-16〜18

仕上げに、スクリプトを見ながらトラック16〜18の音声に**オーバーラップさせて読んでみよう**。タイミングが合うまで繰り返して、ナチュラルスピードで音読できるようになろう。

Task 6

CD 1-16〜18

この音声をスクリプトを見ずに聞いて理解できるか、今後も繰り返し確認するようにしよう。速聴、速解が目標なので、聞き取れない個所、すぐに意味がわからない個所はピンポイントで何度も聞き、音読し、「あいまいな受信」を「発信できるくらい精度の高い受信」に変えていこう。

学習エネルギーをチャージする今日の **格言**

> **You will never "find" time for anything.**
> **If you want time, you must make it.**
>
> Charles Buxton
> （1823〜1871：イギリスの国会議員、作家）
>
> **何をする時間も「見つける」ことはできない。欲しければ、作らねばならないのだ。**

Part 7 基礎トレーニング

4日目 / 20

● ● ● ● 今日は、リーディングセクションのPart 7の基礎トレーニングを行う。まずは例題に挑戦して、その答え合わせをしながらこのパートの解答のポイントを頭に入れよう。

【 例題 】

▶解答：p.61、訳：p.121

Questions 1-4 refer to the following notice.

BULLETIN BOARD
Redwood Arms Condominiums

Regarding waste disposal, the Homeowners' Association (HOA) has approved a plan to contract with Sierra Coast Recycling Co. to have our recyclable plastic, glass and paper collected separately from our ordinary household trash. The advantages of this plan will include lower fees for municipal waste collection services if we can achieve a 25 percent reduction in the volume of non-recycled garbage. If everyone separates glass, paper and plastic from their household waste, and throws these items away in the designated collection bins, we should be able to meet our goal. The result will be a net savings of $150 per household unit per year. All of the necessary preparations have been made. We look forward to your cooperation in the recycling plan, and will post progress reports here every two weeks.
Thank you.

Dick Rogers
HOA Treasurer

(Note: This bulletin board is a service of the Redwood Arms Homeowners' Association [HOA]. All notices must be submitted to the HOA board of directors for approval and posting. To submit a notice for approval, contact HOA board of directors chairperson Gladys Reeves, Unit 1203.)

1. What is one of the main purposes of the notice?
   (A) To help keep nearby beaches clean
   (B) To encourage residents to join volunteer activities
   (C) To purchase less expensive household trash cans
   (D) To shift their disposal habits toward recycling

2. What can be inferred about Dick Rogers?
   (A) He owns at least one of the condominiums in the building.
   (B) He works as a manager at a waste disposal company.
   (C) He studied statistics to get his current job.
   (D) He has served as chairperson of the HOA board.

3. What statement about the Redwood Arms is NOT true?
   (A) Gladys Reeves is in charge of the Homeowners' Association.
   (B) Residents can place their messages on the bulletin board without restraint.
   (C) Recycling bins have already been placed in the disposal area.
   (D) Reducing the amount of trash can lower collection fees.

4. The word "designated" in paragraph 1, line 8, is closest in meaning to
   (A) discarded
   (B) manufactured
   (C) specified
   (D) customized

リーディング問題攻略の基本

重要な基本原則は、**英語の論理構造（結承結）を意識しながら、語順に従ってチャンクごとに意味をとらえ、スピーディーに読んでいくことだ**。ここでもリスニング問題の音読で実践してきた、以下のチェックポイントが役に立つ。

- 1. 言いたいこと（趣旨と目的、書き手と読み手、場所と状況）をつかんでイメージし
- 2. 流れを意識しながら（論理構造と論理展開を踏まえ、接続語に留意して）
- 3. 後戻りせずに英語の語順で
- 4. チャンク（語のかたまり）ごとに区切って意味を把握し
- 5. 文中のメインの主語と述語は何かを意識して
- 6. 繰り返されている語、肯定的・否定的な語などのキーワードに注目する

Part 7 解答のポイント

1つ、あるいは2つの長文を読んで、2～5の設問に答えるのがPart 7だ。設問数は全部で48あり、そのうち後半の20問は、2つの長文を読んで5つの設問に答える形式。1問1分、パート全体を約50分で解き終えたい。効率よく読むためのステップを、前ページで解いた例題を見ながら確認しよう。

Questions 1-4 refer to the following notice. ①

BULLETIN BOARD ②
Redwood Arms Condominiums

② Regarding waste disposal, the Homeowners' Association (HOA) has approved a plan to contract with Sierra Coast Recycling Co. to have our recyclable plastic, glass and paper collected separately from our ordinary household trash. The advantages of this plan will include lower fees for municipal waste collection services if we can achieve a 25 percent reduction in the volume of non-recycled garbage. If everyone separates glass, paper and plastic from their household waste, and throws these items ⑧ away in the designated collection bins, we should be able to meet our goal. The result will be a net savings of $150 per household unit per year. All of the necessary preparations have been made. We look forward to your cooperation in the recycling plan, and will post progress reports here every two weeks.
Thank you.

Dick Rogers ②
HOA Treasurer

(Note: This bulletin board is a service of the Redwood Arms Homeowners' Association [HOA]. All notices must be submitted to the HOA board of directors for approval and posting. To submit a notice for approval, contact HOA board of directors chairperson Gladys Reeves, Unit 1203.) ③

1. What is one of the main purposes of the notice? ④
   (A) To help keep nearby beaches clean
   (B) To encourage residents to join volunteer activities
   (C) To purchase less expensive household trash cans
   (D) To shift their disposal habits toward recycling

2. What can be inferred about Dick Rogers? ④
   (A) He owns at least one of the condominiums in the building.
   (B) He works as a manager at a waste disposal company.
   (C) He studied accounting to get his current job.
   (D) He has served as chairperson of the HOA board.

3. What statement about the Redwood Arms is NOT true? ④
   (A) Gladys Reeves is in charge of the Homeowners' Association.
   (B) Residents can place their messages on the bulletin board without restraint.
   (C) Recycling bins have already been placed in the disposal area.
   (D) Reducing the amount of trash can lower collection fees.

4. The word "designated" in paragraph 1, line 8, is closest in meaning to
   (A) discarded
   (B) manufactured
   (C) specified
   (D) customized

---

① 冒頭の指示文から文書のタイプを確認（文書の目的などの把握に役立つ）
　➡ following notice から、告知文とわかる。

② タイトル、ヘッダー、あて先、差出人、件名、最初のパラグラフの1、2文目、最後のパラグラフの終わりの1、2文などを見て、誰から誰あてで趣旨・目的は何かを把握（2文書型では文書同士の関係も把握）
　➡ タイトルに「掲示板」とあり、その下にマンションの名称が示されている。また、1文目にwaste disposal、Homeowners' Association (HOA)などの語があり、差出人がHOA Treasurerとなっている。分譲マンションの管理組合の会計係が、住人に向けて張り出したごみ処理に関する告知だとわかる。

③ レイアウト（小見出し、大文字、囲みなど）の目立つ個所に注目し、どこに何が書かれているか大まかに把握（5～10秒）。細かく内容を読む必要はない
　➡ ここでは②でチェックしたタイトル以外に目立つ部分はないが、差出人の名前の下のNoteには要注意。設問のヒントが書かれていることが多い。

④ すべての設問にざっと目を通し、問われているポイントから文書の要点を把握、どの問題から解くか決める。設問はヒントが登場する順に並んでいるが、NOTを含

む設問などは原則、消去法で解くため時間がかかる。後回しにしよう
➡ 1.のキーワードはmain purposes。この告知の目的を尋ねている。
2.のキーワードはinferred、Dick Rogers。Dick Rogersに関する情報を尋ねている。
3.のキーワードはstatement、Redwood Arms、NOT true。Redwood Armsに関して尋ねている。
4.は語彙問題なのでキーワード探しは不要。

⑤ 各設問のキーワードを言い換えている表現を、パラグラフの流れを把握しながら探す。is inferred、is impliedなどあいまいな設問は選択肢も参照（2文書型ではAccording toや人物名・組織名などから、参照する文書を判断する）
➡ 1.のmain purposeは文末のWe look forward to your cooperation …と呼応。
2.のDick RogersはHOA Treasurerとなっている。
3.の選択肢のGladysはHOA board of directors chairperson、messages on the bulletin boardはAll notices must be …と言い換えられている。Recycling bins have already …はAll of the necessary preparations …、Reducing the amount of trash …はif we can achieve a 25 percent reductionに対応。

⑥ ヒントがありそうな候補の箇所を見つけたら、その近辺（前後の語句、文全体）を熟読する。複数ある場合は、設問のキーワードを参考に比較して絞り込む
➡ ⑤の言い換えを含む文を熟読しよう。
➡ テスト冊子に線は引けないので、指でヒントとなる箇所を押さえるといい。

⑦ 候補箇所の内容を記述し（言い換え）ている選択肢を選ぶ
➡ 1.のyour cooperation in the recycling planを言い換えているのは(D)。
2.のHOA Treasurerを言い換えているのは(A)。(D)については、Noteに別の名前が記されているので不可。
3.のchairpersonは(A)のin charge ofに、All of the necessary preparations have been made.は(C)に、lower fees … if we can achieve a 25 percent reductionは(D)に対応する。対応する記述がないのは(B)だけ。

⑧ 語彙問題は文脈をチェックし、使われている意味で判断する
➡ すぐに同義語を選択肢から選ばないこと。ここではdesignatedは「指定された」の意味で使われているので、(C)が適している。

Practice

▶解答：p.69〜

それでは、各問題の右ページにある1〜7のステップに従って、解答のポイントで確認した解き方を試してみよう。解答ステップの（　　）に記入しながら、速解の仕方を身に付けよう。全8問で、制限時間は**11分**。

Questions 1-2 refer to the following advertisement.

DASHBOARD CAR RENTAL

Is looking for experienced administrative personnel to manage its new state-of-the-art location at Wayne Central Airport. Both external applicants and candidates from within the company will be given equal consideration for these two career-track positions. The successful applicants will be highly motivated and experienced administrators, capable of managing a large staff in an industry stressing customer service and eager to advance within the company. Knowledge of standard consumer vehicle models will be a distinct advantage. Applicants who successfully complete two rounds of screening interviews will be accepted into a three-week training program. Competitive, negotiable compensation will be offered to the best applicants.

1. What appears to be the most important qualification for the position?
  (A) Skill in organizing and supervising customer service staff
  (B) Extensive experience in producing video advertisements
  (C) An ability to help customers understand legal contract language
  (D) Knowledge of inspecting vehicles for regular maintenance

2. What offer is made in the advertisement?
  (A) Discount of new vehicles
  (B) Possibility of promotion
  (C) Fringe benefits
  (D) Flextime

解答ステップ

1 ▸ 冒頭の指示文から文書のタイプを確認（　　　　　　　　　　　　）

2 ▸ タイトル、ヘッダー、あて先、差出人、件名、最初のパラグラフの1、2文目、最後のパラグラフの終わりの1、2文などを見て、誰から誰あてで趣旨・目的は何かを把握

　（　　　　　　　　　　　　）から（　　　　　　　　　　　　）あて

　趣旨・目的は（　　　　　　　　　　　　　　　　　　　　　　）

3 ▸ レイアウト（小見出し、大文字、囲みなど）の目立つ個所に注目し、どこに何が書かれているか把握

　特にないのでこのステップはパス

4 ▸ すべての設問に目を通し、問われているポイントから文書の要点を把握。解答の順番を決める

　1.のキーワード（　　　　　　　　　　　　　　　　　　　　　　）

　2.のキーワード（　　　　　　　　　　　　　　　　　　　　　　）

5 ▸ 各設問のキーワードを言い換えている表現を、パラグラフの流れを把握しながら探す（is inferred、is impliedなどあいまいな設問は選択肢も参照）

　1.の言い換え（　　　　　　　　　　　　　　　　　　　　　　）

　2.の言い換え（　　　　　　　　　　　　　　　　　　　　　　）

6 ▸ 候補の個所を見つけたら、その近辺を熟読する

　熟読個所を指で押さえ、確認のため下線を引こう（実際のテストでは、問題冊子に書き込みはできないので注意）

7 ▸ 候補個所の内容を記述し（言い換え）ている選択肢を確定する

　1.の解答 Ⓐ Ⓑ Ⓒ Ⓓ　　2.の解答 Ⓐ Ⓑ Ⓒ Ⓓ

4日目

GO ON TO THE NEXT PAGE ▶

Questions 3-5 refer to the following letter.

September 21

Mr. Peter Rutherford
Northeastern Fine Arts Institute
3726 Ashford Drive
Grover, MA   01973

Dear Mr. Rutherford,

Thank you very much for your invitation to participate once again in the institute's municipal charity art auction on October 23, commemorating the 15th anniversary of the founding of the institute. Unfortunately, I will be unable to be in attendance at this year's event since I will be in London on that day to chair an international conference on environmental issues. I do hope that my absence will not pose any inconvenience, and I remain eager to participate in subsequent events — either in person or online — as my schedule permits.

As you know, I am an enthusiastic supporter of the arts in general and of your tireless work for our local fine arts community in particular. I am therefore enclosing a check for $5,000 with this letter to upgrade my membership in the Institute from Contributing Subscriber to Gold Circle Patron. As always, I appreciate your discretion in enabling my donations to remain in the "Anonymous" column in all published listings of donations (i.e., newsletters, art show programs and online communications.)

Please accept my apologies for my inability to attend this year's auction, but be assured of my enduring appreciation and support for your great work.

Sincerely,

Elouise Templeton-Hayes

3. Who most likely is Elouise Templeton-Hayes?
   (A) A popular painter of portraits
   (B) A local realtor
   (C) A specialist in environmental science
   (D) An organizer of an auction

4. What can be inferred from the letter?
   (A) The institute was established two decades ago.
   (B) Ms. Templeton-Hayes has attended a previous auction.
   (C) A newsletter is being prepared for enthusiastic movie fans.
   (D) The institute's Web site needs to be redesigned.

5. Which statement about Ms. Templeton-Hayes is NOT true?
   (A) She is increasing the amount of her regular contribution.
   (B) She is satisfied with the work that the institute has been doing.
   (C) She wants her donations to be made public.
   (D) She intends to participate in future auctions.

解答ステップ

1 ▶ 冒頭の指示文から<u>文書のタイプ</u>を確認（　　　　　　　　　　　　　）

2 ▶ タイトル、ヘッダー、あて先、差出人、件名、最初のパラグラフの1、2文目、最後のパラグラフの末尾などを見て、<u>誰から誰あて</u>で<u>趣旨・目的</u>は何かを把握
　（　　　　　　　　　　）から（　　　　　　　　　　）あて
　趣旨・目的は（　　　　　　　　　　　　　　　　　　　　　）

3 ▶ レイアウトの<u>目立つ個所に注目</u>し、どこに何が書かれているか把握
　特にないのでこのステップはパス

4 ▶ 全設問に目を通し、問われているポイントから文書の<u>要点</u>を把握。解答の順番を決める
　3.のキーワード（　　　　　　　　　　　　　　　　　　　）
　4.のキーワード（　　　　　　　　　　　　　　　　　　　）
　5.のキーワード（　　　　　　　　　　　　　　　　　　　）

5 ▶ 各設問のキーワードを<u>言い換えている表現を、パラグラフの流れを把握しながら探す</u>
　（あいまいな設問は選択肢も参照）
　3.の言い換え（　　　　　　　　　　　　　　　　　　　）
　4.の言い換え（　　　　　　　　　　　　　　　　　　　）
　5.の言い換え（　　　　　　　　　　　　　　　　　　　）

6 ▶ 候補の個所を見つけたら、その<u>近辺を熟読</u>する
　指で押さえ、確認のためそれぞれの熟読個所に下線を引く

7 ▶ 候補個所の内容を記述し<u>（言い換え）ている選択肢</u>を確定する
　3.の解答 Ⓐ Ⓑ Ⓒ Ⓓ　　4.の解答 Ⓐ Ⓑ Ⓒ Ⓓ　　5.の解答 Ⓐ Ⓑ Ⓒ Ⓓ

GO ON TO THE NEXT PAGE

Questions 6-8 refer to the following article.

Travelers looking to go on vacation by car this summer can look forward to more reasonable gasoline prices, according to a survey by Skinner Business Research. The survey of 7,500 gasoline stations across the United States indicated that retail prices have dropped an average of 9.9 cents per gallon over the past three months, with no signs of an impending return to the high prices that had been setting records for the previous three quarters. The lowest statewide average price for regular unleaded gasoline was found in Oklahoma, while the highest prices were recorded in Hawaii. Despite this good news, however, analysts say the lower gasoline prices do not directly affect the fuel surcharges that airlines add to airfares. So no reductions in the surcharges are expected until autumn.

6. What is mentioned about the gasoline prices in the market?
   (A) It has been predicted that they will gradually increase.
   (B) The retail prices have dropped over the last three months.
   (C) The wholesale prices are expected to increase within three months.
   (D) The retail prices decreased over the previous three quarters.

7. According to the article, what is indicated about the situations in Oklahoma and Hawaii?
   (A) The average price for regular leaded gasoline was lowest in Oklahoma.
   (B) The highest gasoline prices were posted in Hawaii.
   (C) The gasoline prices remained stable in both states.
   (D) Hawaiians suffered from outrageous gasoline prices.

8. What is inferred about the surcharges?
   (A) They might be reduced next season.
   (B) Airlines are making great efforts to minimize their running costs.
   (C) The state government has implemented new regulations for surcharges.
   (D) An extensive survey of the surcharges will be conducted in autumn.

解答ステップ

1 ▶ 冒頭の指示文から文書のタイプを確認（　　　　　　　　　　　　）

2 ▶ タイトル、ヘッダー、あて先、差出人、件名、最初のパラグラフの1、2文目、最後のパラグラフの末尾などを見て、誰から誰あてで趣旨・目的は何かを把握
（　　　　　　　　　　　）から（　　　　　　　　　　　）あて
趣旨・目的は（　　　　　　　　　　　　　　　　　　　　　　　）

3 ▶ レイアウトの目立つ個所に注目し、どこに何が書かれているか把握
特にないのでこのステップはパス

4 ▶ 全設問に目を通し、問われているポイントから文書の要点を把握。解答の順番を決める
6.のキーワード（　　　　　　　　　　　　　　　　　　　　　）
7.のキーワード（　　　　　　　　　　　　　　　　　　　　　）
8.のキーワード（　　　　　　　　　　　　　　　　　　　　　）

5 ▶ 各設問のキーワードを言い換えている表現を、パラグラフの流れを把握しながら探す
（あいまいな設問は選択肢も参照）
6.の言い換え（　　　　　　　　　　　　　　　　　　　　　）
7.の言い換え（　　　　　　　　　　　　　　　　　　　　　）
8.の言い換え（　　　　　　　　　　　　　　　　　　　　　）

6 ▶ 候補の個所を見つけたら、その近辺を熟読する
指で押さえ、確認のためそれぞれの熟読個所に下線を引く

7 ▶ 候補個所の内容を記述し（言い換え）ている選択肢を確定する
6.の解答 Ⓐ Ⓑ Ⓒ Ⓓ　7.の解答 Ⓐ Ⓑ Ⓒ Ⓓ　8.の解答 Ⓐ Ⓑ Ⓒ Ⓓ

4日目

解答行動分析リスト

Part 3 と同様に、不正解の原因を次ページからの解答の横の [ ] に記入しよう。

❶ ビジネス文書の文脈がよくわからなかった
❷ 慣れていない文書タイプだった
❸ 文書タイプや誰から誰あてか、趣旨・目的をチェックしなかった
❹ 文書の内容を勘違いした
❺ 設問のポイントがすぐにわからなかった
❻ 選択肢の縦読みをしなかった
❼ 設問の意味を誤解した
❽ 設問を解く順番を間違えた
❾ 長い選択肢のポイント把握に時間がかかった
❿ 選択肢に知らない語句があってうろたえた
⓫ 選択肢を2つに絞った後、迷ってしまった
⓬ 選択肢の内容を勘違いした
⓭ 理由・依頼を示す表現など、設問にかかわるキーワードに注意しなかった
⓮ NOT問題を消去法で解かなかった
⓯ 同義語をすぐに選んでしまった
⓰ チャンク単位で読むのに不慣れだった
⓱ メリハリがない文書の要点把握が難しかった
⓲ ヒントの個所がなかなか見つけられなかった
⓳ 言い換えに気づかなかった
⓴ どちらの文書を読めばよいか迷った
㉑ 文書を読むのに時間をかけすぎた
㉒ 熟読しすぎた
㉓ 完ぺきに理解しようとしすぎた
㉔ 知らない語彙に悩みすぎた
㉕ 理解するため文書を何度も読んでしまった
㉖ 1問に時間をかけすぎた
㉗ 正解を絞り切れずに迷った
㉘ 全問正解にこだわってしまった
㉙ 前の問題をひきずって切り替えられなかった
㉚ 集中力の欠如
㉛ 時間が足りず、適当にマークした
㉜ マークの塗り間違え
㉝ パニックに陥った

Practiceの正解と解説

不正解もしくは解答に時間がかかった設問は、左ページのリストを参照して解答行動を分析しよう。なお、英文の訳はチャンクで区切られているので、後で音読する際に参照すること。

問題1-2は次の広告に関するものです。

Dashboard Car Rental社
では、経験のある管理人員を求めています / Wayne中央空港の最先端を行く新店舗の運営をするための。// 外部からの応募者と社内からの候補者の両方に、出世コースに当たるこれら2つの職に関して同等の考慮がなされます。// 採用される応募者はやる気のある経験豊富な管理者でしょう / 大勢のスタッフを取り仕切る能力があり / 顧客サービスに重点を置く業界で / そして、社内での昇進にも熱意があるでしょう。// 標準的な顧客向け車両モデルに関する知識は / とりわけ有利になるでしょう。// 2度の審査面接を通過した応募者は / 3週間の訓練プログラムへの参加が認められます。// 優遇された、交渉可能な報酬が / 最も優れた応募者には提示されるでしょう。//

●**解答ステップの解答例**
1 広告 **2** レンタカー会社から求職者あて、目的は求人 **4** 1. What、appears、most important qualification、position、2. What、offer **5～7**は解説を参照

1. この職にとって最も重要な資質は何と思われるか。
(A) 顧客サービススタッフを管理・監督する能力
(B) ビデオ広告の製作における幅広い経験
(C) 顧客が法契約用語を理解するのを助ける能力
(D) 定期保守のため車両検査する知識

解説 most important qualificationの言い換えは、タイトル直後のIs looking for experienced administrative personnelと、The successful applicants以降の部分。capable of managing a large staffが (A) と一致する。Knowledge of standard consumer vehicle modelsは特に有利になるとあるが、選択肢に入っていない。

解答 (A) 解答行動の分析 [   ]

2. 広告ではどんな申し出がされているか。
(A) 新車の割引
(B) 昇進の可能性
(C) 福利厚生
(D) フレックスタイム制

解説 offerを言い換えているのはBoth external applicantsの後のbe given equal consideration for these two career-track positionsの部分。ここでのcareerは職業上の成功、出世のことだ。be on the road to a successful[prosperous] career、be on the path to promotion、be on the first trackなども「出世街道にいること」を表す表現。

解答 (B) 解答行動の分析 [   ]

問題3-5は次の手紙に関するものです。

9月21日 // Peter Rutherford様 // Northeastern美術館 // 3726 Ashford Drive // Grover, MA　01973 // Rutherford様 //

お誘いありがとうございます / 貴館で市が開催するチャリティー美術品オークションに再度参加するようにとの / 10月23日に / 貴館創設15周年を記念して。// 残念ながら、私は今年の催しには参加できないでしょう / というのも、その日はロンドンに行く予定なので / 国際会議の議長をするために / 環境問題に関する。// 強く願います / 私の欠席によって何も不都合が生じないことを / そして、今後の催しにぜひ参加したいという気持ちに変わりはありません / 直接であれ、オンラインであれ、私のスケジュールが許せば。// ご存じのとおり、私は芸術一般の熱烈な後援者です / そして、とりわけ地域の美術界のための貴館のたゆまぬ努力への。// ですから5000ドルの小切手をこの手紙に同封しています / 貴館における私の会員ランクを上げるために / 賛助会員からゴールドサークル後援会員へと。// いつも通り / ご配慮くださると助かります / 私の寄付分は「匿名」欄内にとどめていただけるように / 寄付の掲載リストすべてにおいて（すなわち、会報、美術展プログラム、オンライン通信）。// おわび申し上げます / 今年のオークションに参加できないことを / ですが、貴館の努力に対する私の感謝と支援は今後も続きますのでご安心ください。// 敬具 // Elouise Templeton-Hayes //

● 解答ステップの解答例

1 手紙　**2** Elouise Templeton-HayesからPeter Rutherfordあて、目的は招待を断ること
4 3. Who、Elouise Templeton-Hayes　4. What、inferred、letter　5. Which statement、Ms. Templeton-Hayes、NOT true　**5〜7**は解説を参照

3. Elouise Templeton-Hayesは何者だと思われるか。
(A) 人気のある肖像画家
(B) 地元の不動産業者
(C) 環境科学の専門家
(D) オークションの主催者

解説 Unfortunatelyの後に to chair an international conference on environmental issues とある。これが(C)の言い換えに当たる。
解答 (C) 解答行動の分析 [　　　]

4. この手紙から何が言えるか。
(A) この機関は20年前に設立された。
(B) Templeton-Hayesさんは過去のオークションに参加したことがある。
(C) 会報誌は熱心な映画ファンのために用意されている。
(D) この施設のウェブサイトはデザイン変更が必要である。

解説 選択肢(B)の attended a previous auction の言い換えに当たるのが、本文冒頭の participate once again in the institute's municipal charity art auction の部分。過去に参加したことがあるとわかる。
解答 (B) 解答行動の分析 [　　　]

5. Templeton-Hayesさんについて、正しくない文はどれか。
(A) 定期的な寄付額を増やした。
(B) 機関が行う業務に満足している。
(C) 自分の寄付を公にしたがっている。
(D) 今後のオークションに参加する意思がある。

解説 選択肢(C)の wants her donations to be made public が、第2パラグラフ後半の enabling my donations to remain in the "Anonymous" column と矛盾するので、正解となる。
解答 (C) 解答行動の分析 [　　　]

問題6-8は次の記事に関するものです。

この夏、自動車で休暇に出かけようとしている旅行者は / よりお手ごろなガソリン価格が期待できる / Skinner Business Researchの調査によると。// この、アメリカ全土のガソリンスタンド7500カ所の調査は / 小売価格が1ガロン当たり平均9.9セント下落したことを示している / 過去3カ月の間に / 差し当たって高値に戻る兆候もなく / それ(高値)は過去3四半期にわたって記録を更新してきた。// レギュラー無鉛ガソリンの州全体での平均価格の最低は / Oklahomaで見られた / 一方で、最高価格はHawaiiで記録された。// しかしながら、このうれしいニュースにもかかわらず / アナリストたちは低下したガソリン価格は燃料サーチャージには直接影響を与えないと言う / 航空会社が航空運賃に加算する。// よって、秋まではサーチャージの減額は期待できない。//

● 解答ステップの解答例

1 記事 **2** 記者から読者あて、趣旨はガソリン価格 **4** 6. What、mentioned、gasoline prices、7. what、indicated、situations、Oklahoma、Hawaii、8. What、inferred、surcharges **5**～**7**は解説を参照

6. ガソリンの市場価格について何と言及されているか。
(A) 徐々に上昇すると予想されてきた。
(B) 小売価格はここ3カ月で下落した。
(C) 卸売価格は3カ月以内の上昇が予想されている。
(D) 小売価格は過去3四半期の間に下落した。

解説 選択肢(B)のdropped over the last three monthsと同じことを言っているのが、記事前半のretail prices have dropped ... over the past three monthsの個所だ。
解答 (B) 解答行動の分析 [   ]

7. 記事によると、OklahomaとHawaiiの状況について何が示されているか。
(A) レギュラー有鉛ガソリンの平均価格はOklahomaが最低だった。
(B) ガソリンの最高価格はHawaiiで公表された。
(C) 両州のガソリン価格に変動はない。
(D) Hawaii州民は法外なガソリン価格に苦しんだ。

解説 設問のキーワードである地名に注目。選択肢(B)のThe highest gasoline prices ... in Hawaiiと、記事後半のthe highest prices were recorded in Hawaiiは同じ内容を表す。
解答 (B) 解答行動の分析 [   ]

8. サーチャージについて何が示唆されているか。
(A) 次シーズンに減額されそう。
(B) 航空会社は運営経費を最小限に抑えるため大変な努力をしている。
(C) 州政府はサーチャージに対する新たな規制法を施行した。
(D) 秋にはサーチャージの広範な調査が実施されるだろう。

解説 サーチャージにふれているのは最後の部分。no reductions in the surcharges are expected until autumnが、選択肢(A)のreduced next seasonの言い換えになっている。冒頭にthis summerとあるので、次の季節は秋。
解答 (A) 解答行動の分析 [   ]

いよいよ音読を開始しよう！

Task 1

それでは音読に挑戦する。まず、**1)** 英文のすべての区切り (/ と / と //) で区切って音読しよう (**短いチャンク**)。意味をつかみながら読めるようになったら、今度は / で区切らずに**長いチャンク**に挑戦。**2)** トラック22〜24の音声のポーズの部分でリズミカルにリピートしよう (音声は文書のみ)。**3)** きちんとリピートできるようになったら、仕上げに**すべての英文を**長いチャンクで音読しよう。

1. What appears to be the most important qualification / for the position? //
   (A) Skill in organizing and supervising customer service staff //
   (B) <u>Extensive experience / in producing</u> video advertisements //
   (C) <u>An ability to help customers / understand</u> legal contract language //
   (D) <u>Knowledge of inspecting vehicles</u> / for regular maintenance //

2. What offer is made in the advertisement? //
   (A) Discount of new vehicles // (B) Possibility of promotion //
   (C) Fringe benefits // (D) Flextime //

CD 1-22

Dashboard Car Rental /
Is looking for experienced administrative personnel /
to manage its new state-of-the-art location at Wayne Central Airport. //
Both external applicants and candidates / from within the company /
will be given equal consideration / for these two career-track positions. //
<u>The successful applicants / will be highly motivated and experienced administrators, /
capable of managing a large staff / in an industry stressing customer service /
and eager to advance within the company.</u> //
Knowledge of standard consumer vehicle models /
will be a distinct advantage. //
Applicants who successfully complete two rounds of screening interviews /
will be accepted into a three-week training program. //
Competitive, negotiable compensation / will be offered to the best applicants. //

要注意フレーズ

No. 1の選択肢は求人広告の中にも登場する必須フレーズなので、しっかりと音読しよう。トークの中では、長い文だが、The successful applicants ... within the company. を、暗唱できるまで口に出してみよう。必須フレーズ満載の文だ。

3. Who most likely is Elouise Templeton-Hayes? //
   (A) A popular painter of portraits // (B) A local realtor //
   (C) A specialist in environmental science // (D) An organizer of an auction //

4. What can be inferred from the letter? //
   (A) The institute was established two decades ago. //
   (B) Ms. Templeton-Hayes has attended a previous auction. //
   (C) A newsletter is being prepared for enthusiastic movie fans. //
   (D) The institute's Web site needs to be redesigned. //

5. Which statement about Ms. Templeton-Hayes is NOT true? //
   (A) She is increasing the amount of her regular contribution. //
   (B) She is satisfied with the work that the institute has been doing. //
   (C) She wants her donations to be made public. //
   (D) She intends to participate in future auctions. //

1-23

Dear Mr. Rutherford, /

Thank you very much for your invitation / <u>to participate once again in the institute's municipal charity art auction</u> / on October 23, / <u>commemorating the 15th anniversary</u> of the founding of the institute. // Unfortunately, / I will be unable to be in attendance at this year's event / since I will be in London on that day / to <u>chair an international conference</u> / on environmental issues. // I do hope / that my absence will not pose any inconvenience, / and I remain eager to participate in subsequent events / — either in person or online — as my schedule permits. //

As you know, / I am an enthusiastic supporter of the arts in general / and of your tireless work for our local fine arts community in particular. // I am therefore enclosing a check for $5,000 with this letter / to <u>upgrade my membership</u> in the Institute / from Contributing Subscriber to Gold Circle Patron. // As always, / <u>I appreciate your discretion / in enabling my donations to remain</u> in the "Anonymous" column / in all published listings of donations / (i.e., newsletters, art show programs and online communications.) //

<u>Please accept my apologies</u> / for my inability to attend this year's auction, / but <u>be assured of my enduring appreciation</u> and support for your great work. //

Sincerely, / Elouise Templeton-Hayes //

要注意フレーズ!

このトークには、TOEIC に頻出の長めのフレーズが数多く含まれている。下線部の表現をセットとして覚えるつもりで音読しよう。

6. What is mentioned about the gasoline prices in the market? //
   (A) It has been predicted / that they will gradually increase. //
   (B) The retail prices have dropped over the last three months. //
   (C) The wholesale prices <u>are expected to increase</u> within three months. //
   (D) The retail prices decreased <u>over the previous three quarters</u>. //

7. According to the article, / what is indicated about the situations in Oklahoma and Hawaii? //
   (A) The average price for regular leaded gasoline / was lowest in Oklahoma. //
   (B) The highest gasoline prices were posted in Hawaii. //
   (C) The gasoline prices <u>remained stable</u> in both states. //
   (D) Hawaiians <u>suffered from</u> outrageous gasoline prices. //

8. What is inferred about the surcharges? //
   (A) They might be reduced next season. //
   (B) Airlines are making great efforts / to minimize their running costs. //
   (C) The state government has <u>implemented new regulations</u> for surcharges. //
   (D) An extensive survey of the surcharges will be conducted in autumn. //

CD 1-24 🇬🇧

Travelers looking to go on vacation by car this summer /
can look forward to more reasonable gasoline prices, /
according to a survey by Skinner Business Research. //
The survey of 7,500 gasoline stations / across the United States /
indicated that retail prices have dropped an average of 9.9 cents per gallon /
over the past three months, / <u>with no signs of an impending return to the high prices</u> /
that had been setting records for the previous three quarters. //
The lowest statewide average price for regular unleaded gasoline /
was found in Oklahoma, / while the highest prices were recorded in Hawaii. //
Despite this good news, however, / analysts say /
the lower gasoline prices <u>do not directly affect the fuel surcharges</u> /
that airlines add to airfares. //
So <u>no reductions in the surcharges</u> / are expected until autumn. //

要注意フレーズ!

選択肢にもニュースの部分にも、物価の高低やそれに連動した動きに関する表現が数多く盛り込まれている。下線部のフレーズを繰り返し音読して、耳で聞いたときもすぐに理解できるようになろう。

Task 2

CD 1-22~24

CDの音声を聞いて、ポーズの部分で**各チャンクの意味を頭に浮かべよう**（同時通訳の要領で声に出しても可）。ひと通り聞いて、ポーズの間に意味が浮かばなければ、69~71ページの訳をチェックしよう。

Task 3

CD 1-22~24

CDの音声を聞き、**スクリプトを見ないで**ポーズの部分でリズミカルにリピートしよう。

Task 4

CD 1-25~27

仕上げに、スクリプトを見ながらトラック25~27の音声に**オーバーラップさせて読んでみよう**。タイミングが合うまで繰り返して、ナチュラルスピードでの音読に慣れよう。

Task 5

CD 1-25~27

本日の学習を終えた後も、これらのトラックをスクリプトを見ないで聞いて理解できるか、繰り返し確認するようにしよう。

学習エネルギーをチャージする今日の **格言**

> **If we did all the things we are capable of doing, we would literally astonish ourselves.**
>
> Thomas Edison
> （1847~1931：アメリカの発明家、起業家）
>
> **もしわれわれが自分の能力でできることをすべてやったなら、文字通り自分自身に驚愕するだろう。**

Part 7 基本音読

5日目 / 20

今日は、Part 7 の壁の1つであるダブルパッセージ問題に挑戦する。2つの文書を読んで5つの設問に解答するこの形式の、正解のコツを身に付けよう。

Task 1

78〜79ページにある1〜8のステップに従って、(　　) に解答を書き入れながらダブルパッセージ問題に挑戦しよう。

Questions 1-5 refer to the following e-mails.

From: Lydia Rolling <lydrol@eversconsulting.com>
To: Thomas Greene <tgreene@billneting.com>
Subject: Visit

Thank you for your visit yesterday. It was a pleasant surprise to speak in person. I think we were able to clear up a few nagging uncertainties regarding the plan to take a second look at the relationship between our two companies. There was one question that I neglected to ask you. As you know, our information technology and advertising departments currently provide your company with two separate teams of advisors. Each team has its own separate contract and works under separate terms and conditions. As our company moves forward with our reorganization, we would like to integrate these contracts into a single, simplified agreement with a standardized set of conditions. Would you prefer to do this immediately by canceling the current contracts and immediately concluding a new agreement, or wait until they expire two years from now? No immediate decision is needed on this. But it is something that we will need to discuss eventually. I look forward to talking to you again soon.

From: Thomas Greene <tgreene@billneting.com>
To: Lydia Rolling <lydrol@eversconsulting.com>
Subject: Re: Visit

My personal inclination is to opt for your first suggestion. But past experience has shown that it would pose problems for us. Our IT and advertising departments operate very independently, and will very likely have conflicting ideas on how to reorganize their contractual agreements. My advice is therefore to wait for the current contracts to expire. In the meantime, I will start discussions with our IT and advertising departments to come up with a list of areas in which they can agree on new standard contractual terms, and areas in which further negotiations will be necessary. For the time being, please allow me to be your sole contact at our company. I think this will help us keep the process from growing too complicated.

1. What is the purpose of the first e-mail?
   (A) To request revision of the manuscripts
   (B) To cancel an appointment
   (C) To provide an itinerary
   (D) To ask for an opinion

2. What can be inferred from the e-mail exchange?
   (A) Mr. Greene's experience contradicts his personal preference.
   (B) Both Mr. Greene and Ms. Rolling run their own businesses.
   (C) Ms. Rolling is responsible for development of new products.
   (D) Ms. Rolling often visits Mr. Greene on business.

3. When does Mr. Greene think the change should be made?
   (A) This year
   (B) Next year
   (C) In two years
   (D) In five years

4. What does Mr. Greene request Ms. Rolling to avoid?

(A) Discussing the matter with his colleagues
(B) Breaching the latest contract
(C) Signing contracts with other companies
(D) Leaking information to the media

Ⓐ Ⓑ Ⓒ Ⓓ ☐

5. What is indicated about the future?

(A) Mr. Greene's company will merge with Ms. Rolling's company.
(B) Ms. Rolling's department will be split into two divisions.
(C) The two companies will hire the same consulting firm.
(D) Cooperation between the two departments migh be required.

Ⓐ Ⓑ Ⓒ Ⓓ ☐

解答ステップ

1 ▶ 文書タイプを確認：（　　　　　）と（　　　　　　）（冒頭指示文から）

2 ▶ 文書の概要を把握

・①誰から（差出人）　②誰あて（受取人）　③趣旨・目的（件名）をチェック
・タイトル、ヘッダー、レイアウト（小見出し、個条書き、大文字、囲み、イタリック体など）、最初のパラグラフの1、2文目、最後のパラグラフの終わりの1、2文などをチェック

文書1：（　　　　　　　　　）から（　　　　　　　　　）あて
　　　　趣旨・目的は（　　　　　　　　　　　　　　　　　　　　　　　　）

文書2：（　　　　　　　　　）から（　　　　　　　　　）あて
　　　　趣旨・目的は（　　　　　　　　　　　　　　　　　　　　　　　　）

3 ▶ 両文書の関係を把握

（　　　　　　　　　　　　　　　　　　　　　　　　　　　　　　　　）

4 ▶ 要点を把握

・各設問にざっと目を通し、キーワードから要点を把握
・設問で問われているポイントから文書の要点を把握
・問題を解く順番を決定（NOTタイプは最後に解くなど）

1. のキーワード（　　　　　　　　　　　　　　　　　　　）
2. のキーワード（　　　　　　　　　　　　　　　　　　　）

3. のキーワード（　　　　　　　　　　　　　　　　　　　　　　　　　）

4. のキーワード（　　　　　　　　　　　　　　　　　　　　　　　　　）

5. のキーワード（　　　　　　　　　　　　　　　　　　　　　　　　　）

5 ▶ 設問を解くヒントとなる個所を検索
- 各設問のキーワードを言い換えている表現やヒントを、各パラグラフの1、2文を読んで要点を把握しながら、文書中から探す
- According to ... やin the ....、人物・組織名などからどちらの文書（あるいは両文書）を参照するか判断（短い、または読みやすいほうの文書全体を先にざっと読んでおくと判断しやすい）
- パラグラフがない文書は、最初の1、2文と最後の文をしっかり読んだ後、各文のキーワードを意識しながら、全文に素早く目を通す

1. のヒント・言い換え（　　　　　　　　　　　　　　　　　　　　　）

2. のヒント・言い換え（　　　　　　　　　　　　　　　　　　　　　）

3. のヒント・言い換え（　　　　　　　　　　　　　　　　　　　　　）

4. のヒント・言い換え（　　　　　　　　　　　　　　　　　　　　　）

5. のヒント・言い換え（　　　　　　　　　　　　　　　　　　　　　）

6 ▶ ヒントの候補を熟読・比較
候補の個所とその近辺を熟読する。候補が複数ある場合は、設問のキーワードを参考に、読んだ内容を比較して最適な個所を絞り込む。

それぞれの熟読個所を指で押さえ、下線を引こう（実際の試験では引けないので注意）

7 ▶ 候補個所の内容を記述している選択肢を選ぶ

1. の解答　Ⓐ Ⓑ Ⓒ Ⓓ　　2. の解答　Ⓐ Ⓑ Ⓒ Ⓓ　　3. の解答　Ⓐ Ⓑ Ⓒ Ⓓ

4. の解答　Ⓐ Ⓑ Ⓒ Ⓓ　　5. の解答　Ⓐ Ⓑ Ⓒ Ⓓ

8 ▶ 語彙問題は文脈をチェックし、使われている意味で判断する
今回はないのでこのステップは不要

Task 1 の正解と解説

問題1-5は次のメールに関するものです。

文書1
送信者：Lydia Rolling <lydrol@eversconsulting.com> //
あて先：Thomas Greene <tgreene@billneting.com> //
件名：ご訪問 //
昨日はご訪問ありがとうございました。// 直接お話しできたのはうれしい驚きでした。// 付きまとっていたいくつかの不安要素を解決することができたと思います / 2社の関係を見直す計画に関する。// お尋ねし忘れたご質問が1つありました。// ご存じのとおり、弊社の情報技術部と広告部は / 現在、御社に2つの別々のアドバイザーチームを派遣しております。// 各チームはそれぞれ別々に契約し、お仕事をしております / 別々の契約条件下で。// 弊社は組織再編成を進めているため / これらの契約を統合したいと思っております / 諸条件を共通化した、1つの簡素化した契約に。// すぐにそうなさりたいですか / 現在の契約を解除して、すぐに新しい契約を結ぶことで / それとも、今から2年後に契約期限が切れるのを待ちますか。// この件はすぐに判断していただく必要はありません。// しかし、いずれは話し合う必要が出てくる事項です。// また近々お話しできるのを楽しみにしております。//

文書2
送信者：Thomas Greene <tgreene@billneting.com> //
あて先：Lydia Rolling <lydrol@eversconsulting.com> //
件名：Re：ご訪問 //
私の個人的な意向としては、あなたの最初のご提案に従いたいところです。// しかし、過去の経験が示しています / それでは当社に問題が生じそうだと。// 当社の情報技術部と広告部は非常に独立した活動をしています / ですから相いれない意見を持っている可能性が非常に高いのです / 契約内容をどう組み直すかについて。// したがって、現在の契約が期限を迎えるまで待つことをお勧めします。// その間に / 私は自社の情報技術部および広告部と話し合いを始めます / 新しい共通契約条項で彼らが同意できる分野のリストを考え出すために / また、さらなる交渉が必要となりそうな分野とを。// 当面の間は / 私を御社からの唯一の連絡窓口とさせてください。// こうすれば、手順が複雑になりすぎるのを防ぐのに役立つと思います。//

● **解答ステップの解答例**
1 メール、メール **2** 文書1: Lydia RollingからThomas Greeneあて、Greeneが来社したことへの感謝、文書2: Thomas GreeneからLydia Rollingあて、懸念事項の指摘 **3** RollingからGreeneへの問い合わせに対し、Greeneが助言している **4** 1. What, purpose, first e-mail、2. What, inferred, e-mail exchange、3. When, Mr. Greene, change、4. What, Mr. Greene, request, avoid、5. What, indicated, future **5〜7**は解説を参照。

1. 最初のメールの目的は何か。
　(A) 原稿の書き直しを頼むこと
　(B) 面会予約をキャンセルすること
　(C) 旅程表を渡すこと
　(D) 意見を求めること

解説 最初のメールの「目的」を問う全体情報タイプの設問。There was one question that I neglected to ask you. の後、Would you prefer ... or ...? と尋ねている。これを表す選択肢はTo ask for an opinion だ。
解答 (D)

2. メールのやり取りから何が言えるか。
　(A) Greeneさんの経験は彼の個人的な好みと一致しない。
　(B) GreeneさんとRollingさんは2人とも自分で事業を経営している。
　(C) Rollingさんは新製品の開発責任者である。
　(D) Rollingさんは仕事でGreeneさんをよく訪ねている。

解説 漠然とした設問なので、解答の順番は最後に回そう。2通目のメールの冒頭My personal inclination ... past experience has shown that it would pose problems for us が、選択肢(A)のMr. Greene's experience contradicts his personal preference. に当たる。
解答 (A)

3. Greeneさんは、変更をいつすべきだと考えているか。
　(A) 今年
　(B) 来年
　(C) 2年後
　(D) 5年後

解説 設問の主語がMr. Greeneなので、2通目のメールを見る。My advice is therefore to wait for the current contracts to expire. とあるが、いつが期限か記されていないので1通目のwait until they expire two years from now を参照。
解答 (C)

4. GreeneさんはRollingさんに何を避けるよう頼んでいるか。
　(A) この件について自分の同僚と話し合うこと
　(B) 最新の契約に違反すること
　(C) ほかの会社と契約すること
　(D) 情報をメディアに漏らすこと

解説 設問の主語がMr. Greeneなので、2通目のメールを見る。For the time being, please allow me to be your sole contact at our company. の逆の意味の選択肢がDiscussing ... with his colleagues。
解答 (A)

5. 今後について何が示されているか。
　(A) Greeneさんの会社がRollingさんの会社と合併する。
　(B) Rollingさんの部署が2部門に分かれる。
　(C) 2社が同じコンサルティング会社を使う。
　(D) 2部署間の協力が必要になるかもしれない。

解説 今後に関する設問なので、2通目のメールを見る。I will start discussions ... will be necessary. を言い換えた選択肢は、Cooperation between the two departments might be required. となる。
解答 (D)

Practice

▶解答:p.86〜

Task 1の解答ステップを頭に描きながら、ダブルパッセージ問題(合計10問)に取り組もう。制限時間は**10分**。

Questions 1-5 refer to the following article and e-mail.

NEW CARDS TO BEAR PERSONAL HOLOGRAMS – WAYLAND PRINTING

By Rebecca Lewis

Wayland Printing Tech., Inc. on Thursday announced that it has developed a new technology that will make it possible for credit cards to bear three-dimensional holographic images of the cardholder. Credit cards imprinted with identification photos, and with holographic 3-D images have long been popular. But according to Wayland, this is the first time new technology has made it economical to print cards with individual 3-D holographic images generated from I.D. photos of the owner. "This brings credit card security to a new level," said Wayland Spokesperson Gina Rohr. "The images are so realistic, it really is like seeing yourself in the round right there on the card." Wayland plans to begin providing the cards to credit card companies at the end of next month.

From: Lyndon Aames <laames@wpt.com>
To: Rebecca Lewis <rlewis@btimes.com>
Subject: Recent Article

Dear Ms. Lewis,

The article printed in your August 2 morning edition regarding our new credit card technology was generally accurate and informative, and we appreciate your informing the public of this important development. The quote in the story, however, was mistakenly attributed to someone who no longer works with our company. As you no doubt remember, I was the person contacted for the story by telephone, and I recall making the statement quoted in the story.

Please be advised that although Ms. Rohr has worked with us in the past, she has not been affiliated with Wayland Printing for more than two years, and has no connection with this story. We are not demanding a printed correction, but would like to suggest that care be taken in the future to ensure proper attribution of quotes and other information associated with our company. Thank you for your kind attention in this matter.

Sincerely,
Lyndon Aames
Public Relations Department
Wayland Printing Tech., Inc.

1. According to the article, what kind of new products are mentioned?
   (A) Groceries and household items
   (B) Low-cost cards imprinted with the name of a theme park
   (C) 3-D projectors of digitalized films
   (D) State-of-the-art technology of visual authentication   Ⓐ Ⓑ Ⓒ Ⓓ

2. In the article, the word "generated" in line 7, is the closest in meaning to
   (A) created   (B) deposited
   (C) adjusted   (D) updated   Ⓐ Ⓑ Ⓒ Ⓓ

3. What does Mr. Aames point out?
   (A) The public responded to the article quickly.
   (B) Ms. Lewis forgot to confirm that an item is in stock.
   (C) His quote was incorrectly ascribed.
   (D) The stock of commodities has run short.   Ⓐ Ⓑ Ⓒ Ⓓ

4. Which of the following is NOT true?
   (A) Mr. Aames is a spokesperson for Wayland Printing Tech.
   (B) Ms. Lewis is a journalist who reports on business topics.
   (C) Ms. Rohr previously worked at Wayland Printing Tech.
   (D) Ms. Lewis' publication will be required to issue an apology.   Ⓐ Ⓑ Ⓒ Ⓓ

5. How soon will the new products be made available?
   (A) In about a week   (B) In just over a month
   (C) Some time next year   (D) Several years from now   Ⓐ Ⓑ Ⓒ Ⓓ

GO ON TO THE NEXT PAGE

Questions 6-10 refer to the following intra-office memo and e-mail.

ATTN: All Employees

This is a reminder that our companywide semiannual General Meeting is coming up in the cafeteria of the main office building at 2:00 P.M. on June 1. All employees including part-time staff will be expected to attend. Unlike previous General Meetings, in which attendance was merely recommended, you will be required to attend, and exceptions can only be made with written approval from your immediate supervisor or another qualified senior co-worker. We have decided to make these twice-yearly meetings mandatory in order to ensure that they will prove to be as productive and informative as possible. Thank you in advance for your active participation.

Connie Peters
Semiannual Meeting Planning Task Force
Human Resources Dept.

From: Ralph Anderson <randerson@winstwood.com>
To: Connie Peters <conniepeters@winstwood.com>
Subject: Draft Memo

Thank you for sending me a draft of your memo on the meeting before you decided to distribute it. It's generally a well-written memo. But I would like to make a few suggestions. During the five years that I was writing the ACC memos, I learned that the terms "General Meeting" and "main office" should be replaced with the preferred terms "All-Company Conference (or "ACC") and "corporate headquarters." There's no logical justification for this. It's just a matter of company culture, I suppose. Also, you don't need to be so specific about the place and time of day. That information may change. Simply note the date, and then be ready to respond to any requests for scheduling details that you might receive later. Together with this e-mail, I am attaching a copy of your draft in which I have underlined the parts that I suggest you should change. After making these minor edits, please go ahead and distribute it.

Sincerely,
Ralph A.

6. What is the main topic of the memo and e-mail?
    (A) A forthcoming meeting organized for all employees
    (B) The assignment of Connie Peters to a new job
    (C) An upcoming report to be written by Ralph Anderson
    (D) A debate between personnel about managerial positions

7. What procedure has to be followed if employees cannot attend the meeting?
    (A) Sending an e-mail to the chief executive officer
    (B) Participating in a follow-up session
    (C) Submitting a document of authorization to the HR department
    (D) Getting verbal agreement from a supervisor

8. How often do the ACC take place?
    (A) Once a month
    (B) Once every three months
    (C) Once every six months
    (D) Once every year

9. Why have some words in the memo been underlined?
    (A) To suggest areas that should be corrected
    (B) To show the new phrases that have been added
    (C) To point out words consistent with corporate culture
    (D) To put emphasis on the most important statements

10. Who most likely is Ralph Anderson?
    (A) A corporate lawyer checking legal matters
    (B) An editor working for a publishing house
    (C) A colleague with previous relevant experience
    (D) A chair of the committee of marketing strategies

Practiceの正解と解説

英文の訳はチャンクで区切られているので、後で音読する際に参照しよう。

問題1-5は次の記事とメールに関するものです。

文書1

新しいカードに個人のホログラムが入る——Wayland Printing // Rebecca Lewis担当 //
Wayland Printing Tech社は木曜日に発表した / 新技術を開発したと / それは可能にする / クレジットカードにカードの持ち主の3次元ホログラム画像を載せることを。// 本人確認用の写真が印刷されたクレジットカードは / また、ホログラム3D画像を載せたものも前々から一般的だった。// しかしWayland社によると / 新技術によって経済的になったのはこれが初めてだ / 個人の3Dホログラム画像入りカードを印刷するのが / 所有者の本人確認写真から作った（ホログラム画像）。//「これはクレジットカードのセキュリティーを新たな水準に引き上げます」/ Wayland社の広報担当であるGina Rohrは言った。//「画像はとても真に迫っているので / カード上の丸い部分の中に本当に自分自身がいるのを見ているようです」// Wayland社はこのカードをクレジットカード会社に供給し始めることを計画している / 来月末に。//

文書2

送信者：Lyndon Aames <laames@wpt.com> //
あて先：Rebecca Lewis <rlewis@btimes.com> //
件名：先日の記事 //

Lewis様 //
8月2日の貴紙朝刊に掲載された記事は / 弊社の新しいクレジットカード技術に関するもので / 全般に正確で有益でした / そして、この重要な開発を世間に知らしめてくださったことに感謝します。// しかしながら、記事中の引用部は / すでに弊社に勤めていない別人のものとされています。// きっと覚えていらっしゃるでしょうが / この話題の電話取材を受けたのは私でした / そして、自分が記事中に引用された発言をしたことも覚えています。// ご承知おきください、Rohrさんは過去に弊社に勤めていたことはありますが / 2年以上前からWayland Printingには在籍しておらず、/ 今回の話題にはまったく関係ありません。// 訂正記事は要求しません / しかし、今後は注意なさるよう申し上げておきたいと思います / 引用の正しい出所を確認するように / その他、弊社にかかわる情報の。// この件にご対応いただければ幸いです。//
よろしくお願いします。/ Lyndon Aames // 広報部 / Wayland Printing Tech社 //

---

1. 記事によると、どのような新製品が言及されているか。
(A) 日用家庭雑貨
(B) テーマパークの名を印刷した低コストのカード
(C) デジタルフィルムの3D映写機
(D) 最新の視覚的認証技術

解説 設問のキーワードはwhat kind、new products、mentioned。「記事の中で」とあるので、見出しとdeveloped a new technology ....、this is the first time ...の文を参照する。

解答 (D)

2. 記事中の7行目にあるgeneratedに最も意味が近いのは
(A) created（作り出した）
(B) deposited（預け入れた）
(C) adjusted（調整した）
(D) updated（情報を更新した）

解説 individual 3-D holographic images generated from I.D. photos of the ownerの文脈から判断すると、「作られる」の意なので、createdが最も近い。ほかの選択肢はいずれも適さない。
解答 (A)

---

3. Aamesさんは何を指摘しているか。
(A) 世間が記事に素早く反応した。
(B) Lewisさんは、品物の在庫を確認し忘れた。
(C) 彼の言葉が別人のものとされた。
(D) 商品の在庫がなくなった。

解説 キーワードはWhat、Mr. Aames、point out。Aamesという個人名から、すぐにe-mailを参照すると判断する。The quote in the story, however ...以降からHis quote was incorrectly ascribed.が正解とわかる。
解答 (C)

---

4. 次のうち正しくないのはどれか。
(A) AamesさんはWayland Printing Tech社の広報である。
(B) Lewisさんはビジネスの話題を伝えるジャーナリストだ。
(C) Rohrさんは以前、Wayland Printing Techで働いていた。
(D) Lewisさんの出版物は謝罪文を出す必要があるだろう。

解説 キーワードはWhich、NOT true。NOTの設問なので通常は消去法で解くが、ここでは、We are not demanding a printed correctionから直接Ms. Lewis' publication will be required to issue an apology.を選ぶことも可能だ。
解答 (D)

---

5. 新製品はいつ入手可能になるか。
(A) 約1週間後
(B) 1カ月あまり後に
(C) 来年のいつか
(D) 今から数年後

解説 設問のキーワードはHow soon、new products、made available。記事の最後の文のWayland plans to begin ... at the end of next monthから、来月入手可能だとわかる。さらにメールの中のThe article printed in your August 2 morning editionから、記事が掲載されたのが8月2日とわかるので、(A)は不可。
解答 (B)

問題6-10は次の社内連絡票とメールに関するものです。

文書1
あて先：従業員各位 /
再度お知らせします / 半年に一度の全社総会が間もなく行われます / 本社ビルのカフェテリアで / 6月1日の午後2時に。// パートタイムのスタッフを含む全従業員が / 出席することになっています。// これまでの総会とは違い / そこ（これまでの総会）では出席を勧められるだけだったのですが /（今回は）出席が必須となります / そして例外が認められるのは書面による承認がある場合だけです / 直属の上司またはそれ以外のしかるべき上級の同僚からの。// 年に2度の総会への出席義務を課すことにしたのは / 確実にするためです / それら（総会）が可能な限りの生産性と情報伝達力を発揮するように。// 積極的なご参加をよろしくお願いします。//
Connie Peters // 半期総会計画特別委員会 // 人事部

文書2
送信者：Ralph Anderson <randerson@winstwood.com> //
あて先：Connie Peters <conniepeters@winstwood.com> //
件名：連絡票草稿 //
総会に関する社内連絡票の草稿を送ってくれてありがとう / 配布しようとする前に。// 全体的によく書けた社内連絡票です。// しかし、少々提案があります。// ACCの連絡票を書いてきた5年の間に / 私は学びました /「General Meeting」と「main office」という言葉は書き換えた方がいいと / もっと好まれる「All-Company Conference（ACC）」（全社総会）と「corporate headquarters」（本社）という言葉に。// これは理屈で説明のつくものではありません。// 単なる企業文化の問題だと思います。// それから、場所と時間はそんなに詳しく書く必要はありません。// その情報には変更があるかもしれません。// 日付だけを書きましょう / そして、予定の詳細に関する要望に応じられるようにしておきましょう / 後で受けることになるかもしれません。// このメールと一緒に / あなたの草稿のコピーを添付します / その中で、変えたほうがいいと思われる個所に下線を引きました。// この小さな修正を加えたら / どうぞ配布してください。//
よろしく //
Ralph A. //

---

6. 連絡票とメールの主な話題は何か。
(A) 来るべき、全社員向けに準備された会議
(B) Connie Petersの新しい職務への任命
(C) Ralph Andersonが書く予定の今後の報告書
(D) 社員同士の、管理職に関する討論

解説 設問のキーワードはWhat、main topic、memo、e-mail。主題を問う全体情報タイプなので、一番最後に解答すると効率がいい。ただしこの2つの文書では、社員への伝達事項はすべて連絡票に書かれているので、こちらを読むだけでも解答できる。連絡票のsemiannual General Meetingがforthcoming meeting、All employees including part-time staff will be expected to attend.がorganized for all employeesに当たる。

解答 (A)

7. 従業員が会議に参加できない場合、どんな手続きをする必要があるか。
   (A) 最高経営責任者にメールを送る
   (B) 追加講習に参加する
   (C) 承認の書類を人事部に提出する
   (D) 上司から口頭で同意をもらう

> **解説** キーワードはWhat procedure、to be followed、employees、cannot attend、meeting。連絡票のexceptions can only be made ...以降と署名欄のHuman Resources Dept.から正解がわかる。
> **解答** (C)

8. ACCはどのぐらいの頻度で開かれるか。
   (A) 1カ月に1度
   (B) 3カ月に1度
   (C) 6カ月に1度
   (D) 1年に1度

> **解説** キーワードはHow often、ACC、take place。連絡票のsemiannual General Meeting、these twice-yearly meetingsと同じ意味になるのはOnce every six monthsだ。「年に2回」を表す3つの表現を頭に入れよう。
> **解答** (C)

9. 連絡票の単語のいくつかに下線が引かれていたのはなぜか。
   (A) 訂正すべき個所を提案するため
   (B) 追加された新しい語句を示すため
   (C) 企業文化に沿った単語を指摘するため
   (D) 最も重要な記述を強調するため

> **解説** キーワードはWhy、words、memo、underlined。今度はメールを参照する。最後のI am attaching a copy of your draft in which I have underlined the parts that I suggest you should change.から解答がわかる。
> **解答** (A)

10. Ralph Andersonは誰だと思われるか。
    (A) 法律関係をチェックする企業弁護士
    (B) 出版社で働く編集者
    (C) 以前同じ立場を経験した同僚
    (D) マーケティング戦略委員長

> **解説** キーワードはWho、Ralph Anderson。Ralphはメールの送信者だ。送信者とあて先のアドレスの@以降が同じなので、社内メールだとわかる。During the five years that I was writing the ACC memosから、彼が同じ経験をもつ同僚または先輩としてアドバイスしているのは明らか。
> **解答** (C)

いよいよ音読を開始しよう！

Task 2

それでは音読に挑戦する。ダブルパッセージは長いのでここでは設問部分は省くが、以下の手順の3)の項では、設問も必ず音読するようにしよう。
まず、1) 英文をすべての区切り (/と/と//) で区切って音読したら、今度は/は省いて**長いチャンク**に挑戦。2) トラック28〜31の音声のポーズの部分でリピートしよう。3) 意味を促えながら、プロソディーを意識してスピーディーかつリズミカルにリピートできるようになったら、仕上げに設問を含む**すべての英文を**長いチャンクで音読しよう。

CD 1-28

New cards to bear personal holograms // — Wayland Printing //
By Rebecca Lewis //
Wayland Printing Tech., Inc. on Thursday announced /
that it has developed a new technology / that will make it possible /
for credit cards to bear three-dimensional holographic images of the cardholder. //
Credit cards imprinted with identification photos, /
and with holographic 3-D images / have long been popular. //
But according to Wayland, /
this is the first time / new technology has made it economical /
to print cards with individual 3-D holographic images /
generated from I.D. photos of the owner. //
"This brings credit card security to a new level," /
said Wayland Spokesperson Gina Rohr. // "The images are so realistic, /
it really is like seeing yourself / in the round right there on the card." //
Wayland plans / to begin providing the cards to credit card companies /
at the end of next month. //

CD 1-29

From: Lyndon Aames <laames@wpt.com> //
To: Rebecca Lewis <rlewis@btimes.com> // Subject: Recent Article //
Dear Ms. Lewis, // The article printed in your August 2 morning edition /
regarding our new credit card technology / was generally accurate and informative, /
and we appreciate your informing the public of this important development. //
The quote in the story, however, /
was mistakenly attributed to someone / who no longer works with our company. //
As you no doubt remember, /

<u>I was the person contacted for the story by telephone,</u> /
<u>and I recall making the statement quoted in the story.</u> // Please be advised /
that although Ms. Rohr has worked with us in the past, /
she has not been affiliated with Wayland Printing for more than two years, /
and has no connection with this story. //
We are not demanding a printed correction, /
but would like to suggest that care be taken in the future /
to ensure proper attribution of quotes /
and other information associated with our company. //
<u>Thank you for your kind attention in this matter.</u> // Sincerely, /
Lyndon Aames // Public Relations Department // Wayland Printing Tech., Inc. //

5日目

要注意フレーズ！

今回は、記事やメールの特徴である長いセンテンスを繰り返し音読し、そこに含まれる表現を身に付けよう。下線を引いた記事の見出し、カードの説明、メールでの間違いの指摘と締めくくりの言葉に注意！

CD 1-30

ATTN: All Employees //
This is a reminder /
that our companywide semiannual General Meeting is coming up /
in the cafeteria of the main office building / at 2:00 P.M. on June 1. //
All employees including part-time staff / <u>will be expected to attend</u>. //
Unlike previous General Meetings, / in which attendance was merely recommended, /
you <u>will be required to attend</u>, /
and exceptions can <u>only be made with written approval</u> /
<u>from your immediate supervisor</u> or another qualified senior coworker. //
We have decided to make these twice-yearly meetings mandatory /
in order to ensure /
that they will prove to be as productive and informative as possible. //
<u>Thank you in advance for your active participation</u>. //
Connie Peters // Semiannual Meeting Planning Task Force //
Human Resources Dept. //

From: Ralph Anderson <randerson@winstwood.com> //
To: Connie Peters <conniepeters@winstwood.com> //
Subject: Draft Memo //
Thank you for sending me a draft of your memo on the meeting /
before you decided to distribute it. //
It's generally a well-written memo. //
But I would like to make a few suggestions. //
During the five years that I was writing the ACC memos, / I learned that /
the terms "General Meeting" and "main office" should be replaced /
with the preferred terms "All-Company Conference (or "ACC") /
and "corporate headquarters." //
There's no logical justification for this. //
It's just a matter of company culture, I suppose. //
Also, you don't need to be so specific about the place and time of day. //
That information may change. //
Simply note the date, /
and then be ready to respond to any requests for scheduling details /
that you might receive later. //
Together with this e-mail, / I am attaching a copy of your draft /
in which I have underlined the parts that I suggest you should change. //
After making these minor edits, / please go ahead and distribute it. //
Sincerely, // Ralph A. //

要注意フレーズ！

連絡票のほうでは、会社が従業員に通達する際の表現、メールのほうでは、アドバイスをする表現に下線を引いている。どちらもTOEICのリーディングセクションに頻出するので、繰り返し音読しよう。

Task 3
CD 1-28〜31

CDの音声を聞いて、ポーズの部分で各チャンクの意味を頭に浮かべよう（同時通訳の要領で声に出しても可）。一通り聞いて、ポーズの間に意味が浮かばなければ、86〜89ページの訳をチェックしよう。

Task 4
CD 1-28〜31

CDの音声を聞き、スクリプトを見ないでポーズの部分でリズミカルにリピートしよう。

Task 5
CD 1-32〜35

仕上げにスクリプトを見ながら、トラック32〜35の音声にオーバーラップさせて読んでみよう。プロソディーを意識して、スピーディーかつリズミカルに読めるまで繰り返し、ナチュラルスピードでの音読に慣れよう。

Task 6
CD 1-32〜35

本日の学習を終えた後も、これらトラックをスクリプトを見ずに聞いて理解できるか、繰り返し確認するようにしよう。

5日目

学習エネルギーをチャージする今日の **格言**

Every problem is an opportunity for us to grow.
Richard David Bech
（1936〜：アメリカの作家。『カモメのジョナサン』の著者）
すべての問題は私たちが成長するための機会である。

6日目 / 20

Review & Part 1

今日は、今週5日間学習してきた内容の復習と、Part 1 攻略のコツをまとめて学ぶ。復習で定着していないとわかった会話・文書は、必ず再度音読し、CDも繰り返し聞くようにしよう。

Review : Task 1

1～5日目に学習した会話・文書の一部が空所になっているので、指定のトラックを聞いて、ディクテーション（書き取り）してみよう。トラックには会話・文書がまるごと入っているので、該当箇所を聞き逃さないよう注意しよう。

1日目

CD 1-02　▶解答はp.13参照

For Dow Chemical, _____ that can be used to make plastics. The company _____. The Algenol bioreactors _____ to burn coal more cleanly.

2日目

CD 1-13　▶解答はp.43参照

W: Yes, but I'm afraid Ms. Milton is in back-to-back meetings until 4:00 P.M. _____?

M: No, that's all right. Actually, _____ around 5:00 P.M. today. _____? I have some product samples _____ last week.

3日目　　　　　　　　　　　　　　　　　　　🔘 1-17　▶解答はp.52参照

M: I'm afraid _____ with us.
　　But we're here to attend the Insurance Industry Expo, _____
　　_____.

W: OK. In that case, _____ and
　　Robinson Street. _____.

4日目　　　　　　　　　　　　　　　　　　　🔘 1-25　▶解答はp.62参照

The successful applicants _____

_____ within the company. Knowledge of

standard consumer vehicle models _____. Applicants

_____

will be accepted into a three-week training program.

5日目　　　　　　　　　　　　　　　　　　　🔘 1-34　▶解答はp.84参照

All employees _____. Unlike

previous General Meetings, _____, you

will be required to attend, and _____

_____ or another qualified senior coworker.

Task 2

では次に、以下のトラックを聞いてシャドウイング（p.7参照）に挑戦する。プロソディーを意識し、意味を促えながらできるだけ正確にまねよう。英文を見ないで最後まできちんと再生できるか確認し、不十分な場合は繰り返し練習を。

❶ 🔘 1-32　▶解答はp.82参照　　❷ 🔘 1-10　▶解答はp.25〜26参照

Part 1 解答のポイント

テスト冊子に載っている写真に関する4つの英文を聞き、説明として最適なものを選ぶのがPart 1。英文はテスト冊子には印刷されていない。
英文が流れる前に写真を見て、目立つもの（人物、物、風景）に注目し、「だれが」「どこで」「何を」「どうしているか」を把握する。

● チェックするポイント

人（1人）：動作、状態、位置、持ち物、服装、周囲の状況

人（複数）：共通点、相違点、お互いの位置

物・風景：特徴、状態、動き、方向、お互いの位置

＊写真に写っていない人・物を含む選択肢は誤答。「見えていないけれどそうなのかも」など、想像を働かせる必要がある選択肢は選ばない。

＊具体的な表現・名称よりも、抽象的な表現や総称が正解になることが多い。

　例：a guitar ⇒ a musical instrument
　　　a microphone ⇒ a device
　　　a car ⇒ a vehicle
　　　writing a report ⇒ working on a document

＊正解として思いつく語と似た発音を含む選択肢は引っ掛けなので注意。

　例：holding / folding、walking / working

＊Part 1と2では、マークシートの選択肢Aの上に鉛筆を置いて音声を待つ。正解だと思う英文が流れたときだけ、鉛筆をその選択肢に移動させる。音声が終わった時点で鉛筆の置かれている記号を塗る。

● 高得点取得のコツ

選択肢の主語が異なる設問（10問中2、3問程度）をしっかり正解すること。視点がどんどん変わるので、主語を聞き逃さずに写真の内容と比べよう。また、頻出する名詞、動作・状態表現や位置を表す前置詞（句）は音読練習し、耳で聞いたとき瞬時にイメージできるようにしておく。

上級者でも聞き慣れない語や、判断に迷う選択肢が出題されることがある。その場合は消去法で解答するか、適当にチェックして次に進もう。気持ちを切り替えて次に集中することが重要だ。

Part 1 : Task 3

CD 1-36　▶解答：p.100〜

写真を描写する12の英文を聞いて、適切なものを選ぼう。正解は1つとは限らない。終わったら、答え合わせの前に次ページのTask 4に取り組もう。

1.

Ⓐ Ⓑ Ⓒ Ⓓ Ⓔ Ⓕ
Ⓖ Ⓗ Ⓘ Ⓙ Ⓚ Ⓛ

2.

Ⓐ Ⓑ Ⓒ Ⓓ Ⓔ Ⓕ
Ⓖ Ⓗ Ⓘ Ⓙ Ⓚ Ⓛ

3.

Ⓐ Ⓑ Ⓒ Ⓓ Ⓔ Ⓕ
Ⓖ Ⓗ Ⓘ Ⓙ Ⓚ Ⓛ

GO ON TO THE NEXT PAGE

Task 4

今、解答したTask 3に出てきた英文のディクテーションに挑戦する。英文と英文の間に10秒のポーズが設けられているので、このポーズの間に空所を埋めよう。

1. (A) One of the men is _____ the worksite.

   (B) They're _____.

   (C) They're all _____ the same _____.

   (D) Some people are _____.

   (E) People are standing _____.

   (F) The street is _____ boxes.

   (G) One of the men is _____.

   (H) The _____ is being _____.

   (I) The men are _____ some bricks.

   (J) They're _____ the _____.

   (K) They're _____ outside.

   (L) Motorbikes are _____ the wall.

2. (A) The woman's _____ some _____.

   (B) The woman's _____ the board.

   (C) The _____ is _____.

   (D) The woman's _____ her car.

   (E) Pedestrians are _____ the bridge.

   (F) Boxes are _____ on the road.

   (G) Boxes are _____ the table.

   (H) The woman's reading _____ she walks.

   (I) She's _____ the trash can.

   (J) A _____ is being _____.

(K) The woman's _____.

(L) The woman's _____ equipment.

3. (A) The seat _____.
   (B) She's standing _____.
   (C) The woman's _____ some paper.
   (D) The woman's _____ a pet.
   (E) The woman's _____ her arms.
   (F) The door is _____ _____.
   (G) She's _____ her hands.
   (H) The woman's _____ the flowers.
   (I) She's _____ the vase.
   (J) She's _____ her legs.
   (K) The clock is being _____ from the _____.
   (L) The table is _____ magazines.

Task 3 & 4の正解と解説

1.
(A) One of the men is <u>bending over</u> the worksite.
(B) They're <u>mowing the lawn</u>.
(C) They're all <u>putting on</u> the same <u>outfit</u>.
(D) Some people are <u>wearing hard hats</u>.
(E) People are standing <u>in line</u>.
(F) The street is <u>blocked by</u> boxes.
(G) One of the men is <u>directing traffic</u>.
(H) The <u>construction work</u> is being <u>carried out</u>.
(I) The men are <u>piling up</u> some bricks.
(J) They're <u>examining</u> the <u>specimen</u>.
(K) They're <u>working out</u> outside.
(L) Motorbikes are <u>lined up along</u> the wall.

(A) 男性の1人が工事現場越しに身をかがめている。
(B) 彼らは芝生を刈っている。
(C) 彼らは全員同じ服を着ようとしている。
(D) ヘルメットをかぶっている人が何人かいる。
(E) 人々が列に並んでいる。
(F) 通りが箱でふさがれている。
(G) 男性の1人は交通整理をしている。
(H) 工事作業が行われている。
(I) 男性たちはれんがを積み上げている。
(J) 彼らは標本を調べている。
(K) 彼らは屋外で運動をしている。
(L) オートバイが壁に沿って並んでいる。

解説 (A)は、工事現場で体をかがめて作業をしている男性が写っているので正解。(C)の putting onは「着る」という動作を表すので不正解。(D)のwearingは状態を表すので正解。(H) carry outは「～を実行する」で正解。(J)の標本は写っていない。(K) work outは「運動をする」。

解答 (A) (D) (H)　Task 4の解答は英文の下線部を参照

2.
(A) The woman's <u>displaying</u> some <u>produce</u>.
(B) The woman's <u>pointing at</u> the board.
(C) The <u>warehouse</u> is <u>under construction</u>.
(D) The woman's <u>fueling</u> her car.
(E) Pedestrians are <u>crossing</u> the bridge.
(F) Boxes are <u>scattered</u> on the road.
(G) Boxes are <u>stacked beside</u> the table.
(H) The woman's reading <u>as</u> she walks.
(I) She's <u>emptying</u> the trash can.
(J) A <u>traffic signal</u> is being <u>fixed</u>.
(K) The woman's <u>carrying a ladder</u>.
(L) The woman's <u>installing</u> equipment.

(A) 女性は農産物を陳列している。
(B) 女性は掲示板を指差している。
(C) 倉庫は建設中だ。
(D) 女性は車に燃料を入れている。
(E) 歩行者が橋を渡っている。
(F) 箱が路面に散らばっている。
(G) 箱がテーブルの横に重ねられている。
(H) 女性は歩きながら読んでいる。
(I) 彼女はごみ箱のごみを捨てている。
(J) 信号が修理されているところだ。
(K) 女性がはしごを運んでいる。
(L) 女性が機材を設置している。

解説 (A) produceは「農産物」。(C)建設中らしき建物は写っていない。(E)横断歩道を渡っているが橋ではない。(G) besideは「～のそばに」。(H) asは「～しながら」。本は読んでいない。(I) emptyは動詞で「～を空にする」。(K) carryは「運ぶ」で正解。(L) installは「～を設置する」。

解答 (K)　Task 4の解答は英文の下線部を参照

3. (A) The seat has been occupied.
(B) She's standing by herself.
(C) The woman's folding some paper.
(D) The woman's holding a pet.
(E) The woman's folding her arms.
(F) The door is left ajar.
(G) She's clapping her hands.
(H) The woman's watering the flowers.
(I) She's lifting the vase.
(J) She's crossing her legs.
(K) The clock is being removed from the rack.
(L) The table is cluttered with magazines.

(A) 席はふさがっている。
(B) 彼女は1人で立っている。
(C) 女性は紙を折っている。
(D) 女性はペットを抱いている。
(E) 女性は腕組みをしている。
(F) ドアが少し開いている。
(G) 彼女は拍手をしている。
(H) 女性は花に水をやっている。
(I) 彼女は花瓶を持ち上げている。
(J) 彼女は足を組んでいる。
(K) 時計は棚から外されているところだ。
(L) テーブルは雑誌で散らかっている。

解説 (D) holdは「～を抱く」の意で正解。(F) ajarは「半開きで」の意。(I) liftには「＜物＞を持っている、握っている、つかんでいる、～を抱く、～を支える」などの意味がある。

解答 (A) (D)　Task 4の解答は英文の下線部を参照

Task 5

CD 1-37

今度はCDの音声を聞いて、**スクリプトを見ないで**ポーズの部分でリピートしよう。

Task 6

CD 1-38

では仕上げに、CDから流れる日本語訳を聞いて、英語を口に出してみよう（順番はランダム）。とっさに出てこなかったら、英文の意味を確認しながら音読し、Task 5のリピートに再挑戦したり、トラック36の音声をシャドウイングしたりして定着させよう。英語力の精度を上げるため、すぐに正確に言えるようになるまで練習すること！

Task 7

▶解答：p.105〜

最後に、練習問題に挑戦しよう。各写真を描写する英文が、それぞれ8つ流れる。正しい英文の記号をすべてマークしよう。

1.

Ⓐ Ⓑ Ⓒ Ⓓ Ⓔ Ⓕ Ⓖ Ⓗ

2.

Ⓐ Ⓑ Ⓒ Ⓓ Ⓔ Ⓕ Ⓖ Ⓗ

3.

Ⓐ Ⓑ Ⓒ Ⓓ Ⓔ Ⓕ Ⓖ Ⓗ

GO ON TO THE NEXT PAGE

4.

Ⓐ Ⓑ Ⓒ Ⓓ Ⓔ Ⓕ Ⓖ Ⓗ

5.

Ⓐ Ⓑ Ⓒ Ⓓ Ⓔ Ⓕ Ⓖ Ⓗ

Task 7 の正解と解説

1.
(A) The vehicles are parked <u>across from</u> <u>each other</u>.
(B) The road is being <u>paved</u>.
(C) The car is being <u>towed</u> away.
(D) The woman's <u>pulling a cart</u>.
(E) A man's <u>unplugging</u> the electric <u>device</u>.
(F) One of the cars is being parked <u>facing the pole</u>.
(G) The <u>walkway</u> is <u>deserted</u>.
(H) The sheet is being <u>spread over</u> the bench.

(A) 車が向かい合わせに駐車されている。
(B) 道路は舗装されているところだ。
(C) 車がレッカー移動されようとしている。
(D) 女性がカートを引いている。
(E) 男性が電気器具の電源を抜いている。
(F) 1台の車がポールに向かって駐車されようとしている。
(G) 歩道には人けがない。
(H) シートがベンチに広げられようとしている。

解説 (B)道路はpavedな状態だが、現在、舗装作業が行われてはいない。(D)女性もカートも写っていない。(E)男性も電気器具も写っていない。unplugは「線を抜く」の意。(G)歩道には人がいないので正解。be desertedは「人けがない」の意。(H)のベンチは見当たらない。

解答 (G) 下線部は重要表現（以下の設問でも同様）

2.
(A) A painting is <u>hanging on</u> the wall.
(B) The garden is <u>surrounded by</u> a fence.
(C) Plants are <u>placed adjacent to</u> the stairs.
(D) People are <u>leaning over</u> the <u>railing</u>.
(E) The <u>stairs</u> are <u>crowded with</u> people.
(F) A <u>sculpture</u> is in front of the table.
(G) <u>Beverages</u> are <u>being served</u>.
(H) The man's <u>leaning on</u> the desk.

(A) 絵画が壁に掛けられようとしている。
(B) 庭は柵に囲まれている。
(C) 植物が階段のすぐそばに置かれている。
(D) 人々が手すりに寄り掛かっている。
(E) 階段は人で込み合っている。
(F) 彫刻はテーブルの正面にある。
(G) 飲み物が出されているところだ。
(H) 男性が机にもたれている。

解説 (A)絵は写っていないし、(B)庭も写っていない。(C) be adjacent to ～は、「～に隣接して」の意で正解。(D)、(E)人々は写っていない。(F)彫刻は写っていない。(G)給仕する人は写っていない。beverageは「飲み物」。serveは「～を供する」。(H)男性は写っていない。

解答 (C)

3. (A) A man's underline{addressing} the audience from the underline{podium}.
(B) People are standing underline{in a row}.
(C) People are underline{gathering} in a conference room.
(D) The hall is underline{equipped with} a lot of furniture.
(E) One of the women is underline{sweeping} the floor.
(F) The woman's underline{kneeling down} on the floor.
(G) People are underline{arranging} chairs.
(H) One of the men is underline{handing out leaflets}.

(A) 男性が演壇から聴衆に演説している。
(B) 人々が一列に並んでいる。
(C) 人々が会議室に集まっている。
(D) ホールにはたくさんの家具が備わっている。
(E) 女性の1人が床を掃いている。
(F) 女性は床にひざまずいている。
(G) 人々がいすを並べている。
(H) 男性の1人が小冊子を配っている。

解説 (A)演壇で講演している人はいない。(B)、(C)人は右端に1人しか見えず、人々は集まっていない。(D)多くの机、椅子が見えるので正解。(E)、(F)床を掃除したり床にひざまずいている女性はいない。(H)チラシを配っている男性はいない。

解答 (D)

---

4. (A) The cyclists are underline{trying on} helmets.
(B) They're underline{heading} in the same direction.
(C) underline{Pedestrians} are underline{crossing} the road.
(D) They're both underline{walking} on the underline{pier}.
(E) The motorbikes are parked at the underline{curb}.
(F) They're underline{leaning against} the fence.
(G) They're underline{working on} the instrument.
(H) Some workers are underline{digging in} the street.

(A) サイクリストたちがヘルメットを試着している。
(B) 彼らは同じ方向へ向かっている。
(C) 歩行者たちが道路を渡っている。
(D) 彼らは2人とも桟橋の上を歩いている。
(E) オートバイが歩道の縁石に止められている。
(F) 彼らはフェンスに寄り掛かっている。
(G) 彼らは道具の手入れをしている。
(H) 車道を掘っている作業員が何人かいる。

解説 (A) try onは「〜を試着する」の意。(B) head in the same direction は「同じ方向に向かう」の意味で正解。(C)歩行者は写っていない。(E) curbは「縁石」。(F)フェンスは写っていない。(G) work onは「〜に取り組む、修理をする」の意味。(H)作業員は見当たらない。

解答 (B)

5. (A) Some cargo is being unloaded into a truck.
(B) The man's refueling the vehicle.
(C) People are boarding the bus.
(D) Two motorcycles are parked side by side.
(E) The bicycle has been parked on the sidewalk.
(F) The man's putting bricks in a pile.
(G) The vendor is displaying some goods.
(H) The women are distributing handbills.

(A) 積荷がトラックに荷降ろしされようとしている。
(B) 男性は車に燃料補給をしている。
(C) 人々がバスに乗り込んでいる。
(D) 2台のオートバイが隣り合って止めてある。
(E) 自転車は歩道に止められている。
(F) 男性はれんがを山積みにしている。
(G) 露天商人は商品を並べている。
(H) 女性たちはビラを配っている。

解説 (A) unloadは「積み荷を降ろす」。(B) refuelは「燃料を補給する」の意。(D) side by sideは「並んで」の意。写っているのは2台のオートバイではなく、1台の自転車。(E) has been parkedはすでにされている状態なので正解。(F)れんがを積んでいる男性は写っていない。(G)露店商人は見当たらない。(H)ビラを配っている女性たちは見当たらない。

解答 (E)

学習エネルギーをチャージする今日の 格言

Only those who have the patience to do simple things perfectly will acquire the skill to do difficult things easily.

Friedrich von Schiller
(1759〜1805：ドイツの詩人、劇作家)
簡単なことを完ぺきにやる根気強い人たちだけが、
難しいことを難なくこなす能力を身に付ける。

Part 4 基礎トレーニング

7日目 / 20

今週は、リスニングセクションのもう1つの難関、Part 4 の学習から始める。基礎トレーニングはPart 3と同じなので、先週の学習を復習するつもりで取り組もう。

Part 4 解答のポイント

1人の人物によるトーク（説明文）と、その内容に関する3つの設問が読まれる。設問はテスト冊子に印刷されているので、**トークが始まる前に先読みして、キーワードから要点を把握しておく**ことが大切だ。以下の点に注意して、先読みとリスニングを行おう。

○設問の順番と、その設問のヒントがトークに登場する順番は同じことが多い。
○設問はPart 3と同様に、**全体情報タイプ**と**個別情報タイプ**に分けられる（p.33参照）。
○問題番号と一緒に**説明文のタイプ**が読まれるので、聞き取ること。
　例：advertisement、introduction、voice-mail、message、weather forecast、speech、talk
○**冒頭部分が最も重要**なので、確実にキャッチする（話し手、聞き手、話題、目的、場所、状況が特定できる）。
○ストーリーの流れを意識しながら、常識も働かせて理解する。
○Part 3と同様に、マークシートには軽く印を付けるだけにする（p.34参照）。

また、頻出のトピックは**公共放送**、**オリエンテーション**、**紹介**などさまざまだが、ここではハイスコア取得のため、個別情報タイプの設問を中心に、以下のトピックの強化練習をしよう。

● ツアーガイド

乗り物の中で旅の日程を伝えたり、観光地を案内したりするトーク。設問では**訪れる場所**や**時刻**、**禁止事項**、**注意事項**などが問われる。

●電話メッセージ

企業や公共機関の自動受付メッセージや、個人あての留守電では、**吹き込んだ人**と**目的**、それを**聞く人**、**聞いた人のすべきこと**が問われる。

●ニュース

企業の業績や新製品の発表、交通情報などのトークでは、**放送されている時間**、**主な話題**、**新しい点**、**聞き手への影響**が問われる。交通情報では、**工事や迂回路の場所**、**工事などが原因で特定の道路状況になる時刻**などが頻出。

●店内放送

ショッピングモールや商店の中で買い物客向けに流れる放送。その日の**目玉商品**、タイムセールや催し物の**時間・場所**などがよく問われる。

Task 1

▶解答：p.113〜

CDには、**問題番号**⇨**ポーズ1**（8秒）⇨**合図音**⇨**ポーズ2**（20秒）が収録されている。
ポーズ1で**3つの設問**を読み、**ポーズ2**で各設問のキーワードを参考に、【　】の中に「設問で問われている内容」を簡潔に記入しよう（日本語でも英語でも可）。ここでは(A)〜(D)の選択肢は気にしなくてもいい。
終わったら、**答え合わせの前に** Task 2に取り組もう。

1. What is the main topic of the report?
   (A) Relocation of a factory
   (B) Business consolidation
   (C) Corporate withdrawal
   (D) Newcomers to the industry

2. What type of company is MGC Inc.?
   (A) An auto manufacturer
   (B) A software developer
   (C) A financial service company
   (D) A local distributor

3. According to the report, what makes MGC Inc. so successful?
   (A) Its cost-cutting measures
   (B) Its development of new products
   (C) Its hiring of young people
   (D) Its marketing efforts

【1.　　　　　　　　2.　　　　　　　　　　3.　　　　　　　　　　】

4. What is the purpose of the message?
   (A) To explain conference details
   (B) To announce a schedule change
   (C) To discuss travel procedures
   (D) To request help with a marketing process

5. What is Ms. Haslett asked to do?
   (A) Discuss details with the director
   (B) Call him back immediately
   (C) Check on the documents
   (D) Inform everyone about the change

6. Why does the caller thank Ms. Haslett?
   (A) She assisted in his research.
   (B) She showed a keen interest in the project.
   (C) She contacted the airline in advance.
   (D) She provided background information.

【4.　　　　　　　5.　　　　　　　6.　　　　　　　】

7. Who most likely are the tour participants?
   (A) Food retailers
   (B) Sanitation supervisors
   (C) Newly-recruited employees
   (D) Factory Workers

8. Where will the tour begin?
   (A) The exhibit hall
   (B) The assembly line
   (C) A factory-outlet store
   (D) A lecture room

9. What will participants receive at the end of the tour?
   (A) An information package
   (B) A list of items
   (C) Freshly-baked bread
   (D) Discount coupons

【7.　　　　　　　8.　　　　　　　9.　　　　　　　】

111

選択肢のチェックポイント2

選択肢を素早く読むコツを学ぼう（**チェックポイント1**はp. 37参照）。

3. Whatで出来事などを問う設問は、主語⇒動詞＋目的語を縦読みする

What will happen on Wednesday?

(A) The CEO will visit the plant.
(B) A marketing division will be relocated.
(C) A presentation will be held.
(D) A program will change.

まず、選択肢の主語（名詞）を縦読みして違いをつかむ。次にすぐ動詞＋目的語（下線部）も縦読みする。

4. 長い選択肢は「キーワード群」を順番にチェックする

What is indicated about the project?

(A) Mr. Wallace delivered a lecture on an environmental issue.
(B) The shareholders were excited about the success of the new products.
(C) The president promised to make an additional investment.
(D) Ms. Lee has been appointed as director of finance.

長い選択肢では複数の**キーワード群**に注目する。上の例では、まず主語＋述語のセット、Mr. Wallace delivered a lectureの部分を縦読みして違いを把握、それだけで判断できない場合は、下線部にも目を通す。

Task 2

CD 1-12　▶解答：p.113～

Task 1と同じ設問を使って、選択肢を早読みする練習をする。Task 1と同じ音声を聞いて、**ポーズ1**で**3つの設問の選択肢**を読み、**ポーズ2**でポイントを示す選択肢のキーワード語句に**下線を引こう**。

Task 1&2の正解と解説

1. What is the main topic of the report?
(A) Relocation of a factory
(B) Business consolidation
(C) Corporate withdrawal
(D) Newcomers to the industry

レポートの主題は何か。
(A) 工場の移転
(B) 企業の合併
(C) 企業の撤退
(D) 業界への参入者

Task 1： 解答例 話題　全体情報タイプの設問なので、最後に解答すると効率がいい。
Task 2： 解答は赤の下線部参照。まずRelocation、consolidation、withdrawal、Newcomersを縦読みする。

---

2. What type of company is MGC Inc.?
(A) An auto manufacturer
(B) A software developer
(C) A financial service company
(D) A local distributor

MGC社はどんなタイプの会社か。
(A) 自動車メーカー
(B) ソフトウエア開発会社
(C) 金融サービス会社
(D) 地元の代理店

Task 1： 解答例 業種　頻出する設問なので、瞬時に要点がわかるようになろう。
Task 2：選択肢共通のAやAnは読まない。auto、software、financial、localと縦読みする。(D)はlocalだけでは不明確なので、distributorまでチェックする。

---

3. According to the report, what makes MGC Inc. so successful?
(A) Its cost-cutting measures
(B) Its development of new products
(C) Its hiring of young people
(D) Its marketing efforts

レポートによると、何がMGC社に大成功をもたらしているか。
(A) 経費削減策
(B) 新製品開発
(C) 若手の雇用
(D) 販売努力

Task 1： 解答例 原因・手段　「成功」等のキーワードを待ち受けながら聞く。
Task 2：選択肢共通のItsは読まない。cost-cutting、development、hiring、marketingと縦読みすれば、違いが明確になる。不明確な場合は残りの部分もすぐにチェックする。

4. What is the purpose of the message?
 (A) To explain conference details
 (B) To announce a schedule change
 (C) To discuss travel procedures
 (D) To request help with a marketing process

伝言の目的は何か。
(A) 会議の詳細を説明すること
(B) 日程の変更を知らせること
(C) 旅行の手続きを話し合うこと
(D) 販売プロセスで助けを求めること

Task 1：**解答例** 目的
Task 2：伝える内容が重要なので、toの直後の動詞を読む必要はない。

---

5. What is Ms. Haslett asked to do?
 (A) Discuss details with the director
 (B) Call him back immediately
 (C) Check on the documents
 (D) Inform everyone about the change

Haslettさんは何をするよう頼まれているか。
(A) 重役と詳細について話す
(B) 彼にすぐ電話をかけ直す
(C) 書類をチェックする
(D) 変更を全員に知らせる

Task 1：**解答例** Haslettさんへの依頼　依頼表現に注意してトークを聞く。
Task 2：まず動詞＋目的語のセットを縦読みして違いを把握する。

---

6. Why does the caller thank Ms. Haslett?
 (A) She assisted in his research.
 (B) She showed a keen interest in the project.
 (C) She contacted the airline in advance.
 (D) She provided background information.

電話をかけた人物はなぜHaslettさんに感謝しているか。
(A) 彼の調査を手伝ったから。
(B) プロジェクトに強い興味を示したから。
(C) 事前に航空会社に連絡したから。
(D) 背景情報を提供したから。

Task 1：**解答例** 感謝の理由　thank、appreciateなどの表現を待ち受ける。
Task 2：動詞＋目的語のセットをまず縦読みする。

7. Who most likely are the tour participants?
  (A) Food retailers
  (B) Sanitation supervisors
  (C) Newly-recruited employees
  (D) Factory workers

ツアー参加者は誰だと思われるか。
(A) 食品小売業者
(B) 衛生管理者
(C) 新入社員
(D) 工場の従業員

Task 1： **解答例** 参加者　このタイプの設問のヒントは冒頭に登場することが多い。
Task 2：選択肢が短いのですべて読む。

---

8. Where will the tour begin?
  (A) The exhibit hall
  (B) The assembly line
  (C) A factory-outlet store
  (D) A lecture room

ツアーはどこから始まるか。
(A) 展示ホール
(B) 組立ライン
(C) 工場のアウトレット店
(D) 講義室

Task 1： **解答例** 開始場所　hereなどの言葉とともに告げられる。冒頭か最後でふれるパターンが多い。
Task 2：選択肢共通の冠詞は読まない。

---

9. What will participants receive at the end of the tour?
  (A) An information package
  (B) A list of items
  (C) Freshly-baked bread
  (D) Discount coupons

ツアーの最後に参加者は何を受け取るか。
(A) 資料集
(B) 商品リスト
(C) 焼きたてのパン
(D) 割引クーポン券

Task 1： **解答例** 受け取る品　3点攻略法＋1（p.32参照）で、at the endまで押さえて、before finishing the tourなどの言い換え表現を待つ。
Task 2：選択肢が短いので、冠詞以外すべて読む。

Practice

▶解答：p.118〜

1-40〜42

それでは練習問題に挑戦してみよう。CDの音声の冒頭に8秒のポーズを設けているので、この時間を利用して設問・選択肢を先読みしよう。

1. What is the news broadcast mainly about?
   (A) The purchase of medical devices
   (B) A corporate merger
   (C) New drugs for cancer
   (D) The technological development of chemical engineering　Ⓐ Ⓑ Ⓒ Ⓓ ☐

2. How can Williams Limited best be described?
   (A) An American manufacturer of medical devices
   (B) A wholesaler of fertilizers
   (C) A multinational X-ray equipment maker
   (D) A British pharmaceutical company　Ⓐ Ⓑ Ⓒ Ⓓ ☐

3. According to the report, what will happen on April 2?
   (A) Trenton will demonstrate the newly invented machine.
   (B) A collaboration between the two conglomerates will be launched.
   (C) Williams Limited will become a subsidiary.
   (D) The chief executive officer of Trenton will address the media.　Ⓐ Ⓑ Ⓒ Ⓓ ☐

---

4. How many hours will this tour last?
   (A) Two hours
   (B) Three hours
   (C) Four hours
   (D) Five hours　Ⓐ Ⓑ Ⓒ Ⓓ ☐

5. Who most likely is Mr. Aaron Wallace?
   (A) A tour operator
   (B) A sculptor
   (C) A statesman
   (D) A founder of the museum　Ⓐ Ⓑ Ⓒ Ⓓ ☐

6. According to the talk, what will most likely happen toward the end of the tour?
   (A) Visitors will purchase souvenirs.
   (B) A photo taking session will take place.
   (C) Participants will enjoy lunch.
   (D) An auction will be held.　Ⓐ Ⓑ Ⓒ Ⓓ ☐

7. For whom was the message most likely recorded?
   (A) Students of a language school
   (B) Savings tellers
   (C) Consumers calling a financial institution
   (D) College graduates applying for accounting jobs

8. Who would most likely press 3?
   (A) A person who wants to open a savings account
   (B) A customer who already has an account
   (C) A visitor who does not know the location of the center
   (D) An accountant who needs to talk to the division manager

9. According to the message, why might the conversation be recorded?
   (A) To ensure the quality of the service
   (B) To be published in the company's newsletter
   (C) To examine the quality of a production system
   (D) To help in choosing the best candidate

Practiceの正解と解説

Questions 1-3 refer to the following news broadcast. 🇨🇦

In international business news today. Trenton Medical Devices Corporation of the United States announced on February 3 that it plans to purchase British drug manufacturer Williams Limited. A spokesman for Trenton said that the U.S. medical equipment manufacturer would buy all shares in Williams Limited, which will become a wholly-owned subsidiary of Trenton on April 1. He added that Williams Limited specializes in drugs that enhance the effectiveness of medical devices such as X-ray, ultrasound and other systems that produce medical images. He said that new drugs developed by Williams will be used together with Trenton products to help detect and treat cancer and other illnesses more effectively. Trenton's CEO Nancy Lambert will be holding a press conference on a new business scheme on April 2.

問題1-3は、次のニュース放送に関するものです。
今日の国際ビジネスニュースです。アメリカのTrenton医療機器社は2月3日に、イギリスの製薬会社Williams社を買い取ると発表しました。Trenton社の広報担当者が述べたところでは、このアメリカの医療機器メーカーはWilliams社の全株式を買い取るつもりで、同社は4月1日にTrenton社の完全子会社となるでしょう。彼はさらに、Williams社はX線や超音波などの医療用画像を作り出すシステムの効果を高める薬を専門としていると述べました。Williams社で開発された新薬は、ガンなどの病気をより効果的に発見・治療する助けとなるようTrenton製品と一緒に使われるとのことです。Trenton社の最高経営責任者、Nancy Lambertは新事業計画に関する記者会見を4月2日に行う予定です。

---

1. このニュースは主に何に関してか。
  (A) 医療機器の購入
  (B) 企業の吸収合併
  (C) ガンの新薬
  (D) 化学工学の技術発展

解説 全体情報タイプの設問だが、ニュースの場合、冒頭でトピック（主題）が示される。Trenton Medical Devices Corporation … plans to purchase British drug manufacturerがヒント。
解答 (B)

---

2. Williams社の記述として最適なのはどれか。
  (A) アメリカの医療機器メーカー
  (B) 肥料の卸売業者
  (C) X線装置の多国籍メーカー
  (D) イギリスの製薬会社

解説 ヒントが数回登場する。British drug manufacturer Williams Limited、Williams Limited specializes in drugs、new drugs developed by Williamsなどから正解は明らか。
解答 (D)

---

3. この報道によると、4月2日に何が予定されているか。
  (A) Trenton社が、新たに発明した機械の公開実演をする。
  (B) 2つのコングロマリット間の提携が開始される。
  (C) Williams社が子会社になる。
  (D) Trenton社の最高経営責任者がマスコミに発表する。

解説 選択肢が長いので、主語と動詞を縦読みし、必要に応じて目的語も見る。実演か、提携か、子会社化か記者会見か。Trenton's CEO … will be holding a press conference … on April 2.がaddress the mediaと同じ意味になる。
解答 (D)

Questions 4-6 refer to the following announcement. 🇬🇧

Welcome to Leicester Contemporary Art Museum. I'm Ben Hall, a curator of the museum. The four-hour program today is designed to show you well-known pieces in the field of contemporary art. The museum was established 15 years ago by Mr. Aaron Wallace, who presented his personal collection to the local government. Since then, the collection of about 200 artworks has attracted more than 1 million visitors. A special exhibition titled "The Origin and the Future" is currently being held to commemorate its opening and inform you about the history of this museum. Let us start the tour. First, I'll be showing you the section of paintings, and then we'll move on to the sculptures section, then to the section of installations. We will be spending about two hours viewing exhibits. After that, we'll be having a tea break at a cafe located in the museum. Before wrapping up the tour, you will be able to enjoy shopping at our gift shop, where you can purchase a variety of goods such as postcards and T-shirts.

問題4-6は、次のアナウンスに関するものです。
Leicester現代美術館へようこそ。私はBen Hall、当美術館の学芸員です。本日の4時間のプログラムで見ていただくことになっているのは、現代美術の分野でよく知られた作品です。当美術館は15年前に個人コレクションを地方自治体に寄贈したAaron Wallace氏によって創設されました。それ以来、およそ200点の芸術作品からなるコレクションは、100万人以上の来館者を魅了してきました。開館を記念し、この美術館の歴史を皆さんにお伝えするため、「原点と未来」と題された特別展が現在開催中です。ツアーを開始しましょう。最初に絵画部門をご覧いただいて、次に彫刻部門へと進み、その後がインスタレーション部門です。展示品の鑑賞時間は約2時間を予定しています。その後、美術館内のカフェにてティーブレイクを取る予定です。ツアーを締めくくる前には、ギフトショップでのお買い物を楽しんでいただけます。絵はがきやTシャツなどさまざまな商品がご購入いただけます。

4. このツアーは何時間続く予定か。
(A) 2時間
(B) 3時間
(C) 4時間
(D) 5時間

解説 設問のキーワードはHow many hours、this tour, last。ツアー全体の時間を問われているのでfour-hour program todayから正解がわかる。後半のtwo hoursは鑑賞に使う時間。
解答 (C)

5. Aaron Wallace氏は誰だと思われるか。
(A) ツアーの引率者
(B) 彫刻家
(C) 政治家
(D) 美術館の創設者

解説 ツアーガイドの場合、話者は冒頭で名乗る。ここではI'm Ben Hallと名乗っているので、Aaron Wallaceは引率者ではない。The museum was established ... by Mr. Aaron Wallaceがヒント。
解答 (D)

6. このトークによると、ツアーの最後には何が起きると思われるか。
(A) 見学者がお土産を買う。
(B) 写真撮影の時間がある。
(C) 参加者が昼食を楽しむ。
(D) オークションが開催される。

解説 設問のキーワードで重要なのはtoward the end of the tour。トークの中ではBefore wrapping up the tourと言い換えられている。その後にヒントが登場する。
解答 (A)

Questions 7-9 refer to the following telephone message.

Thank you for calling the Bank of Hollingsworth automated customer assistance center. For Spanish-language customer assistance, press 1 now. To open a new checking or savings account, press 2. To make an account balance inquiry or to request other information regarding an existing savings or checking account, press 3. If you would like to speak to a representative in person, please press 9. Please note that your conversation with our customer assistance personnel may be recorded at random to assist us in maintaining the quality of our service. At Bank of Hollingsworth, we're here to serve you.

問題7-9は、次の電話メッセージに関するものです。
Hollingsworth銀行の自動応答お客様サービスセンターにお電話ありがとうございます。スペイン語によるお客様サービスは、ここで1を押してください。新規の当座預金もしくは普通預金の口座開設は、2を押してください。口座残高のご確認、または既存の普通預金もしくは当座預金口座に関するその他のお問い合わせは、3を押してください。担当者と直接お話しになりたい場合は9を押してください。お客様と当行お客様サービス担当者との会話は、当行のサービスの質の維持に役立てるため、無作為に録音される場合がございますのでご注意ください。Hollingsworth銀行は、皆様のお力になるためお待ちしております。

7. このメッセージは誰あてに録音されたと思われるか。
   (A) 語学学校の生徒
   (B) 預金係
   (C) 金融機関に電話をかけた顧客
   (D) 会計業務求職中の大学新卒者

解説 電話メッセージでは、企業のものでも個人のものでも必ず冒頭で名乗る。Thank you for calling the Bank of Hollingsworth automated customer assistance centerから正解は明らか。
解答 (C)

8. 3を押す可能性が最も高いのは誰か。
   (A) 普通預金口座を開設したい人
   (B) すでに口座を持っている顧客
   (C) センターの場所を知らない訪問客
   (D) 部門責任者と話す必要がある会計士

解説 press 1から順番に案内されているので、press 2の後に注意。To make an account balance inquiry ...以降を言い換えているのはA customer who already has an accountだ。
解答 (B)

9. メッセージによると、会話はなぜ録音されるかもしれないのか。
   (A) サービスの質を確保するため
   (B) 企業のニュースレターに掲載するため
   (C) 生産システムの質を検査するため
   (D) 最適な候補者を選ぶのに役立てるため

解説 設問から「会話の録音」に関する情報が告げられるとわかるので、その表現を待ち伏せる。your conversation ... may be recordedの後、to assist us in maintaining the quality of our serviceと理由が説明されている。
解答 (A)

学習エネルギーをチャージする今日の **格言**

If you can dream it, you can do it. Your limits are all within yourself.
Brian Tracy
(1944〜：カナダ出身の自己啓発書の作家)
夢見ることができれば、実現できる。あなたの限界はすべてあなた自身の中にある。

p.58の訳

問題1-4は次の告知に関するものです。
掲示板 / Redwood Armsマンション
ごみ処理に関して、住宅所有者組合（HOA）はSierra Coast Recycling社と契約する計画を承認しました。通常の家庭ごみとは別に、再生可能なプラスチック、ガラス、紙を収集してもらうためです。この計画の利点には、もし再利用されないごみの量の25パーセント削減が達成できたら、市のごみ収集サービス料金を引き下げられることが含まれています。もし皆さんがガラスと紙とプラスチックを家庭ごみと分別し、それらの品目を指定の収集容器に捨てれば、目標に到達できるはずです。その結果は一世帯当たり、年間で正味150ドルの節約になるでしょう。必要な準備はすべて整っています。リサイクル計画への皆さんのご協力に期待しつつ、2週間ごとにここに進捗報告を掲示します。
よろしくお願いします。/ Dick Rogers、HOA会計係
（注：この掲示板はRedwood Arms住宅所有者組合［HOA］のサービスです。すべての掲示物は承認と掲示のため、HOA理事会に提出する必要があります。承認のため掲示物を提出するには、1203号室のHOA理事長Gladys Reevesまでご連絡ください）

1. この告知の主な目的の1つは何か。
(A) 近所の海岸をきれいに保つこと
(B) 居住者にボランティア活動への参加を促すこと
(C) より安価な家庭用ごみ箱を購入すること
(D) ごみ捨て習慣をリサイクルの方向へ転換させること

2. Dick Rogersに関して何が言えるか。
(A) 建物内のマンションを最低1戸所有している。
(B) ごみ処理会社で部長として働いている。
(C) 現在の仕事に就くため統計学を学んだ。
(D) HOA理事会の理事長を務めたことがある。

3. Redwood Armsに関して正しくないのはどれか。
(A) Gladys Reevesは住宅所有者組合の責任者だ。
(B) 居住者は制限なく掲示板にメッセージを張れる。
(C) リサイクル用容器はごみ捨て場に設置済みだ。
(D) ごみの量を減らせば収集料金を下げられる。

4. 第1パラグラフ、8行目のdesignatedに最も意味が近いのは
(A) 捨てられた
(B) 製造された
(C) 指定された
(D) 特注された

Part 4 基本音読

では、Part 4の「音読」に挑戦しよう。漫然と声に出しているだけでは大きな効果は期待できない。16ページのチェックポイントに従って音読し、できれば自分の声を録音して、プロソディーを含めチェックしてみよう。

Practice

CD 2-01〜04　▶解答：p.125〜

音読の前に、その素材となる練習問題に挑戦してみよう。CDの音声の冒頭に8秒のポーズを設けているので、この時間を利用して設問・選択肢を先読みしよう。

1. Where is the announcement most likely being made?
    (A) At an office-supply shop
    (B) At a gym
    (C) At a department store
    (D) At an appliance store

2. What is the main purpose of the announcement?
    (A) To advertise a special time sale
    (B) To mention a new budget plan
    (C) To ensure safety procedures
    (D) To inform customers of an opportunity

3. What does the speaker suggest the listeners do?
    (A) Get a voucher
    (B) Register as a member
    (C) Stop by a reception
    (D) Speak with an athlete

4. What is the report mainly about?
  (A) Details of a construction schedule
  (B) A delay to the start of an automobile race
  (C) The status of local traffic
  (D) The opening of a regional council

5. What is mentioned about the cause of the problem?
  (A) Heavy rain
  (B) A traffic accident
  (C) Damage to the drain pipes
  (D) Partial closure of a road

6. When is the report most likely being heard?
  (A) Early in the morning
  (B) Late in the morning
  (C) Early in the evening
  (D) Late in the evening

7. Who most likely is the speaker?
  (A) A director of a personnel department
  (B) A CEO of a multi-national company
  (C) An international travel agent
  (D) A newly elected ambassador

8. What will the speaker most likely do?
  (A) Pay a visit to overseas production sites
  (B) Apologize for his late arrival
  (C) Recommend downsizing the company
  (D) Nominate an award winner

9. What does the speaker request?
  (A) Scheduling job interviews
  (B) Greater efforts in the months ahead
  (C) Ideas and recommendations
  (D) Revisions to the budget

GO ON TO THE NEXT PAGE

10. Who most likely are the listeners?
(A) Reporters of a TV station
(B) Senior employees of an insurance company
(C) Journalists of a publishing house
(D) Sales representatives of a telecommunication company

11. Why does the speaker mention mistakes?
(A) They may result in dangerous product defects.
(B) They may harm the company's image.
(C) They may damage expensive video equipment.
(D) They may lead to a cancellation of showing of the film.

12. What is scheduled to take place last?
(A) A rehearsal of a theatrical play
(B) An interview with additional instruction
(C) A sales presentation on the product
(D) A press conference by the new CEO

解答行動分析リスト

Practiceで不正解だった設問は、以下から原因を拾い出し、次ページからの解答横の [ ]に番号を記入しよう。

❶ 設問の先読みができなかった
❷ 設問のポイントがすぐにわからなかった
❸ 設問の意味を誤解した
❹ 短い選択肢の先読みをしなかった
❺ 選択肢の縦読みをしなかった
❻ 選択肢の内容を誤解した
❼ 長い選択肢を読みきれなかった
❽ 選択肢に知らない語彙があった
❾ トークの冒頭で状況を把握し損ねた
❿ トークの状況が理解できなかった
⓫ トークの中の知らない語彙に気を取られた
⓬ トークの内容を誤解した
⓭ トークのスピードが速くて把握しきれなかった
⓮ 音の崩れなどがよく聞き取れなかった
⓯ 漠然と聞いてしまった
⓰ 設問の主語に注意して聞かなかった
⓱ 時の副詞句や、理由や依頼を示す表現などに注意しなかった
⓲ 個別情報タイプを優先的に解かなかった
⓳ 1問に時間をかけすぎた
⓴ 言い換えに気づかなかった
㉑ 解答をマークしている間にヒントを聞き逃した
㉒ マークシートを塗り間違えた
㉓ 前の問題をひきずって切り替えができなかった
㉔ 正解を絞りきれず迷った
㉕ 思い込みがあった
㉖ 集中力の欠如
㉗ パニックに陥った

Practiceの正解と解説

英文の訳はチャンクで区切られているので、後で音読する際に参照しよう。

Questions 1-3 refer to the following announcement. 2-01

Good afternoon, ProGoods Department Store shoppers. Have you signed up for your ProGoods Smart Shopper Club membership yet? If you haven't, be sure to ask your cashier when you make your purchase. Smart Shopper Club members receive a 5 percent discount on all purchases, plus access to premium services including free-gift wrapping during the holiday season, pre-approval for installment payment plans, and extra deep discounts on select merchandise. You may also qualify for a ProGoods credit card. Sign up today, and qualify for instant membership with your purchase. Don't miss out on this great opportunity to stretch that holiday shopping budget. Sign up for your membership card today. It's easy, quick and simple. Shop the smart way. Shop at ProGoods.

問題1-3は次のアナウンスに関するものです。
ProGoodsデパートでお買い物中の皆様、こんにちは。// ProGoods買い物上手クラブ会員へのお申し込みはもうお済みですか。// もしまだでしたら / お買い物の際、ぜひレジ係員にお申し付けください。// 買い物上手クラブ会員は / すべてのお買い物で5パーセント割引を受けられます / さらにプレミアムサービスも（受けられます）/ そこに含まれるのは、休暇シーズンの無料ギフト包装、/ 分割払いプランの事前承認、/ それに、限定商品の追加の大幅値引きです。// また、ProGoodsクレジットカードもお持ちいただけます。// 本日お申し込みください / そして、お買い物に使える即時発行の会員権を手に入れてください。// この絶好の機会をお見逃しなく / 休暇の予算を有効利用するためにも。// 会員カードに本日お申し込みください。// 簡単で、素早く、手間いらずです。// 上手にお買い物をしてください。// お買い物はProGoodsで。//

1. このアナウンスはどこで行われていると思われるか。
(A) 事務用品の店で
(B) スポーツクラブで
(C) デパートで
(D) 家電販売店で

解説 キーワードはWhere、announcement、made。「アナウンスの場所」を問う全体情報タイプ。冒頭に注意して、場所を示唆する語句を待つ。ProGoods Department Store ...がヒント。
解答 (C) 解答行動の分析 [　　]

2. このアナウンスの主な目的は何か。
(A) 特別なタイムセールを宣伝すること
(B) 新しい予算案に言及すること
(C) 安全手順を確かにすること
(D) ある機会を顧客に知らせること

解説 設問のキーワードはWhat、purpose、announcement。「アナウンスの目的」を問う全体情報タイプ。会員特典を説明した後、Don't miss out on this great opportunity ...と勧めている。
解答 (D) 解答行動の分析 [　　]

3. 話者は聞き手に何をするよう提案しているか。
(A) 割引券を入手する
(B) 会員登録する
(C) 受付に立ち寄る
(D) 運動選手と話す

解説 キーワードはWhat、speaker、suggest the listeners。「聞き手に求められる行動」を問う個別情報タイプ。命令、依頼、提案などの表現を待つ。Have you signed up ...の後や終盤がヒント。
解答 (B) 解答行動の分析 [　　]

Questions 4-6 refer to the following excerpt from a radio broadcast. 2-02

Good morning drivers in the Willmont County region. This is Marcia Stonewell with your 6 A.M. traffic update. Commuters heading south into the downtown Willmont area on Highway 78 can expect heavy traffic from the North Suburb district, with the usual slowdown at the Aaron Courtney Bridge due to a closed traffic lane. Routine construction is under way there. Traffic slows to walking speed as it passes under the bridge, but soon speeds up again. You'll want to figure on spending an extra 20 minutes on Highway 78 southbound. Elsewhere, traffic is moving smoothly around the region, but it's still early. Tune in every half-hour for the latest traffic. Now, back to the news.

問題4-6は次のラジオ放送の抜粋に関するものです。

Willmont郡地域で運転中の皆さん、おはようございます。// Marcia Stonewellが午前6時の最新交通情報をお伝えします。// 78号線を南下してWillmontの中心部に向かう通勤者には / North Suburb地区から混雑が予想されます / Aaron Courtney橋でのいつもの流れの悪さに加え / 車線閉鎖が原因で。// そこでは定期工事が行われています。// 車の流れは橋の下を通過するところで歩行速度まで落ちます / しかし、すぐにまた速度は上がります。// 20分余計にかかると見ておいたほうがいいでしょう / 78号線の南行きでは。// ほかの場所では、地域全体で交通はスムーズに動いています / しかし、まだ早朝です。// 最新情報は30分ごとにこの周波数でお確かめください。// では、ニュースに戻ります。//

4. このリポートは主に何に関するものか。
(A) 工事予定の詳細
(B) 自動車レースの開始の遅れ
(C) 地域の交通状況
(D) 地方議会の開会

解説 キーワードはWhat、report、about。「リポートの内容」を問う全体情報タイプ。冒頭のdrivers in the Willmont County regionへの呼びかけと、その後の番組紹介に注意しよう。
解答 (C) 解答行動の分析 [　　　]

5. 問題の原因について何が言及されているか。
(A) 大雨
(B) 交通事故
(C) 排水管の損傷
(D) 道路の一部閉鎖

解説 設問のキーワードはWhat、mentioned、cause of the problem。「問題の原因」を問う個別情報タイプ。原因、理由を示す表現(due to、as、because of、since、causeなど)に注意して聞く。heavy trafficの後のdue to a closed traffic laneがヒント。
解答 (D) 解答行動の分析 [　　　]

6. このリポートを聞く可能性が最も高いのはいつか。
(A) 朝早い時間
(B) 午前の遅い時間
(C) 夕方の早い時間
(D) 夜遅い時間

解説 キーワードはWhen、report、heard。「リポートを耳にする時間」について問う個別情報タイプ。時間帯に関する表現を待つ。冒頭のGood morning、6 A.M. traffic updateと、終盤のit's still earlyから早朝であることがわかる。
解答 (A) 解答行動の分析 [　　　]

Questions 7-9 refer to the following talk. 🇬🇧　2-03

As the newly appointed chairman of our company, I would like to offer you all my sincere greetings. I want to let each and every one of you know that I am very excited about working together as a team in the months and years ahead. As you know, we are one of the world's largest electronics manufacturers, with operations in many countries on nearly every continent. This makes it impossible for me to meet and greet each and every one of you in person today. And it is why I have asked your local office to present this video message at a time convenient to you. During the next month, I will be traveling to our major production locations all over the world to learn more about our operations, our strengths, our weaknesses, and our potential for the future. I encourage you all to introduce yourselves when I visit your area, and make any recommendations or share any ideas you see fit.

問題7-9は次のトークに関するものです。
わが社の新任の会長として / 皆さんに心からのごあいさつを申し上げたいと思います。// 皆さん1人ひとりに知っていただきたいのですが / 私は、共に一丸となって働くことを非常に楽しみにしています / この先何カ月も、何年も。// ご存じの通り / わが社は世界でもトップクラスの電気メーカーであり / ほぼすべての大陸の多くの国々に事業所を持っています。// このため、私にとっては不可能となります / 今日、皆さん1人ひとりと直接お会いしてごあいさつすることは。// だからこそ、皆さんの現地オフィスにお願いしておいたのです / 皆さんの都合のいい時にこのビデオメッセージをお見せするようにと。// 来月中に / 私は世界各地の主要な生産拠点を回る予定です / わが社の事業、長所、短所をもっとよく知るために / そして将来の可能性を。// 皆さん、ぜひ自己紹介をしてください / 私が皆さんの地域を訪れた際には / そして、どんな提言でもしてください / あるいは、いいと思うどんなアイデアでも話してください。//

7. 話者は誰である可能性が最も高いか。
(A) 人事部長
(B) 多国籍企業の最高経営責任者
(C) 海外旅行代理業者
(D) 新任の大使

解説 キーワードはWho、is、speaker。「話者」について問う全体情報タイプ。冒頭に注意し、職業や役職などの表現を待つ。chairman of our companyと、world's largest ...以降がヒント。
解答 (B) 解答行動の分析 [　　　]

8. 話者がする可能性が最も高いことは何か。
(A) 海外の生産拠点を訪れる
(B) 到着の遅れを謝る
(C) 会社の規模縮小を提言する
(D) 受賞者を推薦する

解説 キーワードはWhat、speaker、do。「話者の行動」を問う個別情報タイプ。未来表現(I'll、I'm planning to do、I'm supposed to doなど)を待つ。I will be traveling ...以降がヒント。
解答 (A) 解答行動の分析 [　　　]

9. 話者は何を頼んでいるか。
(A) 就職面接の予定を入れること
(B) この先数カ月間の一層の努力
(C) アイデアと提言
(D) 予算の見直し

解説 What、speaker、requestがキーワード。「話者の頼んだ内容」を問う個別情報タイプ。命令、依頼、提案表現を待つ。I encourage you all ... の後に注意。
解答 (C) 解答行動の分析 [　　　]

Questions 10-12 refer to the following excerpt from a talk.

As executives of Overland Insurance Corporation, whenever you speak with a reporter, it is crucial for you to be aware that you are not simply chatting with a friend. You are functioning as the face and the voice of the company. One mistake or miscommunication in such a situation can cause enormous damage to the company. This is why we've been asked to provide you with this half-day media training session. As you can see, our video crew is here to simulate the conditions of a real TV interview, and your video trainer, Mr. Iwata, is a former television reporter. We will begin with a mock interview of five minutes, after which we will review and critique your performance. We will then follow up with a 15-minute interview followed by further discussion and instruction.

問題10-12は次のトークの抜粋に関するものです。
Overland保険会社の幹部として / 記者と話をする場合は常に / 意識することが大変重要です / 友人と何となくおしゃべりしているわけではないのだということを。// 皆さんは、会社の顔と声としての役割を果たしているのです。// そのような場では1つのミスや誤解が / 会社に甚大なダメージを与える可能性があります。// だからこそ私たちが依頼されたのです / 皆さんにこの半日のメディアトレーニング授業を行うようにと。// ご覧のとおり、ここにはわれわれのビデオクルーがいます / 本物のテレビインタビューの状況を模擬体験するためです / そして、ビデオトレーナーのIwataさんは元テレビ記者です。// まずは5分の模擬インタビューから始めます / その後、私たちが皆さんの出来栄えを振り返り批評します。// それから15分のインタビューを行い / さらにディスカッションと説明が続きます。//

10. 聞き手は誰である可能性が高いか。
(A) テレビ局の記者
(B) 保険会社の上層部の社員
(C) 出版社のジャーナリスト
(D) 電気通信会社の営業担当者

解説 キーワードはWho、are、listeners。「聞き手」を問う全体情報タイプ。呼びかけやas（～として）などの表現に注意する。冒頭のAs executives ...以降から解答が可能。
解答 (B) 解答行動の分析［　　　］

11. 話者はなぜミスの話をしたか。
(A) 危険な製品の欠陥をもたらしかねない。
(B) 企業イメージを損ないかねない。
(C) 高価なビデオ機器を壊しかねない。
(D) 映画の上映中止につながりかねない。

解説 Why、speaker、mention mistakesがキーワード。「理由」を問う個別情報タイプ。理由、原因を表す表現を待つ。ヒントのOne mistake or miscommunication ...の後に「これが…の理由です」という意味のThis is why ...が続くため、話の流れを理解しながら聞く必要がある。
解答 (B) 解答行動の分析［　　　］

12. 最後に行われる予定なのは何か。
(A) 舞台劇のリハーサル
(B) インタビューと追加の指示
(C) 製品の営業用プレゼンテーション
(D) 新しい最高経営責任者による記者会見

解説 キーワードはWhat、scheduled、take place、last。4点目のlastが重要だと意識して聞こう。トークの最後のWe will then ...以降がヒントとなる。
解答 (B) 解答行動の分析［　　　］

いよいよ音読を開始しよう！

Task 1

それでは音読に挑戦する。まず、**1)** 英文をすべての区切り（/と/と//）で区切って音読しよう（**短いチャンク**）。意味をつかみながら読めるようになったら、今度は**長いチャンク**に挑戦。**2)** トラック05〜08の音声のポーズの部分でリピートしよう（音声はトークのみ）。**3)** プロソディーを意識してきちんとリピートできるようになったら、仕上げに**すべての英文を**長いチャンクで音読しよう。

1. Where is the announcement / most likely being made? //
　　(A) At an office-supply shop // (B) At a gym //
　　(C) At a department store // (D) At an appliance store //

2. What is the main purpose of the announcement? //
　　(A) To advertise a special time sale // (B) To mention a new budget plan //
　　(C) To ensure safety procedures // (D) To inform customers of an opportunity //

3. What does the speaker suggest the listeners do? //
　　(A) Get a voucher // (B) Register as a member //
　　(C) Stop by a reception // (D) Speak with an athlete //

CD 2-05

Good afternoon, ProGoods Department Store shoppers. //
Have you signed up for your ProGoods Smart Shopper Club membership yet? //
If you haven't, / be sure to ask your cashier / when you make your purchase. //
Smart Shopper Club members / receive a 5 percent discount on all purchases, /
plus access to premium services /
including free-gift wrapping during the holiday season, /
pre-approval for installment payment plans, /
and extra deep discounts on select merchandise. //
You may also qualify for a ProGoods credit card. //
Sign up today, / and qualify for instant membership with your purchase. //
Don't miss out on this great opportunity /
to stretch that holiday shopping budget. //
Sign up for your membership card today. // It's easy, quick and simple. //
Shop the smart way. // Shop at ProGoods. //

要 注 意 フ レ ー ズ !

今回は、選択肢・トークとも**TOEIC**に頻出の動詞を中心とした表現に下線を引いている。動詞と名詞や動詞と前置詞の組み合わせを覚えるつもりで音読しよう。

4. What is the report mainly about?
   (A) Details of a construction schedule // (B) A delay to the start of an automobile race //
   (C) The status of local traffic // (D) The opening of a regional council //
5. What is mentioned about the cause of the problem?
   (A) Heavy rain // (B) A traffic accident //
   (C) Damage to the drain pipes // (D) Partial closure of a road //
6. When is the report most likely being heard?//
   (A) Early in the morning // (B) Late in the morning //
   (C) Early in the evening // (D) Late in the evening //

CD 2-06

Good morning drivers in the Willmont County region. //
This is Marcia Stonewell / with your 6 A.M. traffic update. //
Commuters heading south into the downtown Willmont area on Highway 78 /
can expect heavy traffic from the North Suburb district, /
with the usual slowdown at the Aaron Courtney Bridge /
due to a closed traffic lane. //
Routine construction is under way there. //
Traffic slows to walking speed / as it passes under the bridge, /
but soon speeds up again. //
You'll want to figure on spending an extra 20 minutes /
on Highway 78 southbound. //
Elsewhere, / traffic is moving smoothly around the region, / but it's still early. //
Tune in every half-hour for the latest traffic. //
Now, back to the news. //

要注意フレーズ！

交通情報には特徴的な表現が多い。固有名詞や方角、道路状況など、下線を引いた部分を繰り返し音読して、耳から聞いた際、瞬時に意味がわかるようにしておこう。

7. Who most likely is the speaker? //
   (A) A director of a personnel department // (B) A CEO of a multi-national company //
   (C) An international travel agent // (D) A newly elected ambassador //

8. What will the speaker most likely do? //
   (A) Pay a visit to overseas production sites // (B) Apologize for his late arrival //
   (C) Recommend downsizing the company // (D) Nominate an award winner //

9. What does the speaker request? //
   (A) Scheduling job interviews // (B) Greater efforts in the months ahead //
   (C) Ideas and recommendations // (D) Revisions to the budget //

2-07

<u>As the newly appointed chairman of our company,</u> /
<u>I would like to offer you all my sincere greetings.</u> //
I want to let each and every one of you know /
that I am very excited about working together as a team /
<u>in the months and years ahead</u>. //
As you know, / we are one of the world's largest electronics manufacturers, /
with operations in many countries / on nearly every continent. //
This makes it impossible for me /
to meet and greet each and every one of you in person today. //
And it is why I have asked your local office /
to present this video message / <u>at a time convenient to you</u>. //
During the next month, /
I will be traveling to our major production locations all over the world /
to learn more about our operations, our strengths, our weaknesses, /
and our potential for the future. //
I encourage you all to introduce yourselves / when I visit your area, /
and <u>make any recommendations</u> / <u>or share any ideas you see fit</u>. //

要注意フレーズ

トークはCEOの就任スピーチということで、かなり凝った表現が使われている。CEOになりきって、下線の部分に特に注意しながら堂々と音読しよう。

10. Who most likely are the listeners? //
   (A) Reporters of a TV station //
   (B) Senior employees of an insurance company //
   (C) Journalists of a publishing house //
   (D) Sales representatives of a telecommunication company //

11. Why does the speaker mention mistakes? //
   (A) They may result in dangerous product defects. //
   (B) They may harm the company's image. //
   (C) They may damage expensive video equipment. //
   (D) They may lead to a cancellation of showing of the film. //

12. What is scheduled to take place last? //
   (A) A rehearsal of a theatrical play //
   (B) An interview with additional instruction //
   (C) A sales presentation on the product //
   (D) A press conference by the new CEO //

CD 2-08

As executives of Overland Insurance Corporation, /
whenever you speak with a reporter, / it is crucial for you to be aware /
that you are not simply chatting with a friend. //
You are functioning as the face and the voice of the company. //
One mistake or miscommunication in such a situation /
can cause enormous damage to the company. //
This is why we've been asked /
to provide you with this half-day media training session. //
As you can see, / our video crew is here /
to simulate the conditions of a real TV interview, /
and your video trainer, Mr. Iwata, / is a former television reporter. //
We will begin with a mock interview of five minutes, /
after which we will review and critique your performance. //
We will then follow up with a 15-minute interview /
followed by further discussion and instruction. //

要注意フレーズ！

今回は危機管理に関する少し長めのフレーズを学ぶつもりで音読しよう。トークのほうは１文がかなり長いので、チャンクごとに練習してからセンテンスに挑戦するといい。

Task 2

2-05~08

CDの音声を聞いて、ポーズの部分で**各チャンクの意味を頭に浮かべよう**（同時通訳の要領で声に出しても可）。正確な日本語訳でなくても、おおよその意味が把握できればいい。ポーズの間にわからなければ、125～128ページの訳をチェックしよう。

Task 3

2-05~08

CDの音声を聞いて、**スクリプトを見ないで**ポーズの個所でリピートしよう。

Task 4

2-01~04

仕上げに129～132ページのスクリプトを見ながら、トラック01～04の音声に**オーバーラップさせて読んでみよう**。プロソディーを意識し、タイミングが合うまで繰り返して、ナチュラルスピードでの音読に慣れよう。

Task 5

2-01~04

本日の学習を終えた後も、このトラックをスクリプトを見ずに聞いて理解できるか、繰り返し確認するようにしよう。まず趣旨・目的を把握し、話題に沿って速聴速解を目指す。繰り返し練習することが大切だ。

学習エネルギーをチャージする今日の **格言**

> **Most of the important things in the world have been accomplished by people who have kept on trying when there seemed to be no hope at all.**
>
> Dale Carnegie
> (1888～1955：アメリカの実業家、作家)
>
> **この世で重要なことのほとんどは、何一つ希望が見えないときにも挑み続けた人々によって成されてきた。**

900点突破者たちの体験談(2)
学習法を変え、音読実践で940点達成！

(S.Y.さん　会社員　男性)

880点 → 940点

　私にとっての大きな転機は、セミナーに参加し、CNNニュースを使ったリスニングとリーディングのコツを学んだことでした。

　ネイティブのスピード、論理に近づくためには、英語学習の習慣を根本的に変えること。つまり「英語の語順で、チャンクで区切って、意味を捉えていく。後戻りはしない」——というメソッドに基づいて、英語を聞き、読むようにしました。すると、リスニング力がかなり上がっただけでなく、速読が徐々にできるようになってきたのです。

　この方法に慣れてくると、英語が面白いようにわかり、速く読めるようになりました。おかげで今では、Part 6、7は、文書全体を通読しても、時間内に解答が終わるようになり、読み落としもなくなりました。以前は文全体を読んでから、後戻りして意味や文脈を捉えるという英文解釈的な習慣からなかなか脱却できなかったため、読むスピードが遅く、Part 7を試験時間内に終えることができなかったのです。

　TOEICでは、スピーディーな情報処理能力が求められており、反応時間の遅れがスコアアップの障害になります。私の場合、語彙力のなさが致命的でしたので、TOEIC頻出語をカバーしている単語集を使って、単語の意味が瞬時に頭の中に浮かぶまで繰り返し学習しました。

　ここでもセミナーで教わった語彙学習のコツが役立ちました。リスニング対策の語彙は、CDを何度も聞き、自分でも音読し、文字だけでなく音でも認識することを心がけました。リーディング対策の頻出語も、即座に正確に意味がわかるレベルまで繰り返し覚えました。また、使われている表現をセットで覚えることもしました。

　文法対策では、TOEIC頻出の英文法を、TOEIC対策問題集を解きながら着実にマスター。説明のポイントがわからない場合は、文法書の『総合英語Forest』(桐原書店)を熟読し、あいまいな個所を残さないようにしました。

　今振り返ってみると、900点超えのためには、苦手意識のあるパートを作らないことがとても大切だと思います。また、伸び悩んでいる方には、思い切ってこれまでの学習法を変えてみることをお勧めします。今後はさらに上のスコアを目指して勉強を継続するつもりです。

Part 6 基礎トレーニング

強化パートの最後は、Part 6。本書では、速読と文脈の把握を目標にトレーニングを行う。まずは例題に挑戦しよう。

【例題】

▶解答：p.137

Questions 1-3 refer to the following e-mail.

To: Benjamin Green <bgreen@mailmult.com>
From: Steven Zacchary <szach@cityro.com>
Subject: Order confirmation

Dear Mr. Green,

Thank you for your order of 80 kilos of No. 9 European Mocha Blend coffee, ------- we received by fax earlier today. ------- this is a relatively large order,

1. (A) which
   (B) what
   (C) that
   (D) whenever

2. (A) Since
   (B) Nonetheless
   (C) Because of
   (D) Accordingly

in addition to being your first placed with us, we are eager to ensure your complete satisfaction. The fax we received does not indicate your preferences ------- the roast of the coffee beans, or whether you prefer whole beans or

3. (A) with respect to
   (B) similar to
   (C) regardless of
   (D) in opposition to

ground. Please contact us at your convenience to specify the details of your order.
We are looking forward to hearing from you soon.

Sincerely,

Steven Zacchary
City Roasters Coffee

Part 6 解答のポイント

1つの文書に空所が3カ所あり、各所に入る最も適切な語句をそれぞれ4つの選択肢から選ぶのがPart 6だ。文書は全部で4あるので、設問数は合計12。**1文書1分半から2分、パート全体を6、7分で解き終えたい。**
解答のステップを、例題の解き方を見ながら確認しよう。

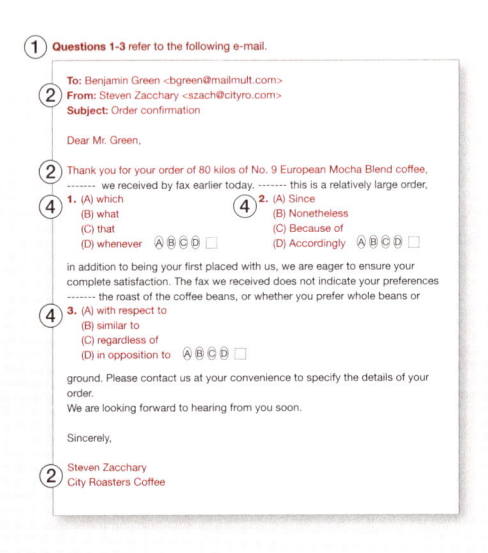

---

① **Questions 1-3** refer to the following e-mail.

② **To:** Benjamin Green <bgreen@mailmult.com>
From: Steven Zacchary <szach@cityro.com>
Subject: Order confirmation

Dear Mr. Green,

② Thank you for your order of 80 kilos of No. 9 European Mocha Blend coffee, -------- we received by fax earlier today. -------- this is a relatively large order,

④ **1.** (A) which
　　(B) what
　　(C) that
　　(D) whenever　Ⓐ Ⓑ Ⓒ Ⓓ ☐

④ **2.** (A) Since
　　(B) Nonetheless
　　(C) Because of
　　(D) Accordingly　Ⓐ Ⓑ Ⓒ Ⓓ ☐

in addition to being your first placed with us, we are eager to ensure your complete satisfaction. The fax we received does not indicate your preferences -------- the roast of the coffee beans, or whether you prefer whole beans or

④ **3.** (A) with respect to
　　(B) similar to
　　(C) regardless of
　　(D) in opposition to　Ⓐ Ⓑ Ⓒ Ⓓ ☐

ground. Please contact us at your convenience to specify the details of your order.
We are looking forward to hearing from you soon.

Sincerely,

② Steven Zacchary
City Roasters Coffee

---

①**冒頭の指示文から文書のタイプを確認**
　➡ following e-mailから、メールだとわかる

②**タイトル、ヘッダー、あて先、差出人、件名、最初のパラグラフの1、2文目、最後のパラグラフの終わりの1、2文などを見て、誰から誰あてで趣旨・目的は何かを把握**
　➡ あて名にBenjamin Green、差出人にSteven Zacchary、件名に「注文の確認」とある。また、署名欄にCity Roasters Coffeeと、Zaccharyの勤める会社の名前がある。「ご注文ありがとうございます」からメールが始まっているので、注文を受けたZaccharyが、内容をGreenに確認することが目的だとわかる。

③**各パラグラフの1、2文目の内容と接続語に注意し、流れをつかみながら文書全体を素早く読む。後戻りせず、語順に従ってチャンク単位で理解すること。**

④**設問にぶつかったら、選択肢を見て問題パターンをチェックする**
　「品詞」を問う問題：空所の前後を見て、文の構造から適切な品詞を判断する。
　「時制」を問う問題：文書の日付、「時」に関する語句やメールの件名、空所を含む

文の前後の流れを見て判断する。
「代名詞」を問う問題：空所のある文、またはその前の文と、メールや手紙の場合は差出人やあて先、件名を参照し、どの名詞を指しているか（人・物・物事など）、どんな働きか（主格、所有格、目的格、所有代名詞、再帰代名詞）を特定する。
「接続語」を問う問題：論理の展開で判断する。空所のある文の前半や後半の節、前後の文、前のパラグラフとの関係を見る。否定や肯定を示す語に注意。
「語彙」を問う問題：空所のある文と前後の文を参照し、言い換えにも注意しつつ文脈から判断。選択肢に知らない語が複数並んでいたら、時間を無駄にせず適当にマークし、次に進む。
「前置詞」を問う問題：知識を尋ねているので、知らない場合は適当にマーク。

➡ 1.は関係代名詞の問題。1文目なので、空所の代名詞が指す名詞は必ず文中にある。we receivedの目的語になる語は、your order。これを言い換えると(A) whichが正解。

2.は接続語の問題。large orderだと言っている個所と、we are eager to ensure …と希望を述べている個所は「理由」を表す接続の語でつながる。because ofの後に節は来ない（名詞が来る）ので、正解は(A) Since。

3.は前置詞(句)を問う問題。preferences と the roastの間に入る語句を選ぶ。文の流れから、「〜に関する」を表す語だとわかるので、正解は(A) with respect to。もしこのフレーズを知らなければ、適当にマークして次の問題に進もう。

⑤ 正解を確定する

訳

問題1-3は次のメールに関するものです。
あて先：Benjamin Green <bgreen@mailmult.com>
差出人：Steven Zacchary <szach@cityro.com> / 件名：ご注文の確認
Green様
No.9 European Mocha Blendコーヒー80キロをご注文いただき、ありがとうございます。本日、ファクスにて承りました。お客様から当店への初めてのご注文であることに加え、比較的大口のご注文ですので、十分ご満足いただけるよう確実を期したいと願っております。いただいたファクスには、コーヒー豆の焙煎についてのお好みや、豆と粉末のどちらをご希望かが記載されていませんでした。ご都合のよろしいときに、注文の詳細の指定のため、ご連絡いただけますでしょうか。/ お返事をお待ちしております。/
敬具 / Steven Zacchary / City Roasters Coffee /

● 選択肢の訳
1. 訳は割愛
2. (A)【接続詞】〜なので (B)【副詞】それにも関わらず (C)【前置詞句】〜のために (D)【副詞】それゆえに
3. (A) 〜に関して (B) 〜に似ている (C) 〜に関わらず (D) 〜に反して

Practice

▶解答：p.143〜

それでは、各問題の右ページにある1〜5のステップに従って、実際に解答してみよう。全6問で、制限時間は6分。

Questions 1-3 refer to the following advertisement.

Good Eating Annual Healthy Dessert Contest

Share your ideas on good eating and help make the world a healthier place! Send us your favorite low-calorie dessert recipe together with a short explanation or interesting anecdote. All entries will be judged by ------- panel of expert

    1. (A) its
       (B) her
       (C) our
       (D) their

chefs and dietitians, and the top 15 recipes will be ------- in the January

    2. (A) featured
       (B) participated
       (C) donated
       (D) accepted

edition of *Good Eating* magazine. The winner of the first prize will receive a complete set of *Good Eating* kitchen accessories and a three-year premium membership of the *Good Eating* Gourmet Club, ------- two runners-up will

    3. (A) while
       (B) which
       (C) what
       (D) when

receive a free one-year subscription to *Good Eating* magazine. Don't miss out on this excellent opportunity to share your unique cooking style.

解答ステップ

1 ▶ 冒頭の指示文から文書のタイプを確認（　　　　　　　　　　）

2 ▶ タイトル、ヘッダー、あて先、差出人、件名、最初のパラグラフの1、2文目、最後のパラグラフの終わりの1、2文などを見て、誰から誰あてで趣旨・目的は何かを把握

（　　　　　　　　　　）から（　　　　　　　　　　）あて

趣旨・目的は（　　　　　　　　　　　　　　　　　　　　　　）

3 ▶ 各パラグラフの1、2文目の内容と接続語に注意し、流れをつかみながら文書全体を読む

4 ▶ 設問にぶつかったら、まず選択肢をチェックする

1.は（　　　　　　　　　　）を問う問題

解き方は（　　　　　　　　　　　　　　　　　　　　　　　　）

2.は（　　　　　　　　　　）を問う問題

解き方は（　　　　　　　　　　　　　　　　　　　　　　　　）

3.は（　　　　　　　　　　）を問う問題

解き方は（　　　　　　　　　　　　　　　　　　　　　　　　）

5 ▶ 正解を確定する

1.の解答 Ⓐ Ⓑ Ⓒ Ⓓ　　2.の解答 Ⓐ Ⓑ Ⓒ Ⓓ　　3.の解答 Ⓐ Ⓑ Ⓒ Ⓓ

Questions 4-6 refer to the following memorandum.

ATTN: All Employees

Summer is almost here, and that means it's time to begin planning for the annual company picnic and summer outing. As in previous years, this year's event will be held at the Tynan River Recreation Area within Grand Falls National Park. ------- the event is still more than two months away, we want to begin planning

4. (A) However
   (B) Although
   (C) Due to
   (D) Meanwhile   Ⓐ Ⓑ Ⓒ Ⓓ ☐

early to make this year's outing the most spectacular ever.
Each year, we have succeeded in attracting increased attendance from employees' family members, ------- have expressed particular appreciation for

5. (A) who
   (B) whose
   (C) which
   (D) whoever   Ⓐ Ⓑ Ⓒ Ⓓ ☐

the child-friendly activities we have organized. We would like to continue to encourage this trend by planning more fun events, and are therefore -------

6. (A) soliciting
   (B) influencing
   (C) impressing
   Ⓐ Ⓑ Ⓒ Ⓓ ☐   (D) infringing

suggestions and pledges to volunteer.
If you have any ideas on how we can make this the best annual picnic and summer outing ever, please contact us in the Public Relations Office at your earliest convenience.

Cheryl Fields
Coordinator, 17th Annual Company Picnic and Summer Outing

解答ステップ

1 ▶ 冒頭の指示文から文書のタイプを確認（　　　　　　　　　　）

2 ▶ タイトル、ヘッダー、あて先、差出人、件名、最初の段落の1、2文目、最後のパラグラフの終わりの1、2文などを見て、誰から誰あてで趣旨・目的は何かを把握

　（　　　　　　　　　　）から（　　　　　　　　　　）あて

　趣旨・目的は（　　　　　　　　　　　　　　　　　　　　　）

3 ▶ 各パラグラフの1、2文目の内容と接続語に注意し、流れをつかみながら文書全体を読む

4 ▶ 設問にぶつかったら、まず選択肢をチェックする

　4.は（　　　　　　　　　）を問う問題

　解き方は（　　　　　　　　　　　　　　　　　　　　　　　）

　5.は（　　　　　　　　　）を問う問題

　解き方は（　　　　　　　　　　　　　　　　　　　　　　　）

　6.は（　　　　　　　　　）を問う問題

　解き方は（　　　　　　　　　　　　　　　　　　　　　　　）

5 ▶ 正解を確定する

　4.の解答　Ⓐ Ⓑ Ⓒ Ⓓ　　5.の解答　Ⓐ Ⓑ Ⓒ Ⓓ　　6.の解答　Ⓐ Ⓑ Ⓒ Ⓓ

解答行動分析リスト

Practiceで正解できなかった、もしくは解答に時間がかかりすぎた設問については、以下のポイントから原因を拾い出し、次ページからの解答横の[　　]に記入しよう。

❶ ビジネス文書の文脈がよくわからなかった
❷ 慣れていない文書タイプだった
❸ 文書タイプや誰から誰あて、趣旨・目的をチェックしなかった
❹ 文書の内容を勘違いした
❺ 設問のポイントがすぐにわからなかった
❻ 設問を解く順番を間違えた
❼ 選択肢に知らない語句があってうろたえた
❽ 選択肢を2つに絞った後、迷ってしまった
❾ 選択肢の内容を勘違いした
❿ チャンク単位で読むのに不慣れだった
⓫ 文書にメリハリがなく、要点把握が難しかった
⓬ ヒントの個所がなかなか見つけられなかった
⓭ 文書を読むのに時間をかけすぎた
⓮ 熟読しすぎた
⓯ 完ぺきに理解しようとしすぎた
⓰ 知らない語彙に時間をかけすぎた
⓱ 理解するため何度も読んでしまった
⓲ 1問に時間をかけすぎた
⓳ 正解を絞りきれずに迷った
⓴ 全問正解にこだわってしまった
㉑ 前の問題をひきずって切り替えられなかった
㉒ 集中力の欠如
㉓ 時間が足りず、適当にマークした
㉔ マークの塗り間違え
㉕ パニックに陥った

Practiceの正解と解説

英文の訳はチャンクで区切られているので、後で音読する際に参照しよう。

問題1-3は次の広告に関するものです。
*Good Eating*毎年恒例のヘルシーデザート・コンテスト //
おいしい料理に関するあなたのアイデアを広く伝えて、/ 世界をより健康的な場所にする手助けをしましょう！// あなたのお気に入りの低カロリーデザートのレシピをお送りください / 短い説明や楽しい逸話と一緒に。// すべての参加作品は、熟練シェフと栄養士からなる当社の委員会による審査を受け / 上位15位までのレシピは、*Good Eating*誌1月号で取り上げられます。// 優勝者に贈られるのは、*Good Eating*台所用品一式と、/ *Good Eating*グルメクラブの3年間のプレミアムメンバーシップで、/ 2名の準優勝者に贈られるのは、*Good Eating*誌の1年間の無料購読権です。// あなただけの料理法を広く知らせる絶好の機会を、どうかお見逃しなく。//

● 解答ステップの解答例

1 広告　**2** Good Eating誌から一般の人あて、趣旨・目的はコンテスト参加者の募集
4 1. 代名詞　解き方：空所のある文、またはその前の文を参照し、どの名詞を指しているかとどんな働きをしているかを特定、2. 語彙　解き方：空所のある文と前後の文を参照し、言い換えに注意しつつ文脈から判断、3. 接続語　解き方：空所のある文の前半や後半の節を見て、論理展開で判断
3、5は解説を参照

1. 訳は割愛

解説 コンテスト参加者の募集広告で、Send us your ... recipeから主催が広告主だとわかる。judged by ------- panel of expert chefs and dietitiansの前に、主催者以外は登場していないので、正解は明らか。
解答 **(C)** 解答行動の分析 [　　　　　]

2. (A)【他動詞】〜を特集する
(B)【自動詞】参加する
(C)【他動詞】〜に寄付する
(D)【他動詞】〜を受け入れる

解説 the top 15 recipes will be ------- in the January edition of *Good Eating* magazineという空所の前後を読めば、「magazineに特集で掲載される」という意のfeaturedが適しているとわかる。
解答 **(A)** 解答行動の分析 [　　　　　]

3. 訳は割愛

解説 空所のある文に目を通すと、The winner of the first prizeとtwo runners-upが対比して述べられていることがわかる。こういう場合に使われるのはwhile（一方）だ。
解答 **(A)** 解答行動の分析 [　　　　　]

問題4-6は次の社内メモに関するものです。
従業員の皆さんへ //
夏はもうすぐそこです / つまり、毎年恒例の社員ピクニックと夏期の遠出の計画を始める時期だということです。// 昨年と同様、/ 今年のイベントが開催されるのも、Tynan Riverレクリエーションエリアです / Grand Falls国立公園内の。// イベントはまだ2カ月以上先ですが、/ 早めに計画を始めて、今年の遠出をこれまでで最も素晴らしいものにしたいと思っています。//
毎年、/ ますます多くの従業員のご家族の皆様にご参加いただいていますが、/ そういった方々がとりわけ高く評価してくださるのが、私たちが計画した、子どもにぴったりの活動です。// この流れを後押しすべく、より楽しいイベントを企画することで / ご提案や、ボランティアとして加わってくださるメンバーを募集しております。//
どうすれば、今回の年次ピクニックと夏期の遠出を過去最高のものにできるか、何かアイデアをお持ちでしたら、/ 広報室まで早急にご連絡ください。//
Cheryl Fields / 第17回年次社員ピクニック及び夏期の遠出コーディネーター //

● 解答ステップの解説例

1 社内メモ　**2** 広報室から従業員あて、趣旨・目的は社員ピクニックのアイデア募集
4 4.接続語　解き方：空所のある文の前半や後半の節を見て、論理展開で判断、5. 代名詞　解き方：空所のある文、またはその前の文を参照し、どの名詞を指しているかとどんな働きをしているかを特定、6. 語彙　解き方：空所のある文と前後の文を参照し、言い換えに注意しつつ文脈から判断　**3、5**は解説を参照

4. (A)【副詞】しかしながら
(B)【接続詞】〜であるけれども
(C) 〜のために
(D)【副詞】一方では

解説　空所のある節とその後ろの節の流れに注目して判断する。キーワードに注目するとわかりやすい。前半のstill more than two months awayと後半のwant to begin planning earlyから逆接の関係と判断できる。
解答　(B) 解答行動の分析 [　　　　　　　]

5. 訳は割愛

解説　文頭のEach yearから読むと、空所の直前のemployees' family membersが先行詞だとわかる。この先行詞を受けて主語となれるのはwhoのみ。
解答　(A) 解答行動の分析 [　　　　　　　]

6. (A)【他動詞】〜を求める
(B)【他動詞】〜に影響を与える
(C)【他動詞】〜に感銘を与える
(D)【他動詞】〜を破る

解説　空所の前後の文脈で判断する。前にlike to continue to encourage this trend、後ろにsuggestions and pledges to volunteerとあるので、それらをつなぐ「求める」という意味をもつsolicitが正解。
解答　(A) 解答行動の分析 [　　　　　　　]

いよいよ音読を開始しよう！

Task 1

それでは音読に挑戦する。まず、**1**) 英文をすべての区切り (/と/と//) で区切って音読しよう (**短いチャンク**)。意味をつかみながら読めるようになったら、今度は**長いチャンク**に挑戦。**2**) トラック09、10の音声のポーズの部分でリピートしよう。**3**) きちんとリピートできるようになったら、**仕上げにもう一度**、長いチャンクで音読しよう。

CD 2-09

Good Eating Annual Healthy Dessert Contest //

Share your ideas on good eating / and help make the world a healthier place! //
Send us your favorite low-calorie dessert recipe /
together with a short explanation / or interesting anecdote. //
All entries will be judged / by our panel of expert chefs and dietitians, /
and the top 15 recipes will be featured in the January edition /
of *Good Eating* magazine. //
The winner of the first prize /
will receive a complete set of *Good Eating* kitchen accessories /
and a three-year premium membership / of the *Good Eating* Gourmet Club, /
while two runners-up will receive a free one-year subscription /
to *Good Eating* magazine. //
Don't miss out on this excellent opportunity /
to share your unique cooking style. //

要注意フレーズ！

この英文には、コンテストの特徴的な表現が盛り込まれている。イベントの告知などにも登場するフレーズなので、丸ごと覚えるつもりで下線部を音読しよう。

ATTN: All Employees //
Summer is almost here, / and that means it's time to begin planning /
for the annual company picnic and summer outing. //
As in previous years, /
this year's event will be held at the Tynan River Recreation Area /
within Grand Falls National Park. //
Although the event is still more than two months away, /
we want to begin planning early /
to make this year's outing the most spectacular ever. //
Each year, / we have succeeded in attracting /
increased attendance from employees' family members, /
who have expressed particular appreciation /
for the child-friendly activities we have organized. //
We would like to continue to encourage this trend /
by planning more fun events, /
and are therefore soliciting suggestions and pledges to volunteer. //
If you have any ideas /
on how we can make this the best annual picnic and summer outing ever, /
please contact us in the Public Relations office / at your earliest convenience. //
Cheryl Fields /
Coordinator, 17th Annual Company Picnic and Summer Outing //

要注意フレーズ！

動詞を中心としたフレーズを、前置詞や目的語との組み合わせに注意しながら音読しよう。「2カ月も先」、「これまでで最も素晴らしいもの」、「早急に」なども、即座に英語で言えるように繰り返し練習を。

Task 2

2-09~10

CDの音声を聞いて、ポーズの部分で**各チャンクの意味を頭に浮かべよう**（同時通訳の要領で声に出しても可）。ポーズの間にわからなければ、143~144ページの訳をチェックしよう。

Task 3

2-09~10

CDの音声を聞いて、**スクリプトを見ないで**ポーズの部分でリピートしよう。

Task 4

2-11~12

仕上げに145~146ページのスクリプトを見ながら、トラック11~12の音声に**オーバーラップさせて読んでみよう**。プロソディーに注意しながらタイミングが合うまで繰り返して、ナチュラルスピードでの音読に慣れよう。

Task 5

2-11~12

本日の学習を終えた後も、これらトラックをスクリプトを見ずに聞いて理解できるか、繰り返し確認するようにしよう。

学習エネルギーをチャージする今日の **格言**

> **Let me tell you the secret that has led me to my goal.**
> **My strength lies solely in my tenacity.**
>
> Louis Pasteur
> （1822~1895：フランスの生化学者、細菌学者）
>
> 私に目標達成をもたらした秘密をお教えしよう。私の強みはただひたすら粘り強さにあるのだ。

4カ国発音を攻略する！ Vol.2
オーストラリア英語編

イギリス連邦（The Commonwealth of Nations）のメンバーであるオーストラリアの英語は、アメリカ英語よりイギリス英語に近い。オーストラリアならではの発音もあるので、しっかりチェックしよう。

❶ 語尾の /r/ は発音されないことが多い

❷ 二重母音 /ei/ が /æi/ になる

米語・イギリス英語の /ei/（二重母音）が /æi/ の発音になる。

	came	date	face	mail	same	take	today
米	kéim	déit	féis	méil	séim	téik	tədéi
豪	kǽim	dǽit	fǽis	mǽil	sǽim	tǽik	tədǽi

❸ 母音の後ろの /t/ 音と /d/ 音が似た発音になる

イギリス英語では、/t/ 音と /d/ 音は明確に発音するが、オーストラリア英語では米語と同様にいずれも弱 /d/ 音になる。

	metal	medal
英	métl	médl
豪	mé(d)l	mé(d)l

❹ 米語の /i:/ 音が /ei/ の発音になる

	meet	team
米	mí:t	tí:m
豪	méit	téim

それでは以下の会話をCDで聞いた後、色文字の部分を意識しながら音読しよう。

2-13

W: Did you check the mail today? I've been expecting a package from Zimmerman Metal, and it was supposed to come yesterday.

M: Oh, it came this morning. I didn't know who it was for, because they only put our company name on the label. Isn't Zimmerman the same company that you're going to talk with face to face next week?

W: Yes, I'm going to meet their development team about the project we're working on. These are materials I need to check out before the meeting.

M: Okay, I'll ask John to take the box up to your office in a couple of minutes. It's pretty heavy!

会話の訳

W: 今日、郵便物をチェックした？ Zimmerman Metalからの小包をずっと待ってるの。昨日着くはずだったんだけど。
M: ああ、けさ来たよ。誰あてかわからなかったんだ、ラベルに会社名しかなかったから。そのZimmermanって、君が来週直接話すことになっている会社？
W: ええ、今取りかかっているプロジェクトに関して、先方の開発チームと会うの。これは会議前にチェックしなければならない資料なのよ。
M: 了解、例の箱を君のオフィスにすぐに持って行くようJohnに頼むよ。すごく重いんだ！

Part 6 基本音読

10日目 / 20

今日は、Part 6で最も難関となるDiscourse Markerの設問を中心に取り上げる。例題に挑戦した後、Practice、音読の順に学習を進めよう。

【例題】

▶解答：p.152

Questions 1-3 refer to the following book summary.

An Inventory of Innovation
By Sam K. Pierce

This book will be of immense interest to anyone ------- enjoys stories of

1. (A) whoever
 (B) whose
 (C) who
 (D) whom Ⓐ Ⓑ Ⓒ Ⓓ ☐

success. It includes 12 well-told accounts of how people from all walks of life took fresh new ideas and turned them into winning business plans. But this is not, -------, a how-to book. Chock-full of good practical advice as it is, it will

2. (A) under consideration
 (B) so to speak
 (C) besides
 (D) nonetheless Ⓐ Ⓑ Ⓒ Ⓓ ☐

naturally be of great use to those who are thinking about starting a business. But the fact remains that these are stories about people. And they are told with such heart, sensitivity and wit that it will be a compelling read in terms of how others take on challenges, overcome obstacles and struggle to succeed in the end. -------, Mr. Pierce's book is inspiring, uplifting, and practically useful.

3. (A) For instance
 (B) By the way
 (C) Instead
 (D) In brief Ⓐ Ⓑ Ⓒ Ⓓ ☐

Discourse Markerの種類

Discourse markerは「話の道筋を示すために使われる語句」のことで、接続詞、接続副詞や前置詞句などがある。選択肢に下記のようなDiscourse markerが並んでいたら、空所のある文と前後の文を読み、論理展開や流れを把握して判断しよう。

1. 追加
    additionally、in addition、also、besides、furthermore、moreover（さらに、加えて、そのほかに）

2. 矛盾・比較・対照・対比
    however、nevertheless、nonetheless、still、all the same（しかしながら）、conversely（逆に）、on the contrary（反対に）、on the other hand（一方）、whereas、while（〜だが一方）、instead（それどころか）、in contrast、by contrast（それと対照的に）

3. 結果・結論
    as a result、as a consequence、in consequence、consequently、thus、therefore、accordingly、hence（したがって、その結果）、finally、in the end、at last、lastly（ついに、やっと）、eventually（ゆくゆくは、やがては）、ultimately、in the long run（最終的に、結局）、in conclusion、in summary、in a word、in short、in brief、in short（要するに）

4. 類似
    likewise、also、similarly（同様に）

5. 例示
    for instance、for example（たとえば）

6. 言い換え
    that is (to say)、in other words（すなわち）

7. 強調
    in particular、particularly、especially、above all（特に）、as a matter of fact、in fact、actually（事実上、実際は）、obviously、evidently（明らかに）、specifically（もっと正確に言えば）

8. その他
    otherwise（さもなければ）、incidentally、by the way（ところで）、meanwhile（そうしている間に）、at the same time（同時に）、apparently、seemingly（一見すると）、as a rule、in general、generally、generally speaking、by and large、on the whole、roughly speaking、broadly speaking、all in all、in all、altogether、taken altogether（概して）、that is why（そういうわけで）、at any rate、in any event、at all events、in any case、anyhow、anyway（とにかく）、so to speak（いわゆる）

例題の正解と解説

英文の訳はチャンクで区切られている。音読する際に参照しよう。

問題1-3は次の本の要約に関するものです。
『革新の在庫目録』// Sam K. Pierce 著 //
本書は、成功談好きには非常に興味深いだろう。// ここに収録されているのは、巧みに語られた12の物語である / さまざまな分野の人々が、いかにして斬新なアイデアを取り入れて、それらを素晴らしいビジネスプランにしたかという。// しかし本書は、いわゆるハウツー本ではない。// 実践的な助言そのものがぎっしりと詰まっていて、/ 当然、起業を考えている人には、大いに役立つであろう。// しかし、これらが人々の物語であることに変わりはない。// しかも、豊かな愛情と感性、ウィットを持って描かれているため、/ 非常に説得力のある読み物でもある / ほかの人々が、どのように挑戦し、障害を乗り越えたのかに関する / そして最終的に成功を収めるため奮闘しているか(に関する)。// つまり、Pierce氏の本は感動的で、気持ちを盛り上げてくれる、極めて実用的な一冊である。//

---

1. 訳は割愛

解説 関係代名詞の問題を解く際にチェックするのは3点。①どの名詞を指しているか(人・物・事など)と②働き(主格・所有格・目的格)。③前置詞＋関係代名詞の選択肢がある場合は、関係代名詞のところで分けた2つの文を考える。最初の文には、関係代名詞が指す可能性がある名詞としてThis book、immense interest、anyoneがある。後の文のenjoys stories of successの主語になれるのはanyoneのみだ。**解答** (C)

---

2. (A) 検討中で
(B) いわゆる
(C)【副詞】その上
(D)【副詞】それにもかかわらず

解説 まず空所のある文とその前の文との論理展開をチェックする。前の文は本の特徴の紹介で、空所のある文はBut this is not, -------, a how-to book.となっている。Butはnonethelessと意味が重なる。besidesも「追加」なので不適。under considerationは文脈に合わない。その語がなくても文の意味が成立し、言い換えを表すso to speakが正解。**解答** (B)

---

3. (A) 例えば
(B) ところで
(C)【副詞】その代わりに
(D) 要するに

解説 前の文からの論理展開に注目する。they are told with such heart, sensitivity and wit that it will be a compelling read in terms of how others take on challenges ...という前文の内容を、空所の後ではMr. Pierce's book is inspiring, uplifting, and practically useful.と、要点をまとめて言い換えている。下線部に注目すると論理展開がわかりやすい。**解答** (D)

Practice

▶解答：p.155〜

それではDiscourse Markerに注意しながら、練習問題に挑戦しよう。全6問で、制限時間は4分。

Questions 1-3 refer to the following article.

Local businesses in the Slayton Heights district are hoping that a new convention center in the nearby downtown area will bring in more customers. Real estate developers have proposed numerous plans for a downtown convention center in recent decades. -------, polls show that a majority of

1. (A) Otherwise
   (B) Namely
   (C) For instance
   (D) Additionally   Ⓐ Ⓑ Ⓒ Ⓓ ☐

residents favor such a project. -------, such plans have run into opposition

2. (A) Still
   (B) Hence
   (C) Specifically
   (D) Despite   Ⓐ Ⓑ Ⓒ Ⓓ ☐

from environmentalist groups warning of potential damage to the adjacent wetland area. The design for a new "Green Convention Center," -------, has

3. (A) moreover
   (B) in order that
   (C) on the other hand
   (D) by and large   Ⓐ Ⓑ Ⓒ Ⓓ ☐

incorporated advice from environmentalists from the beginning, and appears likely to become a reality within about three years.

Questions 4-6 refer to the following e-mail.

From: Natalie Thomas <nthomas@workingsnet.mail.com>
To: Jason Evans <jevans@workingsnet.mail.com>
Subject: Presentation Advice

Thanks very much for meeting with me earlier today about our upcoming presentation. I certainly do appreciate your advice.
------- I have no shortage of confidence in the content of my material, this is,
4. (A) Nevertheless
   (B) Even though
   (C) Instead
   (D) In spite   Ⓐ Ⓑ Ⓒ Ⓓ ☐
as you know, my first appearance before the board of directors. So it means a lot to me to be able to adjust my style and presentation in keeping with your knowledge and experience in this area.
I think I'm all ready to go, ------- one nagging uncertainty. This may sound like
   5. (A) except for
      (B) in place of
      (C) with respect to
      (D) in exchange for   Ⓐ Ⓑ Ⓒ Ⓓ ☐
a small matter, but sometimes details are important. The meeting room isn't really all that big. But it does have an audio system. Given your impression of my speaking voice, and the preferences of the board members, would you advise using the microphone and speakers? -------, simply relying on my
   6. (A) Lastly
      (B) Conversely
      (C) Unlikely
Ⓐ Ⓑ Ⓒ Ⓓ ☐   (D) In particular
voice alone might make a better impression. What are your thoughts? I would appreciate it if you could give me some quick feedback.

Sincerely,
Natalie T.

Practiceの正解と解説

英文の訳はチャンクで区切られている。後で音読する際に参照しよう。

問題1-3は次の記事に関するものです。
Slayton Heights地区の地元経済界は / 近隣の商業地区の新たなコンベンションセンターが、さらに多くの客を呼び込んでくれることを期待している。// 不動産開発業者は計画を数多く提案してきた / ここ数十年、商業地区のコンベンションセンターの。// さらに、世論調査によると、住民の大半はこういった計画を歓迎している。// しかしこの種の計画は、環境保護グループの反対を受けてきた / (彼らは)近くの湿地帯地域にダメージを与える危険性があると警告している。// 他方、新たな「Green Convention Center」のデザインは、/ 当初から環境保護活動家からの助言を取り入れてきたので、/ 3年以内には実現する可能性が高そうだ。//

---

1. (A)【副詞】さもなければ
(B)【副詞】すなわち
(C) たとえば
(D)【副詞】さらに

解説 空所のある文とその前の文の論理展開を確認しよう。キーワードに注目し、語句が表現している内容が肯定的なニュアンス（＋）か、否定的なニュアンス（－）か考えてみる。前の文はproposed numerous plans（＋）、空所の文はfavor such a project（＋）なので、追加の意味のAdditionallyを入れると最も自然な展開となる。

解答 (D)

---

2. (A)【副詞】しかしながら
(B)【副詞】その結果
(C)【副詞】すなわち
(D)【前置詞】～にも関わらず

解説 キーワードに注目して論理の流れを調べる。前の文はfavor such a project（＋）で、空所のある文はrun into opposition（－）なので、逆接の意味のStillが論理展開として自然。

解答 (A)

---

3. (A)【副詞】さらに
(B) ～するように
(C) 他方では
(D) 概して

解説 ここでもキーワードに注目して論理の流れを調べる。前の文のrun into opposition from environmentalist groupsと、空所を含む文のincorporated advice from environmentalists from the beginning, and...become a reality within about three years. の下線部を見ると、空所には「したがって」または「他方で」のいずれかが入る流れになっていることがわかる。選択肢中で該当するのはon the other handのみ。

解答 (C)

問題4-6は次のメールに関するものです。
差出人：Natalie Thomas <nthomas@workingsnet.mail.com>
あて先：Jason Evans <jevans@workingsnet.mail.com> // 件名：プレゼンテーションの助言 //
先ほどは、今度のプレゼンテーションのことでご面会くださいましてありがとうございました。// ご助言をいただき、誠に感謝しております。//
資料の内容には自信があるのですが、/ ご存じのとおり、私が重役の前に出るのは今回が初めてです。// ですから、私にとってスタイルやプレゼンテーションを調整することはとても意義があります / あなたのこの分野における知識や経験に沿って。//
準備は万端だと思いますが / ただ1つ、なかなか消えない不安があります。// 小さなことと思われるかもしれませんが / 細部が重要なこともあります。// 会議室はそれほど大きくありません。// しかし、オーディオシステムが備え付けられています。// 私の話す声についてのあなたのご感想や、重役の方々の好みを考慮すると、/ マイクとスピーカーを使ったほうがいいと思われますか。// 逆に、自分の声のみで話したほうが、/ より良い印象を与えるかもしれないとも思います。// あなたはどうお考えでしょうか。// 早急にご意見をお聞かせ願えれば幸いです。// 敬具 / Natalie T. //

---

4. (A) 【副詞】しかしながら
   (B) 〜ではあるけれども
   (C) 【副詞】それどころか
   (D) in spite of（〜にもかかわらず）の一部

解説 空所のある文の前半はno shortage of confidence（＋）、後半はmy first appearance ...（−）なので、論理展開は「〜ではあるけれども」の意のEven thoughが自然。
解答 (B)

---

5. (A) 〜を除けば
   (B) 〜の代わりに
   (C) 〜に関して
   (D) 〜と交換に

解説 空所を含む文の前半all ready to goはプラスの情報、後半のone nagging uncertaintyはマイナス情報なので、対比、または逆接の論理展開になる。選択肢の中ではexcept forが最適。
解答 (A)

---

6. (A) 【副詞】ついに
   (B) 【副詞】逆に
   (C) 【副詞】ありそうもなく
   (D) 特に

解説 前の文のusing the microphone and speakersと、空所のある文のsimply relying on my voice aloneは、論理展開として逆接または対比なので、Converselyが正解。simplyに注目するとわかりやすい。
解答 (B)

Task 1

それでは音読に挑戦する。まず、**1)** 英文をすべての区切り (/と/と//) で区切って音読しよう (**短いチャンク**)。意味をつかみながら読めるようになったら、今度は**長いチャンク**に挑戦。**2)** トラック14、15の音声のポーズの部分でリピートしよう。**3)** プロソディーを意識してリピートできるようになったら、**仕上げにもう一度**、長いチャンクで音読しよう。

CD 2-14

Local businesses in the Slayton Heights district /
are hoping that a new convention center in the nearby downtown area /
will bring in more customers. //
Real estate developers have proposed numerous plans /
for a downtown convention center in recent decades. //
Additionally, / <u>polls show that a majority of residents favor such a project</u>. //
Still, / such plans <u>have run into opposition from environmentalist groups</u> /
<u>warning of potential damage to the adjacent wetland area</u>. //
The design for a new "Green Convention Center," on the other hand, /
<u>has incorporated advice from environmentalists</u> from the beginning, /
and appears likely to become a reality / within about three years. //

10日目

要注意フレーズ!

ニュースのトピックとして頻出なのが、新しい施設の建設と、それが近隣に与える影響の分析。この記事には、住民の意向、環境保護団体の反対など、TOEICでおなじみの語彙・表現が多数登場する。下線部の長めのフレーズ・文に特に注意しよう。

From: Natalie Thomas <nthomas@workingsnet.mail.com> //
To: Jason Evans <jevans@workingsnet.mail.com> //
Subject: Presentation Advice //
Thanks very much for meeting with me earlier today / about our upcoming presentation. //
<u>I certainly do appreciate your advice.</u> //
Even though I have no shortage of confidence in the content of my material, / this is, as you know, my first appearance before the board of directors. //
So <u>it means a lot to me</u> / <u>to be able to adjust my style and presentation</u> / <u>in keeping with your knowledge and experience in this area</u>. //
I think I'm all ready to go, / except for one nagging uncertainty. //
This may sound like a small matter, / but sometimes details are important. //
The meeting room isn't really all that big. //
But it does have an audio system. //
Given your impression of my speaking voice, / and the preferences of the board members, / would you advise using the microphone and speakers? //
Conversely, / simply relying on my voice alone / might make a better impression. //
What are your thoughts? //
<u>I would appreciate it if you could give me some quick feedback.</u> //
Sincerely, / Natalie T. //

要注意フレーズ！

感謝や要望を伝えるメールも頻出する。このメールでは、感謝に続き、自分の考えの表明と助力の要請が行われている。下線部は特に書き言葉特有の表現なので、繰り返し口に出して覚えよう。

Task 2

2-14〜15

CDの音声を聞いて、ポーズの部分で**各チャンクの意味を頭に浮かべよう**（同時通訳の要領で声に出しても可）。ポーズの間にわからなければ、155〜156ページの訳をチェックしよう。

Task 3

2-14〜15

CDの音声を聞いて、**スクリプトを見ないで**ポーズの部分でリピートしよう。

Task 4

2-16〜17

仕上げに157〜158ページのスクリプトを見ながら、トラック16、17の音声に**オーバーラップさせて読んでみよう**。プロソディーを意識しながらタイミングが合うまで繰り返し、ナチュラルスピードでの音読に慣れよう。

Task 5

2-16〜17

本日の学習を終えた後も、これらトラックをスクリプトを見ずに聞いて理解できるか、繰り返し確認するようにしよう。

学習エネルギーをチャージする今日の **格言**

> The people who get on in this world are the people who get up and look for the circumstances they want, and, if they can't find them, make them.
>
> George Bernard Shaw
> （1856〜1950：アイルランド出身の劇作家、劇評家）
>
> この世界で成功するのは、立ち上がっておのれの求める環境を探し、そして見つからない場合にはそれを作り出す人間だ。

11日目 / 20

チャレンジ Reading!

今日は、普段耳から聞いて解答しているPart 3、4を音読しながら解くという少し変わったトレーニングを行う。「たまたま設問には正解したけれど、実はきちんと聞けていなかった」部分がいつまでも残っていると、さらなるスコアアップは望めない。精読ならぬ精聴の力を付けるため、以下の手順で挑戦してみよう。

Task 1

▶解答：p.168〜

このTaskでは、Part 3の会話2つ、Part 4のトーク2つを取り上げる。
各会話、トークについて、以下の要領で解いていこう。

STEP 1：設問を音読する

まず、p.161の1〜3の設問をすべて音読する。音読は一度だけで、なるべくナチュラルスピードに近い速さで行う（この時点では選択肢は読まない）。

STEP 2：会話orトークを音読する

ページをめくって、p.163のQuestions 1-3の会話を一度だけ音読する。こちらもできるだけナチュラルスピードに近い速さで。冒頭部分は人物、趣旨、話題、状況、場所などが把握できるので特に注意しよう。設問の解答を探しつつ、チャンクで意味を把握しながら読んでいく。キーワードをキャッチしながら音読すること。

STEP 3：設問と疑問詞を再度音読して解答する

さらにページをめくって、p.165の1〜3の設問と選択肢を一度だけ順番にすべて音読し、正解をマークしていく。この際、絶対に前のページの会話を見ないこと。

以上のSTEPを、4〜6、7〜9、10〜12についても行っていく。
全問解答し終えたら、Task 2に進もう。

1. What is the man's job?
   (A) A cashier
   (B) A sales clerk
   (C) An accountant
   (D) A librarian

2. What does the woman ask about?
   (A) Whether she should go to the Children's Section
   (B) Whether her I.D. card has expired
   (C) Whether her CD is overdue
   (D) Whether the procedure will take much time

3. What does the man imply?
   (A) He will be working at a registration office next week.
   (B) The woman has to settle the payment.
   (C) The books for young children are available at a different department.
   (D) The woman should return goods at Counter Five.

4. What is the woman asking about?
   (A) Lawn and garden care
   (B) Office building maintenance
   (C) Inspection of a property
   (D) A travel schedule

5. What is true about the woman's business?
   (A) It was established recently.
   (B) It is a subsidiary of West Valley Landscaping.
   (C) It is located near a baggage claim area in the airport.
   (D) It won't remain open until late at night tonight.

6. What will the man do?
   (A) Ring up again to schedule an appointment
   (B) Visit the woman's office tomorrow
   (C) Decide whether to accept the estimate
   (D) Present a bill for past services

7. What is the report mainly about?
   (A) New services in the airline industry
   (B) Changes in transportation costs
   (C) Plans for purchasing new aircrafts
   (D) Extra fuel charges added to airfares

8. What is good about the new services?
   (A) All the seats are equipped with in-flight movie monitors.
   (B) The airfare has been greatly discounted for frequent fliers.
   (C) More menu choices have been offered.
   (D) The luggage compartment has been enlarged.

9. Who is Emma Gilbert?
   (A) An inspector
   (B) An airline employee
   (C) A journalist
   (D) An interior decorator

10. What kind of company is most likely providing this message?
    (A) A computer electronics company
    (B) A telecommunications company
    (C) A pharmaceutical company
    (D) An electric power company

11. What has to be done to receive information about a printer?
    (A) Press the number 1
    (B) Press the number 2
    (C) Press the number 3
    (D) Press the number 9

12. According to the message, what are the club members asked to do?
    (A) Update their personal information
    (B) Inform a representative of their club number
    (C) Give details of their new order
    (D) Sign up for the conference

Questions 1-3 refer to the following conversation.

W: Hi, I'd like to return these books and this audio CD. //
   The books are from the Children's Section of the library. //
   Can I return them here at the main desk? //
M: Certainly. // That'll be no problem. // Thank you. //
   May I see your I.D. card, please? //
W: Actually, / I had a card made when I borrowed the books and CD. //
   But I'm afraid I forgot to bring it with me today. //
   Is that going to be a problem? //
M: Not at all. // I can get the information by scanning the items. //
   Just a moment, please. //
   ... It seems the CD is past due. // So there'll be a fee of $1.25 on that one. //
   Here's a receipt and bill, / and you can pay at the cash register /
   right there at Counter Five. //

Questions 4-6 refer to the following conversation.

W: Hello, I'm calling to ask about your landscaping services. //
   We have a commercial property on Airport Boulevard /
   near the West Valley Mall, /
   and we're looking for someone who can handle the basic maintenance /
   and upkeep of the lawn, trees, and garden. //
M: Thank you for calling West Valley Landscaping. //
   We'd be glad to take care of everything you need. //
   I can have one of our professional landscape designers /
   visit you this afternoon if you're available. //
W: Actually, tomorrow morning around 10 would be best for us. //
   We're closing early today. //
M: That's fine. // I can visit you myself at 10 tomorrow /
   to look at the property and give you an estimate. //

Questions 7-9 refer to the following news report.

And now for today's business news. //
Discount airlines are responding to customers /
who want more comfort and perhaps a little bit of luxury /
without sacrificing affordability of a low-cost fare. //
In recent decades, low-cost airlines have become an important alternative /
for travelers who want the cheapest airfares they can find. //
Budget airlines such as RedJet, ValuFly and AirCommute /
have achieved popularity and profitability by placing more emphasis /
on economy, speed and convenience than on comfort or luxury. //
But all three of these popular discount airlines /
are now introducing new premium services. //
All three premium services charge 10% to 12% more than basic airfare, /
and offer more spacious seating and enhanced meal options. //
For example, according to ValuFly spokesperson Emma Gilbert, /
ValuFly's new "Premium Class" is less expensive than its own First Class service /
and the enhanced services of most other airlines, /
but it also provides more comfort than other basic services. //

....

Questions 10-12 refer to the following telephone message.

Thank you for calling / the Gibson Corporation Customer Assistance Center. //
All of our customer assistance specialists / are currently helping other customers, /
and will be with you in a moment. // The estimated wait time is 4 minutes /
although it may actually be much shorter. // While you wait, /
please help us prepare to assist you by refining your inquiry. //
For information about a software product, press 1. //
For information about a computer product, press 2. //
To inquire about peripheral equipment, press 3. //
To repeat these menu choices, press 9. //
If you are a Gibson Corporation Preferred Customer Club member, /
please prepare to provide our service representative with your I.D. number. //
Thank you for waiting. // Your call will be taken momentarily. //

1. What is the man's job?
(A) A cashier
(B) A sales clerk
(C) An accountant
(D) A librarian   Ⓐ Ⓑ Ⓒ Ⓓ ☐

2. What does the woman ask about?
(A) Whether she should go to the Children's Section
(B) Whether her I.D. card has expired
(C) Whether her CD is overdue
(D) Whether the procedure will take much time   Ⓐ Ⓑ Ⓒ Ⓓ ☐

3. What does the man imply?
(A) He will be working at a registration office next week.
(B) The woman has to settle the payment.
(C) The books for young children are available at a different department.
(D) The woman should return goods at Counter Five.   Ⓐ Ⓑ Ⓒ Ⓓ ☐

4. What is the woman asking about?
(A) Lawn and garden care
(B) Office building maintenance
(C) Inspection of a property
(D) A travel schedule   Ⓐ Ⓑ Ⓒ Ⓓ ☐

5. What is true about the woman's business?
(A) It was established recently.
(B) It is a subsidiary of West Valley Landscaping.
(C) It is located near a baggage claim area in the airport.
(D) It won't remain open until late at night tonight.   Ⓐ Ⓑ Ⓒ Ⓓ ☐

6. What will the man do?
(A) Ring up again to schedule an appointment
(B) Visit the woman's office tomorrow
(C) Decide whether to accept the estimate
(D) Present a bill for past services   Ⓐ Ⓑ Ⓒ Ⓓ ☐

7. What is the report mainly about?
   (A) New services in the airline industry
   (B) Changes in transportation costs
   (C) Plans for purchasing new aircrafts
   (D) Extra fuel charges added to airfares   Ⓐ Ⓑ Ⓒ Ⓓ ☐

8. What is good about the new services?
   (A) All the seats are equipped with in-flight movie monitors.
   (B) The airfare has been greatly discounted for frequent fliers.
   (C) More menu choices have been offered.
   (D) The luggage compartment has been enlarged.   Ⓐ Ⓑ Ⓒ Ⓓ ☐

9. Who is Emma Gilbert?
   (A) An inspector
   (B) An airline employee
   (C) A journalist
   (D) An interior decorator   Ⓐ Ⓑ Ⓒ Ⓓ ☐

---

10. What kind of company is most likely providing this message?
   (A) A computer electronics company
   (B) A telecommunications company
   (C) A pharmaceutical company
   (D) An electric power company   Ⓐ Ⓑ Ⓒ Ⓓ ☐

11. What has to be done to receive information about a printer?
   (A) Press the number 1
   (B) Press the number 2
   (C) Press the number 3
   (D) Press the number 9   Ⓐ Ⓑ Ⓒ Ⓓ ☐

12. According to the message, what are the club members asked to do?
   (A) Update their personal information
   (B) Inform a representative of their club number
   (C) Give details of their new order
   (D) Sign up for the conference   Ⓐ Ⓑ Ⓒ Ⓓ ☐

Task 2

▶解答:p.168〜

下欄の正解を踏まえて会話とトークを再度音読し、正解のヒントとなる文に下線を引こう。

Task 3

2-18〜21

CDのナチュラルスピードの音声を聞いて、会話・トークの設問のヒントがきちんと聞き取れるかどうか、確認しよう。この際、スクリプトは見ないこと。

設問の正解

1. (D)　2. (A)　3. (B)　4. (A)　5. (D)　6. (B)
7. (A)　8. (C)　9. (B)　10. (A)　11. (C)　12. (B)

Task 1&2 の正解と解説

※Task 2の解答は、解説のヒントを参照。

問題1-3は次の会話に関するものです。　　　　　　　W: 🇺🇸　M: 🇦🇺　2-18

W: どうも。この本と音声CDを返却したいのですが。// 本は、図書館の子ども向けセクションから借りたものです。// こちらのメインデスクでも返却できますか。//
M: もちろんです。// 問題ありません。// ありがとうございます。// IDカードを見せていただけますか。//
W: 実は、/ この本とCDを借りたときにカードを作っていただきました。// でも、今日は忘れてしまったようなんです。// だめでしょうか。//
M: まったく問題ありませんよ。// 品物をスキャンすれば、情報がわかります。// 少々お待ちください。// ……どうやらCDは返却期限を過ぎているようですね。// ですから、料金が1ドル25セントかかります。// こちらが受領書と請求書です / レジでお支払いいただけます / あちらの5番カウンターで。//

1. 男性の職業は何か。
 (A) レジ係
 (B) 店員
 (C) 経理担当者
 (D) 司書

解説 設問のキーワードはWhat、is、man's job。「男性の職業」を問う全体情報タイプ。職業に関する表現を待つ。
冒頭の女性のI'd like to …という発言からat the main desk?と、男性のCertainly. That'll be no problem.がヒントとなる。
解答 (D)

2. 女性は何について尋ねているか。
 (A) 彼女が子ども向けセクションに行くべきかどうか
 (B) 彼女のIDカードが失効しているかどうか
 (C) 彼女のCDが期限切れかどうか
 (D) 手続きに長い時間がかかるかどうか

解説 キーワードはWhat、woman、ask about。「女性の質問内容」を問う個別情報タイプ。女性の発言に注意して質問の表現を待とう。
The books are from the Children's Section … at the main desk?がヒント。
解答 (A)

3. 男性は何を示唆しているか。
 (A) 彼は来週、登録所で仕事をする。
 (B) 女性は料金を支払わなければならない。
 (C) 子ども向けの本は別の部署で入手できる。
 (D) 女性は5番カウンターで品物を返却すべきだ。

解説 キーワードはWhat、man、imply。「男性が示唆すること」を問う個別情報タイプ。男性の発言に注意する。
It seems the CD is past due. So there'll be a fee of $1.25 on that one.がヒント。
解答 (B)

問題4-6は次の会話に関するものです。　W: 🇦🇺　M: 🇨🇦　2-19

W: もしもし、そちらの造園サービスについて伺いたくてお電話しました。// Airport Boulevardに商業用不動産を持っているのですが / West Valley Mallの近くの / 基本的なメンテナンスをしてくれる方を探しているんです / それに芝生、木、庭の維持を。
M: West Valley Landscapingにお電話いただき、ありがとうございます。// すべてのご要望を喜んで承ります。// プロの造園設計家を1人、/ そちらのご都合がよろしければ、今日の午後にも派遣することができますよ。
W: そうですね、こちらは明朝10時ごろが、最も都合がいいんです。// 今日は早じまいするので。//
M: わかりました。// 明日10時に私が伺い / 不動産を拝見して見積もりを出しましょう。//

4. 女性は何について尋ねているか。
 (A) 芝生と庭の手入れ
 (B) オフィスビルの維持
 (C) 不動産の視察
 (D) 旅行スケジュール

解説 キーワードはWhat、woman、asking about。「女性の質問内容」を問う個別情報タイプ。女性の発言に注意。
ヒントは we're looking for someone who can handle the basic maintenance and upkeep of the lawn, trees, and garden. の部分。
解答 (A)

5. 女性の会社について正しいのは何か。
 (A) 最近設立された。
 (B) West Valley Landscapingの子会社である。
 (C) 空港の手荷物受取所の近くにある。
 (D) 今日は夜遅くまでは開いていない。

解説 キーワードはWhat is true、woman's business。「正誤」を問う個別情報タイプ。女性の発言に注意して会社に関する情報を待つ。
We're closing early todayがヒント。
解答 (D)

6. 男性はこれから何をするか。
 (A) 予約を入れるために電話をかけ直す
 (B) 明日、女性のオフィスを訪れる
 (C) 見積もりを受け入れるかどうか決断する
 (D) 過去の業務の請求書を渡す

解説 キーワードはWhat、man、do。「男性の行動」を問う個別情報タイプ。男性の発言に注意して未来表現を待つ。
I can visit you myself at 10 tomorrowがヒント。
解答 (B)

問題7-9は次のニュース報道に関するものです。

さて、次は今日のビジネスニュースです。// 格安航空会社が顧客に応えています / 彼ら（顧客）はさらなる快適さと、場合によっては少々のぜいたくを求めています / 低料金の手軽さを犠牲にせずに。// ここ何十年か、低料金の航空会社は重要な選択肢になっています / 見つけられる最安料金を求めている旅行者にとって。// RedJet, ValuFly, AirCommuteといった格安航空会社は / より力点を置くことで人気と採算性を獲得しました / 快適性や豪華さ以上に経済性とスピードと便利さに。// しかし、こうした人気のある格安航空会社の3社全部が / 現在、新たなプレミアムサービスを導入しています。// 3社のプレミアムサービスはどれも基本航空料金に10パーセントから12パーセント上乗せします / そして、より広い座席とランクアップした料理のオプションを提供します。// たとえば、ValuFly社の広報担当者、Emma Gilbertによれば / ValuFlyの新「プレミアムクラス」は自社のファーストクラスよりも安いのです / そしてほかの大半の航空会社の豪華なサービスよりも / しかし、基本サービスより上の快適さを提供するとのことです。//

7. この報道は主に何に関するものか。
- (A) 航空業界の新サービス
- (B) 輸送コストの変化
- (C) 新しい航空機の購入計画
- (D) 航空料金に加算される追加燃料費

解説 「報道内容」を問う全体情報タイプ。
Discount airlines ... a little bit of luxury without sacrificing affordability of a low-cost fare. 以降の、now introducing new premium services、provides more comfort than other basic servicesなどから正解がわかる。butなどの話題の転換を示す語句に注意。その後に必ず重要な情報が登場する。
解答 (A)

8. 新サービスの長所は何か。
- (A) 全座席に機内映画のモニターが装備されている。
- (B) 頻繁に利用する人には航空料金が大幅に値引きされた。
- (C) 提供されるメニューの選択肢が増えた。
- (D) 荷物室が拡張された。

解説 キーワードはWhat、good、new services。「新サービスの長所」を問う個別情報タイプ。長所を述べる個所を待つ。
offer more spacious seating and enhanced meal optionsがヒント。広いのは座席なので(D)は不正解だ。
解答 (C)

9. Emma Gilbertは誰か。
- (A) 調査員
- (B) 航空会社の社員
- (C) ジャーナリスト
- (D) 内装装飾家

解説 設問全体がキーワード。Emmaの「職業」を問う個別情報タイプだ。Emma Gilbertという固有名詞を待つ。
according to ValuFly spokesperson Emma Gilbertがヒントとなる。広報担当者は社員なので、An airline employeeが正解。
解答 (B)

問題10-12は次の電話メッセージに関するものです。 2-21

お電話ありがとうございます / Gibson社お客様サービスセンターです。// 当社のお客様サービス専門員は全員 / 現在ほかのお客様の対応をしております / ですので、もう少々たってからのお取り次ぎとなります。// 予想される待ち時間は4分です / ただし、実際にはそれよりずっと短くなることもございます。// お待ちの間 / お問い合わせ内容を分類することで、サービスに備えるのにご協力ください。// ソフトウエア製品に関する情報は1を押してください。// コンピューター製品に関する情報は2を押してください。// 周辺機器に関するお問い合わせは3を押してください。// このメニュー選択を繰り返すには9を押してください。// もしあなたがGibson社お得意様クラブ会員でしたら / サービス担当者に会員番号を伝えられるようご準備ください。// お待ちいただきましてありがとうございます。// お客様の通話を間もなくお受けいたします。//

10. このメッセージを流しているのはどんな会社と思われるか。
(A) コンピューター機器の会社
(B) 電気通信会社
(C) 製薬会社
(D) 電力会社

解説 キーワードはWhat kind of company、providing、this message。「会社の業種」を問う全体情報タイプ。通常は冒頭に注意して聞くが、このトークではCustomer Assistance Centerとしかわからない。
その後のsoftware product、computer product、peripheral equipmentがヒントになる。
解答 (A)

11. プリンターの情報を得るためには何をしなければならないか。
(A) 1番を押す
(B) 2番を押す
(C) 3番を押す
(D) 9番を押す

解説 設問をきちんと読むこと。「行動」を問う個別情報タイプ。
To inquire about peripheral equipment, press 3.がヒント。printerは周辺機器に含まれる。
解答 (C)

12. メッセージによると、クラブ会員は何をするよう求められているか。
(A) 個人情報を更新する
(B) クラブ会員番号を担当者に知らせる
(C) 新規注文の詳細を述べる
(D) 会議の出席申し込みをする

解説 キーワードはwhat、club members、asked to do。「クラブ会員に求められる行動」を問う個別情報タイプ。依頼表現を待とう。
please prepare to provide our service representative with your I.D. numberがヒント。
解答 (B)

Task 4

2-18〜21

会話とトークの意味をしっかりつかんだら、スクリプトを見ないで再度音声を聞いて、内容を確認しよう。

Task 5

▶解答：p.176〜

今度は、会話・トークを1度だけ音読して**概要をキャッチする**トレーニングを行う。
まずConversation 1を音読し、p.174の**会話の概要を示した文**の空所を補充する。この際、p.172の英文は見ないこと。冒頭に特に注意して、人物、趣旨、話題、状況、場所などを把握しながらチャンクで読もう。キーワードから内容をつかむようにする。
続いて、Conversation 2、Talk 1、Talk 2についても音読⇒空所補充を行おう。

Conversation 1

M: Kate, have you decided who you're going to choose / for this year's best employee award? // I'm still wondering who to vote for. // I always have trouble making up my mind about it. //

W: I totally understand what you mean, Tony. // Frankly, it's not an easy decision, /especially because we can't possibly know the details / of everyone's job performance. // And the only available data sources for reference / are the employee performance records / on the company's official nomination list. //

M: I know. // And the point is that some contributions toward the company / can't be evaluated purely by sales performance, right? // I mean what about someone who comes up with the idea to implement precautionary measures / against damage to our firm, / or someone who proposes a novel idea / that facilitates the success of a new product? // I think they should be assessed properly as well. //

Conversation 2

M: Susan, have you completed your article / about the Water Festival in June? // The due date for it is the 15th, isn't it? // That's in two days — / the same day as my concert. //

W: I know, I know. // There's no need to add to the pressure, John. // I've been working as hard as I can / to keep up with the deadline. // But the thing is, / the marketing division hasn't provided us / with the details of their plan for this issue yet. // I'm still waiting for their draft. //

M: Is there anything I can do to help? //

W: Thanks. // If I need any technical assistance, / I'll let you know. //

M: Well, should we put off the editorial meeting then? // I know the editor is looking forward to hearing from you / about the content and layout of your piece though. //

W: Yes. // Would you mind informing him / about the postponement of the meeting? // I think he'll understand the situation. //
But either way, / I'll contact the marketing division again / to get an update on what's going on there. // I hope the delay in my work doesn't interfere with you / going to the concert on Friday, though. //

Talk 1: A news broadcast
Share prices remained steady overall / on the Central Stock Market Tuesday. //
An announcement of official government unemployment figures /
indicated that unemployment increased last month. //
And that news combined with general fears of an overall economic decline /
caused share prices to fall. // But, according to a separate report later in the day, /
most large banks and other financial firms /
are preparing to announce strong business results / for the past half-year. //
That encouraged buying of shares in the financial sector, /
and analysts say the positive mood spread throughout the market /
during afternoon trading. //
The result was a recovery in the average share price / from morning declines. //

Talk 2: An announcement
I can sum up your midday traffic report today by saying, /
"No news is good news." //
An accident that occurred early this morning on McArthur Drive /
south of Creek Street /
was cleared up about an hour ago, /
and traffic has begun flowing smoothly there again. //
This morning's usual bumper-to-bumper traffic on Highway 9 /
has also cleared up, /
and there are no major problems on the main highways. //
Routine road construction is blocking traffic /
on westbound 45th Avenue at Rollins Street. //
But a detour is in place, / and no congestion is occurring in the area. //
So the upshot of it is, / if you're planning to go out on the road today, /
now would be a good time, / before the afternoon rush begins. //

概要

音読した内容を思い出しながら、空所を埋めよう（1語とは限らない）。　　▶解答：p.176〜

Conversation 1

1. Speakers: (　　　) and (　　　)
2. Their relationship: (　　　　　　　)
3. Topic: How to (　　　　) this year's (　　　　　　　).
4. Kate's problem: She (　　　　　　　　　　) to decide.
5. Tony's problem: The (　　　　　　　) system is (　　　　　　).
6. Who are not assessed properly?: The originator of implementation of the
   (　　　　　　　　　　　) , proposers of (　　　　　　　)

Conversation 2

1. Place: (　　　　) (publishing company)
2. Speakers: (　　　) and (　　　)
3. Their relationship: (　　　　　　　)
4. Topic: A (　　　　) in the completion of an (　　　　)
5. The deadline of Susan's job: The day after tomorrow, on the (　　)th.
6. The reason that she can't finish it: The (　　　　　　) division hasn't provided her with the (　　　　　　　).
7. John's suggestion: (　　　　) the editorial meeting
8. Susan's request: Inform the (　　　　) of the (　　　　　　　) of the meeting.
9. When will Susan contact John?: When she needs his (　　　　　　).
10. What will John do on Friday?: Go to the (　　　　　).

174

Talk 1: A news broadcast

1. Speaker: (   )
2. Listeners: (   )
3. Topic: (   ) climate
4. Current Share prices: (   )
5. Last month's unemployment figures: (   )
6. Business results of the major financial institutions: (   )
7. Mood of the stock market in the afternoon: (   )

Talk 2: An announcement

1. Speaker: (   ) reporter
2. Listeners: (   )
3. Topic: (   )
4. The on-the-air time of this broadcast: (   )
5. The accident site: (   ) south of Creek Street
6. The heavy traffic area in the morning: (   )
7. The construction site: Westbound (   ) at Rollins Street
8. The best time to drive today: Now before the (   )

Task 5 の正解と解説

Conversation 1 M: 🇦🇺 W: 🇬🇧   2-22

M: Kate、誰を選ぶかもう決めたかい / 今年の最優秀社員賞に。// 僕はまだ誰に投票するか悩んでいるんだ。// これを決めるのにはいつも苦労するんだよな。//

W: あなたの言っていること、すごくよくわかるわ、Tony。// 正直、選ぶのは簡単じゃないわ / 特に私たちは詳細を知ることができないから / みんなの仕事ぶりの。// しかも、唯一参考にできる情報源が、/ 社員業績記録だけだもの / 会社が公式に出している候補者リストの。//

M: だよね。// 問題なのは会社への貢献というのは、/ 純粋に営業成績だけじゃ判断できないという点だよね。// つまり、こんな人はどうなるのか、予防措置を講じるというアイデアを思いついた人 / 会社へのダメージに対する / または斬新なアイデアを出した人 / 新製品の成功を助けるような。// 彼らだって、きちんと評価されるべきだよな。//

● 概要の解答例と訳

1. Tony、Kate（話者：TonyとKate）、2. Colleagues（2人の関係：同僚）、3. choose、best employee（話題：今年の最優秀社員をどうやって選ぶか）、4. doesn't have enough data（Kateの問題：彼女には、決めるための十分なデータがない）、5. evaluating、not fair（Tonyの問題：評価システムが公正でない）、6. precautionary measures、novel ideas（きちんと評価されていないのは誰か：予防措置の実施を思いついた人、斬新なアイデアを提案した人）

Conversation 2 M: 🇬🇧 W: 🇨🇦   2-23

M: Susan、記事は完成したかい？ / 6月のWater Festivalについての。// 締切は15日だよね？ // あと2日だ。// 僕のコンサートと同じ日。//

W: わかってる、わかってる。// プレッシャーを加えてくれなくて結構よ、John。// 私は精一杯働いてきたわ / 締切に間に合わせるために。// でも実は、/ 販売部門がまだ提供してくれていないの / この話題についての彼らの計画の詳細を。// まだ、彼らの草稿を待っているのよ。//

M: 僕に手伝えることは何かある？//

W: ありがとう。// 技術面で手伝ってもらいたいことがあったら、/ 連絡するわ。//

M: ああ、それなら編集会議を延期したほうがいいかな。// 編集長が君からの報告を楽しみにしているのは知っているけど / 君の記事の内容とレイアウトについて。//

W: ええ。// 彼に伝えてもらえる？ / 会議の延期を。// 彼も状況を理解してくれると思う。// でもどちらにしろ / もう一度販売部門に連絡して / あちらの進捗状況についての最新情報を聞くわ。// 私の仕事の遅れが、あなたの妨げにならないといいのだけれど / 金曜日にコンサートへ行くのに。//

● 概要の解答例と訳

1. Office（場所：オフィス〈出版社〉）、2. John、Susan（話者：JohnとSusan）、3. Colleagues（2人の関係：同僚）、4. delay、article（話題：記事の完成の遅れ）、5. 15（Susanの仕事の締切：明後日、15日）、6. marketing、details of their plan（彼女が作業を終えられない理由：販売部門がまだ彼女に計画の詳細を提供していない）、7. Put off（Johnの提案：編集会議を延期する）、8. editor、postponement（Susanの依頼：編集長に会議の延期を伝える）、9. technical assistance（SusanがJohnに連絡するのはいつか：彼からの技術面での援助が必要になったとき）、10. concert（Johnは金曜日に何をするか：コンサートへ行く）

Talk 1: ニュース放送 🇨🇦

2-24

株価は全般に堅調のままでした / 火曜日の中央株式市場では。// 政府による失業者数の公式な発表が / 先月の失業者が増加したことを示しました。// そして、そのニュースが経済全体の下降に対する全般的な不安と相まって / 株価の下落を招きました。// しかし、同日遅くの別の報道によると / 大手銀行やそのほかの金融機関のほとんどが / 好調な業績発表の用意をしています / 過去半年間の。// それが金融分野で株式の買いを後押ししました / そのためアナリストたちは市場全体に好感ムードが広がったと言います / 午後の取引で。// その結果が、平均株価の回復でした / 午前の下落からの。//

● 概要の解答例と訳
1. Newscaster（話者：ニュースキャスター）、2. Audience（聞き手：視聴者）、3. Economic（話題：経済情勢）、4. Remained steady（現在の株価：堅調を維持）、5. Increased（先月の失業者数：増加）、6. Strong（大手金融機関の業績：好調）、7. Positive（午後の株式市場のムード：好感）

Talk 2: アナウンス 🇦🇺

2-25

今日正午の交通情報は、次の言葉で総括することができます /「ニュースがないのは良いニュース」。// McArthur大通り沿いで、今朝早く起きた事故は / Creek通りの南側でしたが / 1時間ほど前に処理を終えました / そして、そこの交通はまた順調に流れ始めています。// 今朝の、9号線恒例ののろのろ渋滞は / これも解消しました / そして主要自動車道には大きなトラブルはありません。// 定期道路工事で通行止めになっています / 45番大通り西行きは、Rollins通りとの交差点で。// けれど、迂回路が用意されています / ですから、この付近で混雑は起きていません。// ですから、結論として / もし今日車でお出掛けの予定があるのでしたら / 今がいいタイミングでしょう / 午後のラッシュが始まる前に。//

● 概要の解答例と訳
1. Traffic（話者：交通情報リポーター）、2. Audience（聞き手：視聴者）、3. Traffic report（話題：交通情報）、4. Midday（この番組の放送時間：正午）、5. McArthur Drive（事故現場：McArthur大通り沿い、Creek通り南側）、6. Highway 9（朝の渋滞場所：9号線）、7. 45th Avenue（工事現場：45番大通り西行き、Rollins通りとの交差点）、8. afternoon rush（今日車で出掛ける最良の時間：午後のラッシュの前である今）

学習エネルギーをチャージする今日の **格言**

> That which we persist in doing becomes easier,
> not that the task itself has become easier,
> but that our ability to perform it has improved.
>
> Ralph Waldo Emerson
> （1803〜1882：アメリカの評論家、哲学者、詩人）
>
> われわれがやり通すことは簡単になる。課題自体が簡単になるのではなく、われわれの遂行する能力が向上するのだ。

12日目 / 20

Review & Part 2

12日目の今日は、5日間学習してきた内容を復習した後、Part 2攻略のコツをまとめて学ぶ。復習で定着していないとわかった会話、トーク、文書は、プロソディーに注意して、リズミカルかつスピーディーにもう一度音読するようにしよう。

Review: Task 1

7〜11日目に学習した会話・トーク・文書の一部が空所になっているので、指定のトラックを聞いて、ディクテーション（書き取り）してみよう。トラックには会話・トーク・文書がまるごと入っているので、該当箇所を聞き逃さないよう注意しよう。

7日目

CD 1-40　▶解答はp.118参照

A spokesman for Trenton _____
_____ Williams Limited, _____
_____ of Trenton on April 1. He added that
Williams Limited _____
_____ such as X-ray, ultrasound and other systems _____
_____.

8日目

CD 2-01　▶解答はp.125参照

You may also qualify for a ProGoods credit card. _____
_____.
Don't miss out _____
_____. _____.
It's easy, quick and simple. _____. Shop at ProGoods.

178

9日目

CD 2-12 ▶解答はp.146参照

Although _____, we want to begin planning early _____. Each year, _____
_____, who have expressed particular appreciation _____.

10日目

CD 2-16 ▶解答はp.157参照

Real estate developers _____
_____. Additionally, _____
_____. Still, _____
_____
_____
_____.

11日目

CD 2-18 ▶解答はp.163参照

W: But I'm afraid I forgot to bring it with me today. _____
_____?
M: Not at all. _____. Just a moment, please. ... _____. So there'll be _____. Here's a receipt and bill, _____
_____ at Counter Five.

● Task 2

では次に、以下のトラックを聞いてシャドウイングに挑戦する。プロソディーを意識し、意味を促えながらできるだけ正確にまねよう。スクリプトを見ないで最後まできちんと再生できるか確認し、不十分な個所は繰り返し練習を。

❶ **CD 2-02** ▶解答はp.126参照   ❷ **CD 2-17** ▶解答はp.158参照

Part 2 解答のポイント

質問と、それに対する3つの応答例が読まれるのがPart 2の形式。質問も応答例もテスト冊子には印刷されていない。最も重要なのは集中力だ。基本戦略は次の3点。

❶ 冒頭に集中する（Wh-、How、Yes/No疑問文、否定疑問文などを確認）
❷ 設問に登場したキーワードを含む選択肢は原則として避ける
❸ Wh疑問文に対しては通常Yes/Noで答えない

応答が直接的でも、間接的でも、意味がかみ合って会話として成り立つなら正解として選ぼう。主な設問のタイプは以下のとおり。

●WH疑問文

Where、Whoなど、5W1Hの疑問詞で始まる質問。Yes/Noでは通常答えないので選ばないこと。また、質問に登場したキーワードやそれに類似した単語を含む選択肢は引っ掛けの場合が多い。

●Yes/No疑問文

Are you、Do youなどで始まる通常疑問文、Aren't youなどで始まる否定疑問文、..., don't you? などで終わる付加疑問文の3つを指す。基本的にはYes/Noを用いた返答が正解だが、Yes/Noで答えていなくても、会話として成り立てば正解になる。

●質問でない疑問文

疑問文の形をしていても、実際には「提案」「勧誘」「依頼」「命令」の意味で使われている表現。返答は、「応じる決まり文句」か「断る理由」になる。Yes/Noでの返答も、時には正解になる。

●選択疑問文

A or B の形でどちらを選ぶかを問う疑問文。比べられている部分が短い語句の場合と、長い節（主語と述語）の場合がある。質問に登場したキーワードを含む選択肢も正解になる可能性があるので注意。Yes/Noで始まる返答は不正解。

●陳述

疑問文の形をしていない、相手からの反応を期待するコメント。質問や提案ではないので返答パターンが多様になる。会話としてかみ合う選択肢を選ぶようにしよう。

p.96のマークシートの塗り方も確認しておこう。

Part 2: Practice

CD 2-26 ▶解答：p.182〜

質問とそれに続く3つの応答を聞いて、最も適切なものを1つ選ぼう。

1. Mark your answer on your answer sheet.   Ⓐ Ⓑ Ⓒ ☐

2. Mark your answer on your answer sheet.   Ⓐ Ⓑ Ⓒ ☐

3. Mark your answer on your answer sheet.   Ⓐ Ⓑ Ⓒ ☐

4. Mark your answer on your answer sheet.   Ⓐ Ⓑ Ⓒ ☐

5. Mark your answer on your answer sheet.   Ⓐ Ⓑ Ⓒ ☐

6. Mark your answer on your answer sheet.   Ⓐ Ⓑ Ⓒ ☐

7. Mark your answer on your answer sheet.   Ⓐ Ⓑ Ⓒ ☐

8. Mark your answer on your answer sheet.   Ⓐ Ⓑ Ⓒ ☐

9. Mark your answer on your answer sheet.   Ⓐ Ⓑ Ⓒ ☐

10. Mark your answer on your answer sheet.   Ⓐ Ⓑ Ⓒ ☐

Practiceの正解と解説

1. Where are we supposed to deliver goods?
(A) It shouldn't be much longer.
(B) Thank you. It was a very quick delivery.
(C) You should ask Ben.

どこに品物を配達することになっていますか。
(A) そう長くはかからないはずです。
(B) ありがとう。とても迅速な配達でした。
(C) Benに尋ねてください。

解説 冒頭のWhereを聞き取り、場所に関する返答を待つ。(C)は場所について直接答えていないが、意味がかみ合うので正解。(A)は時間に関する返答。(B)はdeliveryを使った引っ掛けだ。
解答 (C)

---

2. Are you coming to the movie with us this Friday night?
(A) Yes, it was a smart career move.
(B) As soon as possible.
(C) Who are you going with?

今週金曜の夜に私たちと映画に行く？
(A) ええ、賢明な転職でした。
(B) できる限り早く。
(C) 誰と一緒に行くんですか。

解説 冒頭のAre youからYes/No疑問文と判断し、「来るか否か」を述べている選択肢を待つ。疑問文に対して疑問文で答えている(C)にはキーワードのcomingが使われているが、会話として意味がかみ合うので正解。(A)はmoveを使った引っ掛け。(B)は応答として不自然。
解答 (C)

---

3. There is a leak in the ceiling of the conference room.
(A) I have some fluorescent lights in the stock room.
(B) Should I call the maintenance department?
(C) No, turn off the lights when you leave.

会議室の天井が雨漏りしているんです。
(A) 倉庫に蛍光灯が何本かあります。
(B) 保守部門に電話したほうがいいですか。
(C) いいえ、離れる際は照明を消してください。

解説 陳述の「状況描写」問題だ。(A)と(C)はroom、leaveを使った引っ掛け。(B)は問題の解決策を提示していて、意味がかみ合うので正解。 **解答** (B)

4. Why don't you take a rest before going back to work?
(A) I think it probably would be best.
(B) Because I didn't have enough time.
(C) I can't adjust this backrest.

仕事に戻る前に、休憩を取りませんか。
(A) それが多分ベストだと思います。
(B) 十分な時間がなかったので。
(C) この背もたれが調整できません。

解説 Why don't you[we] ...?は「提案・勧誘」の表現。応じる決まり文句や断る理由が正解になる。「なぜ？」の意ではないので(B)は不可。(C)はrestとbackを使った引っ掛け。

解答 (A)

ポイント Why don't you[we] ...?、How about ...?、What about ...?、What do you say to ...?、Shall we ...?、Let's ...などに対して、応じる場合はSure.、Sounds good[great].、That's a great[good] idea.、Why not?、I'd love to.などが正解。断る場合は、Sorry,...、I'm sorry, ...、I'm afraid ...、I'd love to, but ...、Unfortunately, ...などが正解になる。

---

5. Wouldn't it make more sense to split the profit?
(A) It depends on how the sales figures are.
(B) No, it has the highest percentage gain.
(C) I'll make one for you too.

利益を分け合うほうが納得がいきませんか。
(A) 売り上げの数字次第ですね。
(B) いいえ、その利益の割合が最も高いのです。
(C) あなたにも１つ作りますね。

解説 冒頭から否定疑問文と判断。Would it make more sense to split the profit?と同じと考える。(B)はprofitから想起されるgainを使って誤答を誘っている。(C)はmakeを使った引っ掛け。 **解答** (A)

ポイント 否定疑問文や付加疑問文への応答のコツは、①質問の要点・返答の仕方は通常の疑問文と同じと考える、②否定・付加の個所を日本語に訳して判断しない、③Yes/Noの応答は、応答者の視点から見て肯定であればYes、否定ならNoになる。
例：1) Do you like watching movies?　2) Don't you like watching movies?　3) You like watching movies, don't you?　4) You don't like watching movies, do you?に対して、好きならYes, I do.(= I like watching movies.)、好きでないならNo, I don't.(= I don't like watching movies.)

---

6. How many laptop PCs are in the latest shipment?
(A) All of them were wrapped securely.
(B) Twice a month, I suppose.
(C) Enough to fulfill our order.

一番最近の荷物にノートパソコンは何台入っていましたか。
(A) すべてしっかりと包装されていました。
(B) 月に２回だと思います。
(C) 注文どおりの数です。

解説 How manyと数を聞いている。(A)はlaptopと似た発音のwrappedを使った引っ掛け。(B)はHow oftenに対する応答だ。 **解答** (C)

7. What do you say to a game of tennis next weekend?
(A) I heard it was a fantastic game.
(B) I'm afraid I'm supposed to participate in a seminar.
(C) Yes, what you said was convincing.

来週末にテニスの試合なんてどうですか。
(A) 素晴らしい試合だったと聞きました。
(B) 残念ながら、セミナーに出ることになっていて。
(C) はい、あなたのおっしゃったことは信用できました。

解説 What do you say to …?は「提案・勧誘」の表現。断るときの決まり文句＋理由などが正解となる。(A)はgame、(C)はyouとsaidを使った引っ掛け。**解答** (B)

---

8. Is Kim still in the meeting or has she gone out for lunch?
(A) Yes. I heard that too.
(B) She didn't tell us anything.
(C) Do we have to postpone the meeting?

Kimはまだ会議中ですか、それともお昼を食べに出ましたか。
(A) ええ。私もそれを聞きました。
(B) 彼女は私たちには何も言いませんでした。
(C) 会議を延期する必要がありますか。

解説 節と節の選択疑問文は長いので、何が比較されているかキーワードから把握する。ここではstillとgone out。(A)はYesで答えているので不可。(C)はmeetingを使った引っ掛け。
解答 (B)

ポイント 選択疑問文への返答の5パターン
Should we hold a meeting in May or in June? には、以下のように答えられる。
①AかBの選択結果：May would be better for me. / I prefer June.
②どちらでも構わない：Either is fine with me. / It doesn't matter to me.
③相手に選択を任せる：It's up to you.
④いずれも好ましくない：Sorry, neither month is suitable for me.
　　　　　　　　　　Do you have any other choices?
　　　　　　　　　　Both months are bad for me.
⑤今決めかねる：I can't decide at the moment.
　　　　　　　I have to ask about our guest's availability first.

---

9. You like walking around the park near the office, don't you?
(A) No, she usually drives to work.
(B) Just about an hour or so.
(C) Yes, I enjoy it as an exercise.

あなたは会社のそばの公園を歩くのが好きですよね。
(A) いいえ、彼女は普段は車で通勤しています。
(B) せいぜい1時間くらいです。
(C) はい、運動として楽しんでいます。

解説 文末のdon't youから付加疑問文だとわかる。Do you like walking …?と同じと考えよう。(A)、(B)はいずれも応答として意味がかみ合わない。**解答** (C)

10. I was hoping to have a briefing from Mr. Akimoto today but he's out.
(A) Ms. Jacobson can also do it for you.
(B) She made a brief address on behalf of her division.
(C) There are some in the warehouse.

Akimotoさんから簡単な説明を受けたかったのに、彼は外出中です。
(A) Jacobsonさんもあなたに説明できますよ。
(B) 彼女は部署を代表して短いスピーチを行いました。
(C) 倉庫にいくらかあります。

解説 (B)はbriefを使った引っ掛け。(C)は意味がかみ合わない。 **解答** (A)

Task 3

1〜10の設問について、質問と正解の選択肢を音読し、頭にしっかり入れよう。

Task 4

CD-2-27、28

仕上げにロールプレイに挑戦する。トラック27には**質問部分のみ**が収録されているので、その後のポーズの部分で**正解の選択肢**を読もう。次のトラック28には、**正解の選択肢**のみが収録されている。今度は設問番号の後のポーズで**質問**を読み上げ、応答を聞き取ろう。
どちらもシチュエーションを思い浮かべて感情を込め、自分の言葉として話しているつもりで取り組もう。意味を促え、プロソディーを意識することも忘れずに。

Task 5

2-29

最後に、練習問題に挑戦しよう。各質問に対し、それぞれ5つの応答が流れる。正解が複数含まれているので、正しい応答の記号をすべてマークしよう。

1. Mark your answer on your answer sheet.　　Ⓐ Ⓑ Ⓒ Ⓓ Ⓔ ☐

2. Mark your answer on your answer sheet.　　Ⓐ Ⓑ Ⓒ Ⓓ Ⓔ ☐

3. Mark your answer on your answer sheet.　　Ⓐ Ⓑ Ⓒ Ⓓ Ⓔ ☐

4. Mark your answer on your answer sheet.　　Ⓐ Ⓑ Ⓒ Ⓓ Ⓔ ☐

5. Mark your answer on your answer sheet.　　Ⓐ Ⓑ Ⓒ Ⓓ Ⓔ ☐

Task 5 の正解と解説

1. Could you tell us how you'd promote the new automobile?
(A) No, I couldn't get a promotion then.
(B) Certainly. Could you see the images on the screen?
(C) We began to develop a low-emission car.
(D) Yes, here's a copy of my plan.
(E) It's right over there.

その新車をどうやって宣伝するか、教えていただけますか。
(A) いいえ、その時は昇進できませんでした。
(B) もちろんです。スクリーンの画像をご覧いただけますか。
(C) 低排出ガス車の開発を始めました。
(D) はい、こちらが私のプランのコピーです。
(E) ちょうどあちらになります。

解説 Could you ...?は「依頼・命令」の表現。決まり文句で応じている(B)と、意味がかみ合う(D)が正解となる。(C)はautomobileから想起されるcarを使った引っ掛け。
解答 (B)、(D)

---

2. Alison gave a great presentation at the press conference, didn't she?
(A) It was a great present for her.
(B) You bet. All participants seemed to be impressed.
(C) No, I can't go to the conference.
(D) Yes, we really enjoyed it.
(E) That's what I heard.

Alisonは記者会見で素晴らしいプレゼンをしたんでしょう?
(A) それは彼女にとって素晴らしいプレゼントでした。
(B) そのとおり。参加者は全員感心したようでした。
(C) いいえ、会議には行けないんです。
(D) はい、本当に堪能しました。
(E) そう聞いています。

解説 付加疑問文。Did Alison give ...?という疑問文と同じと考える。応答として意味がかみ合うのは、肯定的に答えている3つの選択肢。
解答 (B)、(D)、(E)

---

3. Please let me know when you have your itinerary.
(A) Sure. Will I call your mobile phone?
(B) I'm glad to hear that.
(C) In last week's assembly, I think.
(D) No, I didn't tell you.
(E) As soon as we receive it.

旅程がわかったらお知らせください。
(A) もちろん。携帯に電話しましょうか。
(B) それを聞いてうれしいです。
(C) 先週の集まりで、だと思います。
(D) いいえ、あなたには言いませんでした。
(E) 受け取り次第すぐに。

解説 陳述の依頼表現。質問の内容をしっかりと頭に入れ、応答がかみ合っているかどうか判断しよう。
解答 (A)、(E)

4. Do we have enough files, or should I order some more?
(A) We plan to file a complaint today.
(B) Yes, in the supply room.
(C) We still have plenty.
(D) No, we have a large stock.
(E) I picked it up yesterday morning.

ファイルは足りていますか、もうちょっと注文しますか。
(A) 今日、苦情を申し立てる予定です。
(B) はい、備品倉庫の中に。
(C) まだたくさんありますよ。
(D) いいえ、在庫がたくさんあります。
(E) 昨日の朝にそれを取ってきました。

解説 選択疑問文のキーワードから何が比較されているか把握する。have enoughとorderをしっかり聞き取ること。(A)はfileを使った引っ掛け。(B)はYes、(D)はNoで答えているので不可。質問と応答の意味がかみ合うかどうか確認しよう。

解答 (C)

5. Why is the negotiation being delayed?
(A) Yes, but it should be longer.
(B) The conditions haven't been met.
(C) Lay it on the floor.
(D) I don't know the details.
(E) No, we were at the negotiating table.

なぜ交渉は長引いているのですか。
(A) はい、しかしもっと長くなるでしょう。
(B) 条件が折り合わないんです。
(C) 床に置いてください。
(D) 詳細はわかりません。
(E) いいえ、われわれは交渉のテーブルに着いていました。

解説 Whyで理由を尋ねている。(A)はYes、(E)はNoで答えているので不可。(C)と(E)は音の引っ掛けにもなっている。(D)のように「わからない」と答えるパターンも、意味がかみ合えば正解となる。

解答 (B)、(D)

学習エネルギーをチャージする今日の **格 言**

> **If I miss one day's practice, I notice it.**
> **If I miss two days, the critics notice it.**
> **If I miss three days, the audience notices it.**
>
> Ignacy Jan Paderewski
> （1860〜1941：ポーランドのピアニスト・作曲家・首相）
> **1日練習を休むと自分でわかる。2日休むと批評家にわかる。3日休むと聴衆にわかる。**

4カ国発音を攻略する！ Vol.3

カナダ英語編

カナダ英語は「北米英語」のカテゴリーに含まれており、基本的に米語とほぼ同じと考えていいだろう。ただし、オーストラリア同様、イギリス連邦（The Commonwealth of Nations）のメンバーであるため、イギリス英語の影響も多少ある。

❶ 米語と同じく語尾の/r/は発音する

❷ 米語/ɔː/がカナダ英語では/ɑː/

特に「子音＋a＋子音」の形の場合に、違いは顕著だ。

	call	fall	tall	talk
米	kɔ́ːl	fɔ́ːl	tɔ́ːl	tɔ́ːk
加	kɑ́ːl	fɑ́ːl	tɑ́ːl	tɑ́ːk

＊米語でも/ɑː/と発音されることはある

それでは以下の会話をCDで聞いた後、色文字の部分を意識しながら音読しよう。

CD 2-30

M: Hi, Beth. Do you have time to talk for a second?

W: Sure, Nick. What's going on? You sound a little serious. I hope nothing is wrong.

M: Well, actually, I just got a call from my wife. I guess our son was in the playground at school, and he had a pretty bad fall. They think his leg might be broken. Would it be possible for me to go down to the hospital and make sure everything's OK?

W: Oh, I'm really sorry to hear that. Yes, of course. Go make sure he's all right. We can handle things here until you get back.

p.188の訳

M: やあ、Beth。ちょっと話す時間、あるかな。
W: もちろんよ、Nick。どうしたの？ 何か深刻な感じね。困ったことじゃないといいけど。
M: いや、実は妻から電話があってね。学校の校庭でだと思うんだけど、息子がひどい転び方をしたんだ。脚が折れているかもしれないって。病院に行って、どんなことになっているか見てきても構わないかな。
W: まあ、それはお気の毒に。ええ、もちろん。息子さんの様子を見てきてちょうだい。あなたが戻ってくるまで、ここは何とかできると思うわ。

13日目 / 20

Part 3 応用音読

3週目は、応用音読ということで、実際のTOEICテストよりも難易度の高い問題に挑戦して、実力アップを図る。会話のスピードや長さ、設問数が増えているので、心して取りかかろう。

Practice

CD 2-31〜33　▶解答：p.193〜

それでは難易度の高い問題に挑戦する。CDの音声の冒頭に8秒のポーズを設けているので、この時間を利用して設問・選択肢を先読みしよう。

1. Where has the man been?
   (A) At a company picnic at Greenway Seaside Park
   (B) In the public relations department
   (C) At the offices of a client company
   (D) At a community environment event

2. How often are the activities carried out?
   (A) Every month
   (B) Every three months
   (C) Every four months
   (D) Every year

3. What activity is planned?
   (A) Safety inspections
   (B) Volunteering a subscription
   (C) Participating in emergency services
   (D) Cleaning up trash

4. Why is the man pleased?
   (A) His résumé looks promising.
   (B) Some of the candidates have strong work experience.
   (C) The personal interviews are going well.
   (D) The company's growth is increasing.

   Ⓐ Ⓑ Ⓒ Ⓓ ☐

5. What is implied about the head of the organization?
   (A) She will be attending a meeting at 2:30.
   (B) She is forming a new committee.
   (C) She will go over the final candidates' CVs.
   (D) She will conduct interviews in the conference room.

   Ⓐ Ⓑ Ⓒ Ⓓ ☐

6. What will most probably happen this afternoon?
   (A) The man will attend a press conference.
   (B) The CEO will come around for inspection.
   (C) A judging committee will be met.
   (D) Personal interviews will be conducted.

   Ⓐ Ⓑ Ⓒ Ⓓ ☐

GO ON TO THE NEXT PAGE

7. What are the speakers mainly discussing?
   (A) Notification of an upcoming meeting
   (B) Corrections to the minutes
   (C) A search for state-of-the-art auditing technology
   (D) Strengthening the company information network

8. Who most likely is the man?
   (A) A systems engineer
   (B) The head of the organization
   (C) A securities analyst
   (D) A prosecutor

9. What is implied about the woman?
   (A) She is capable of dealing with the new project.
   (B) She thinks M&A doesn't work well.
   (C) She is an experienced architect.
   (D) She has little time for the new venture.

10. What is implied about the staff members?
   (A) They work in the telecommunications industry.
   (B) They will be replaced by specialists.
   (C) They always give quick feedbacks to their superiors.
   (D) They seem to be aware of the necessity of updating the system.

11. What is inferred about the woman's responsibility?
   (A) She has to make a statement regarding her suggestion.
   (B) She is required to reorganize workflow to avoid scheduling conflicts.
   (C) She has to make a cost analysis of the printing system.
   (D) She is required to digitize documents.

Practiceの正解と解説

1-3　**2-31**　M: 🇺🇸　W: 🇦🇺

M: I've just been talking to the people in the public relations department about our community service program. It seems they have an annual event planned for next month.
W: Oh, really? I assume it's another volunteer activity. What are we going to be doing this year?
M: We're going to encourage volunteers to help with Community Environment Day. We'll help pick up trash in Greenway Seaside Park. Their goal is to get 100 staff members to volunteer, but so far only 40 have signed up.
W: I suppose you can make that 41. I'll join in. But I think they should be more aggressive about publicizing it within the company, don't you think so?

M: 今、広報部の人たちと話してきた / 地域奉仕プログラムについて。// どうやら来月、毎年恒例の行事があるらしい。//
W: あら、そうなの？// きっとまた別のボランティア活動ね。// 今年は何をする予定なの？//
M:『地域環境デー』を援助するボランティアを募集するよ。// Greenway Seaside公園でのゴミ拾いを手伝うんだ。// 目標は100人のボランティアスタッフを集めることらしいけれど、/ 今のところ、参加の意思を表明しているのは40人だけなんだ。//
W: 41人にしていいわよ。// 私も参加するわ。// それにしても、社内での宣伝活動をもっと積極的にするべきだと思うわ、そう思わない？//

1. 男性はどこに行っていたのか。
　(A) Greenway Seaside公園での会社のピクニックに
　(B) 広報部に
　(C) 取引先のオフィスに
　(D) 地域環境イベントに

解説　設問のキーワードはWhere、man、been。「場所」を問う個別情報タイプ。男性の発言に注意して聞く。冒頭のI've just been ... がヒント。
解答 (B)

2. 活動はどれくらいの頻度で行われているか。
　(A) 毎月
　(B) 3カ月ごと
　(C) 4カ月ごと
　(D) 毎年

解説　キーワードはHow often、activities、carried out。「頻度」を問う個別情報タイプ。annual eventがヒントとなっている。
解答 (D)

3. どんな活動が計画されているか。
　(A) 安全の点検
　(B) 寄付の申し出
　(C) 救急サービスへの参加
　(D) ゴミの掃除

解説　短い設問なので全体がキーワード。「行動」を問う個別情報タイプ。未来表現に注意しよう。予定を尋ねる女性の質問に、We'll help pick up trash ... と答えている個所がヒント。
解答 (D)

4-6　2-32　W: 🇺🇸　M: 🇨🇦

W: Where are we with recruiting new personnel for our department? Have you looked through all the application forms yet?

M: Well, we're done screening candidates based on résumés now. Dozens of people applied for the job. In fact, some of the candidates look quite promising and have some impressive work histories. I think their capabilities will definitely be conducive to the growth of the company. It looks as though advertising the position in a major financial newspaper was really a worthwhile idea.

W: You can say that again. Can you make sure to brief me on the people who will be coming in for the final screening? We'll have to conduct personal interviews with them soon.

M: Sure. Why don't we hold a quick meeting this afternoon, say, around 2:30 p.m., to go through the list of candidates? We can book conference room 9. Oh, and by the way, the CEO wants to review the candidates' files prior to our official decision as well. Our committee doesn't need her final approval normally, but this is an exception.

W: 私たちの部署の新しい人材の募集は、どこまで進んでいるかしら。// もう願書には全部目を通した？//

M: ああ、履歴書による候補者の選抜を終えたところだよ。// 何十人もが、この職に応募してきた。// そして、候補者のうち何人かは、極めて有望なようだし、/ 素晴らしい職歴の持ち主だ。// 彼らの能力は間違いなく直結してくると思う / わが社の成長に。// 大手経済紙で求人をしたのは、/ とてもいいアイデアだったようだね。//

W: まさにそのとおり。// 忘れずに私に説明してね / 最終選抜に来る人について。// すぐに彼らと個人面接をしなければならないのでしょうから。//

M: そうだね。// それなら、ちょっとした会議をしてはどうかな、今日の午後、たとえば2時30分ごろ、/ 候補者のリストを確認するために。// 第9会議室を予約できるよ。// ああ、それから、/ CEOも候補者のファイルを確認したがっている / 正式な決定の前に。通常、われわれの委員会は最終承認を受ける必要はないが、/ 今回は例外だ。//

4. 男性が喜んでいるのはなぜか。
   (A) 彼の履歴書が有望なようだ。
   (B) 志願者の中に素晴らしい職歴の持ち主がいる。
   (C) 個人面接がうまくいっている。
   (D) 会社の成長率が増加している。

解説 短い設問なので全体がキーワードだ。「理由」を問う個別情報タイプ。男性の発言内の感情表現や肯定的な内容を示す語句を待つ。some of the candidates look ...の個所がヒント。

解答 (B)

5. 組織の長について何が示唆されているか。
 (A) 彼女は2時30分の会議に出席する。
 (B) 彼女は新しい委員会を組織している。
 (C) 彼女はこれから最終候補者の履歴書を確認する。
 (D) 彼女はこれから会議室で面接を行う。

解説 キーワードはWhat、implied、head of the organization。「示唆」を問う個別情報タイプ。CEOやpresidentなど、組織のトップを指す語を待つ。the CEO wants to review ...がヒント。

解答 (C)

---

6. 今日の午後何が起きると思われるか。
 (A) 男性が記者会見に出席する。
 (B) CEOが視察に訪れる。
 (C) 審査委員会が開かれる。
 (D) 個人面接が行われる。

解説 キーワードはWhat、happen、this afternoon。「出来事」を問う個別情報タイプ。未来の時や行動を示す表現を待つ。通常、設問は会話中にヒントが登場する順に並べられているが、ここでは5の設問のヒントより前に6の設問のヒントがあるので注意。また、今後の出来事・行動に関する設問のヒントは、通常会話の最後に登場する。この場合はそのセオリーも守られていないので、難易度の高い問題となっている。Why don't we hold a quick meeting this afternoon ...以降がヒントとなる。

解答 (C)

M: Wendy, thank you for joining the board meeting. Let me get straight to the point. I'd like you to be in charge of a new project. It concerns our computer system. We want to establish an efficient computer networking system for our company. The board have unanimously agreed that you are the most appropriate person to lead the project. Can you take this new responsibility?

W: Certainly, sir. It's actually perfect timing for me, since I've just finished an extensive report on our company's overall productivity. I can fully focus on the new project. Could you give me a bit more detail on it?

M: Great, that's good to hear. Our objective is to renew the existing systems and integrate them. As you realize, each department has its own computer system and there isn't much compatibility between the different systems. We need something more unified and standardized to be competitive in the food market.

W: I see what you're saying. To be honest, what you've just said is in tune with my thinking. I'm sure that most of our staff members also share your opinion. May I ask what steps you had in mind in order to go forward without wasting any time?

M: I'd like you to make a quick analysis first on the advantages and disadvantages of the current system, and to do some research on what would be best for our company. Can you make a presentation on your evaluation along with a proposal in about 10 days?

M: Wendy、役員会議に参加してくれてありがとう。// 早速だが、本題に入らせてもらおう。// 君に、新たなプロジェクトを担当してもらいたい。// コンピューターシステムについてのプロジェクトだ。// わが社のために、効率的なコンピューターネットワークシステムを構築したいんだ。// 役員会はすでに、満場一致で合意しているよ、/ 君がこのプロジェクトを率いるのに最も適した人物だということにね。// この新たな任務を果たしてくれるかな？//

W: もちろんです。// 実のところ、私にとって絶好のタイミングなんです / ちょうど、わが社の総合的な生産性について膨大な報告書を仕上げたところなので。// 新しいプロジェクトに完全に集中することができます。// もう少し詳しいことをお聞かせ願えますか。//

M: よかった、それを聞いてうれしく思うよ。// われわれの目標は、現行のシステムを刷新し、統合することだ。// 君も気づいているだろうが、/ それぞれの部署が独自のコンピューターシステムを採用していて、/ 異なるシステム間の互換性があまりない。// もっと統合された、標準化されたものが必要だ / 食品業界で競争力を持つためには。//

W: わかります。// 本当に、今おっしゃったことは、私の考えと正に一致しています。// きっと、ほとんどの社員も同じ意見だと思います。// どのような手順をお考えか、伺ってもよろしいでしょうか。/ 一刻も無駄にせずに進めるために。//

M: まずは君に、現行のシステムの長所と短所について、ざっと分析してもらいたい。/ そして、わが社にとってどのようなものが最良か、調査してもらいたい。// 君の評価についてプレゼンしてもらうことはできるかな？/ 提案とともに、10日ほど後に。//

7. 話者は主に何について話しているか。
  (A) 次の会合についての通知
  (B) 議事録の訂正
  (C) 最先端の会計監査テクノロジーについての調査
  (D) 会社の情報ネットワークの強化

解説 設問のキーワードはWhat、speakers、discussing。「話題」を問う全体情報タイプ。冒頭に留意して聞き取る。We want to establish an efficient computer networking system以降、システム構築に関して繰り返し述べられている。
解答 (D)

---

8. 男性は誰だと思われるか。
  (A) システム・エンジニア
  (B) 組織のトップ
  (C) 証券アナリスト
  (D) 検察官

解説 キーワードはWho、is、man。「人物」を問う全体情報タイプ。男性の発言に注意して、職業を示す表現を待つ。thank you for joining the board meeting以降、取締役会を代表しての発言が続く。女性の応答もヒント。**解答** (B)

---

9. 女性について何が示唆されているか。
  (A) 新たなプロジェクトを担当する能力がある。
  (B) M&A（合併・買収）がうまくいかないと考えている。
  (C) ベテランの建築家だ。
  (D) 新事業に割く時間はほぼない。

解説 キーワードはWhat、implied、womanで、「示唆」を問う個別情報タイプ。設問の主語が女性なら、普通は女性の発言に注意して聞くが、implied aboutの場合は両方の発言に注意しなければならない。The board have unanimously agreed ...以降がヒント。**解答** (A)

---

10. 社員について何が示唆されているか。
  (A) 電気通信業界で働いている。
  (B) 専門家たちに取って代わられる。
  (C) いつも上司に対して迅速なフィードバックを行う。
  (D) システムをアップデートする必要性を感じているようだ。

解説 キーワードはWhat、implied、staff members。9と同じく「示唆」を問う個別情報タイプ。「職員たち」を示す語句を待つ。男性のWe need something more unified ...という発言を、I'm sure that most of our staff members also share your opinion.と女性が肯定していることがヒント。会話の流れをつかんでいないと解けない難問だ。**解答** (D)

---

11. 女性の責務について、何が示唆されているか。
  (A) 自分の提案について発表しなければならない。
  (B) 日程がかち合わないように仕事の進行を再編する必要がある。
  (C) 印刷システムのコスト分析をしなければならない。
  (D) 書類を電子化するよう求められている。

解説 キーワードはWhat、inferred、woman's responsibility。これも「示唆」を問う個別情報タイプ。命令・依頼表現や責任を示すresponsible、duty、task、are supposed to do、in charge of、have to do、should doなどの語句を待つ。男性はI'd like you to ...以下で女性の仕事内容を指示し、Can you make a presentation ...?と聞いている。**解答** (A)

13日目

いよいよ音読を開始しよう！

Task 1

それでは音読に挑戦する。まず、**1)** 英文をすべての区切り（/と/と//）で区切って音読しよう（**短いチャンク**）。意味をつかみながらリズミカルかつスピーディーに読めるようになったら、今度は**長いチャンク**に挑戦。**2)** トラック34〜36の音声のポーズの部分でリピートしよう（音声は会話のみ）。**3)** プロソディーを意識しながらきちんとリピートできるようになったら、仕上げに**すべての英文を**長いチャンクで音読しよう。

1. Where has the man been? //
   (A) At a company picnic / at Greenway Seaside Park //
   (B) In the public relations department //
   (C) At the offices of a client company // (D) At a community environment event //
2. How often are the activities carried out? //
   (A) Every month // (B) Every three months // (C) Every four months // (D) Every year //
3. What activity is planned? //
   (A) Safety inspections // (B) Volunteering a subscription //
   (C) Participating in emergency services // (D) Cleaning up trash //

CD 2-34

M: I've just been talking to the people in the public relations department /
about our community service program. //
It seems they have an annual event / planned for next month. //

W: Oh, really? // I assume it's another volunteer activity. //
What are we going to be doing this year? //

M: We're going to encourage volunteers /
to help with Community Environment Day. //
We'll help pick up trash in Greenway Seaside Park. //
Their goal is to get 100 staff members to volunteer,/
but so far only 40 have signed up. //

W: I suppose you can make that 41. // I'll join in. //
But I think they should be more aggressive /
about publicizing it within the company, don't you think so? //

要注意フレーズ！

社内行事に関する下線のセンテンスを、繰り返し音読してマスターしよう。下線以外に、pick up trash、only 40 have signed up、I suppose、I'll join inなどのフレーズにも注意。

4. Why is the man pleased? //
   (A) His résumé looks promising. //
   (B) Some of the candidates / have strong work experience. //
   (C) The personal interviews are going well. //
   (D) The company's growth is increasing. //

5. What is implied about the head of the organization? //
   (A) She will be attending a meeting at 2:30. //
   (B) She is forming a new committee. //
   (C) She will go over the final candidates' CVs. //
   (D) She will conduct interviews / in the conference room. //

6. What will most probably happen this afternoon? //
   (A) The man will attend a press conference. //
   (B) The CEO will come around for inspection. //
   (C) A judging committee will be met. //
   (D) Personal interviews will be conducted. //

CD 2-35

W: Where are we with recruiting new personnel for our department? //
   Have you looked through all the application forms yet? //
M: Well, we're done screening candidates / based on résumés now. //
   Dozens of people applied for the job. //
   In fact, some of the candidates look quite promising /
   and have some impressive work histories. //
   I think their capabilities will definitely be conducive /
   to the growth of the company. //
   It looks as though advertising the position / in a major financial newspaper /
   was really a worthwhile idea. //
W: You can say that again. // Can you make sure to brief me on the people /
   who will be coming in for the final screening? //
   We'll have to conduct personal interviews with them soon. //
M: Sure. //
   Why don't we hold a quick meeting this afternoon, / say, around 2:30 p.m., /
   to go through the list of candidates? //
   We can book conference room 9. //
   Oh, and by the way, /
   the CEO wants to review the candidates' files /
   prior to our official decision as well. //
   Our committee doesn't need her final approval normally, /
   but this is an exception. //

要注意フレーズ！

求人に関する表現の宝庫。設問の選択肢がすべてセンテンスになっているので、下線部のフレーズに気をつけてしっかりと音読しよう。会話のほうで、選択肢の表現がどう言い換えられているかにも注意。

7. What are the speakers mainly discussing? //
    (A) Notification of an upcoming meeting //
    (B) Corrections to the minutes //
    (C) A search for state-of-the-art auditing technology //
    (D) Strengthening the company information network //

8. Who most likely is the man? //
    (A) A systems engineer //
    (B) The head of the organization //
    (C) A securities analyst //
    (D) A prosecutor //

9. What is implied about the woman? //
    (A) She is capable of dealing with the new project. //
    (B) She thinks M&A doesn't work well. //
    (C) She is an experienced architect. //
    (D) She has little time for the new venture. //

10. What is implied about the staff members? //
    (A) They work in the telecommunications industry. //
    (B) They will be replaced by specialists. //
    (C) They always give quick feedbacks / to their superiors. //
    (D) They seem to be aware of the necessity / of updating the system. //

11. What is inferred about the woman's responsibility? //
    (A) She has to make a statement regarding her suggestion. //
    (B) She is required to reorganize workflow / to avoid scheduling conflicts. //
    (C) She has to make a cost analysis of the printing system. //
    (D) She is required to digitize documents. //

2-36

M: Wendy, thank you for joining the board meeting. //
Let me <u>get straight to the point</u>. //
I'd like you to <u>be in charge of</u> a new project. //
It concerns our computer system. //
We want to establish an efficient computer networking system for our company. //
The board <u>have unanimously agreed</u> /
that you are the most appropriate person to lead the project. //
Can you <u>take this new responsibility</u>? //

W: Certainly, sir. // It's actually perfect timing for me, /
since I've just finished an extensive report on our company's overall productivity. //
I can fully focus on the new project. //
Could you <u>give me a bit more detail on it</u>? //

M: Great, that's good to hear. //
Our objective is to renew the existing systems / and integrate them. //
<u>As you realize</u>, / each department has its own computer system /
and there isn't much compatibility between the different systems. //
We need something more unified and standardized /
<u>to be competitive in</u> the food market. //

W: I see what you're saying. //
To be honest, / what you've just said <u>is in tune with</u> my thinking. //
I'm sure that most of our staff members also <u>share your opinion</u>. //
May I ask what steps you <u>had in mind</u> /
in order to go forward without wasting any time? //

M: I'd like you to <u>make a quick analysis</u> first /
<u>on the advantages and disadvantages of</u> the current system, /
and to do some research on what would be best for our company. //
Can you make a presentation on your evaluation /
along with a proposal in about 10 days? //

13日目

要注意フレーズ！

設問の選択肢には、リーディングセクションでも役立つフレーズが多く含まれている。下線部を覚えるつもりで音読しよう。会話のほうはビジネス的な表現に下線を引いているので、声に出しながら意味をしっかりと確認すること。

Task 2

CD 2-34〜36

CDの音声を聞いて、ポーズの部分で**各チャンクの意味を頭に浮かべよう**（同時通訳の要領で声に出しても可）。ポーズの間にわからなければ、193〜197ページの訳をチェックしよう。

Task 3

CD 2-34〜36

CDの音声を聞いて、**スクリプトを見ないで**ポーズの部分でリピートしよう。

Task 4

CD 2-31〜33

仕上げに198〜201ページのスクリプトを見ながら、トラック31〜33の音声に**オーバーラップさせて読んでみよう**。プロソディーを意識しながら、リズミカルなナチュラルスピードでの音読に慣れよう。

Task 5

CD 2-31〜33

本日の学習を終えた後も、このトラックをスクリプトを見ずに聞いて理解できるか、繰り返し確認するようにしよう。

学習エネルギーをチャージする今日の　格言

A problem is a chance for you to do your best.

Duke Ellington
(1899〜1974：アメリカのジャズのピアノ奏者)

困難はベストを尽くすためのチャンス。

900点突破者たちの体験談（3）
900点突破のカギは効果的な音読！

（M. O. さん　会社員　男性）

875点 → 950点

　独学で875点を取得し、「もうすぐ900点に届くかな」と勉強を継続していましたが、スコアが頭打ちになり、一種のスランプに陥っていました。さまざまな教材を試し、いろいろ自分でも試行錯誤しましたが、なかなかトンネルを脱出できません。電車内や自宅で四六時中英語を聞いたり、本で音読やシャドーイングが良いことを知り、実践してみたりしましたが、効果をあまり実感できませんでした。そのころ、小山先生のTOEIC対策講座に参加して、自分の伸び悩みの理由がわかりました。

　今にして思えば、私のやり方は聞き流すことが中心で、シャドーイングも内容には注意をあまり向けず、発音を正確にまねすることに力点を置いていたのです。意味を把握しながらの音読は、まったくやっていませんでした。そこで、チャンクで理解しながら、リピーティング中心の音読練習をした後、リスニング教材を聞くようにしたところ、徐々に理解度が増してくるのが実感できました。

　また、自分には不要と感じていたTOEIC攻略本にも本気で取り組みました。英語力ではなくコツのようなものでスコアアップを目指すのは邪道と考えていたのですが、セミナーの指定テキストになっていた『新TOEICテスト直前の技術』（アルク）を使用してみたところ、自分のこれまでの解法に誤りがあったことに気づき、また、「なるほどそうだったのか」という発見にもたくさん出合いました。

　Part 2における「キーワードを避けるテクニック」、Part 5の「選択肢から読む方法」などを知り、勝手な思い込みのせいでスコアが伸び悩んでいた面もあったのだとわかりました。単なるコツではなく、基本的なTOEICの特徴や効果的な解法は本来知っているべきであり、実力を発揮するのにも必要だと思います。

　950点を取得した今は、背景や状況をイメージし、意味を把握しながら、リズミカルに感情を込めて、登場人物になったつもりで行う「なりきり音読」を毎日実践しています。また、アドバイスされたとおり、インプットとアウトプットを重視し、リスニングセクションとリーディングセクションの学習を、毎日5分でも欠かさずに実践することを自分に課しています。

Part 7 応用音読

14日目 / 20

今日は、Part 7の応用音読に挑戦する。問題の英文は本番よりかなり難易度が高いが、「高地トレーニング」に挑むつもりで速読して解こう。

Practice

▶解答：p.211〜

英文を読み、それに関する設問の解答として最も適切なものを1つずつ選ぼう。
合計11問の解答時間は**11分**。

Questions 1-3 refer to the following e-mail.

From: Frederick Kenner <fkenner@netcoxnet.com>
To: Marsha Root <marshar@grelandcom.com>
Subject: Remittance of Payment
Date: June 12

This is in response to your inquiry of May 19 regarding our remittance dated April 28 of $542.98 to cover the final payment for office equipment delivered to us from your Palmdale branch store the previous month. Our records show that although this amount was remitted to your company by the agreed deadline of May 1, it was mistakenly transferred to the wrong account, No. 87387287 at Firmington Bank & Trust, under the account name "Greland Co., Inc." I spoke with the accounting department at your corporate headquarters on June 10, and they informed me that each Greland Office Supply branch store receives payments from customers at its own separate bank account. Our error was that we should have remitted the payment to Firmington Bank & Trust account No. 13204800 under the account name "Greland Co. Palmdale Branch Office." The person I spoke to in accounting said that she would transfer the money to your account the following day. If you have not received it, please contact her directly: Kerrie Macy, Greland Main Office, extension 4747. I apologize for any inconvenience.

Sincerely,
Frederick Kenner

1. What is indicated about Frederick Kenner?
   (A) He accidentally made his payment to the wrong bank.
   (B) He bought and paid for some office furniture.
   (C) He plans to open a new account at Firmington Bank & Trust.
   (D) He received a refund for overpayment to Greland Co.

2. When was the merchandise delivered to Mr. Kenner's company?
   (A) March
   (B) April
   (C) May
   (D) June

3. What was Kerrie Macy expected to do?
   (A) Transfer funds from one bank account to another
   (B) Issue a corrected invoice to Marsha Root
   (C) Visit the Palmdale Branch Office in a few days
   (D) Call the bank to ask whether Mr. Kenner has paid

Questions 4-6 refer to the following article.

LOCAL RETAIL CONSULTANT FINDS NEW WORK ON THE WEB

Steve Nelson grew up helping his father run his neighborhood grocery store here in the Ridgeborough area. Although he never went into the retail business himself, he always had a particular talent for making business more efficient. On the basis of his experience, he came to realize success in business depends on cost, speed, and quality of products. Since then, as an entrepreneur, he has been particularly focusing on giving customers easy access to products, and eventually he devised his own strategies for increasing the efficiency of ordering and payment systems by simplifying the procedures. Now he runs Nelson & Sons Direct Marketing Consultants, which advises Internet Web sites on how to cut down on the phenomenon of shoppers who fill their virtual shopping carts, only to abandon them when they reach the check-out procedure. "Most of these potential customers give up when they are surprised by unexpectedly high shipping costs, or troublesome registration and payment procedures," he said, adding that he can advise companies on how to design Web sites to guide customers on through the payment process without losing them to impatience or various common distractions of the Internet age.

4. What is the purpose of the article?
   (A) To announce the latest sales performance of an enterprise
   (B) To notify readers of the content of an inaugural speech
   (C) To describe legal procedures regarding how to set up a joint venture
   (D) To profile a corporate executive

5. According to the article, who most likely is Steve Nelson?
   (A) The owner of a successful grocery store
   (B) An advisor to Internet regulatory authorities
   (C) A mid-level manager at a cargo shipping company
   (D) A CEO of a consulting firm

6. What is the main function of Steve Nelson's work?
   (A) To reduce the amount of unpaid bills
   (B) To mediate labor-management disputes
   (C) To increase employee performance
   (D) To eliminate inefficiency

Questions 7-11 refer to the following e-mails.

From: cservice@shoppingxyz-amicom.com
To: Phillip Hall <phall@rcoxnet.com>
Subject: Important Notice to ShoppingXYZ Customers (Please do not reply to this message)

AN IMPORTANT NOTICE FOR ALL OF OUR CUSTOMERS
ShoppingXYZ.com
Your Online Shopping Mall

    At ShoppingXYZ.com, we are dedicated to providing you with absolute safety and security, in addition to the ultimate in bargains and variety. This is why we thought you should know that our security team has recently detected a series of attempts at "phishing" — fraudulent attempts by unauthorized parties to coax personal information from consumers by impersonating legitimate Web sites like ShoppingXYZ.com.
    We can assure you that as of now, no personal information of any of our customers has been compromised. We would, however, like to remind you to exercise caution whenever attempting to access our Web site or conduct transactions online. In particular, please be aware that we never, under any circumstances, ask you for information such as your address, phone number, social security number or credit card number before you have properly logged in using your username and password. Please follow these simple steps whenever logging on to access your ShoppingXYZ.com account:

1) Confirm that the address "www.shoppingxyz.com/login" appears at the top of your Web browser.
2) Never provide more information than your username and password when initially logging on to the Web site.
3) Confirm that the message "Welcome to ShoppingXYZ.com, (your username)" appears on the welcome page after you submit your password.

If you experience any irregularities, DO NOT disclose any information, and immediately contact us at cservice@shoppingxyz-amicom.com.

From: Phillip Hall <phall@rcoxnet.com>
To: Customer Service <cservice@shoppingxyz-amicom.com>
Subject: "Phishing" Attempt

Dear Customer Service,

I was recently doing some Internet shopping, when I decided to access your Web site. I entered my shoppingXYZ.com password and ID, and looked at a few products before I had to turn off my computer and leave the house to run some errands. This was prior to receiving your warning of "phishing" attempts, and I did not notice whether the correct address appeared at the top of my Web browser, or whether the proper "welcome" message appeared. Since then, I have read your warning. Just to be safe, I have canceled my account with shoppingXYZ.com, and opened a new one with a different username and password. Will it be possible for you to confirm whether any of my private information was compromised? Please advise at your earliest convenience.

Many thanks,

Phillip Hall

7. What is the main purpose of the first e-mail?
   (A) To offer special discounts for frequent shoppers
   (B) To apologize for compromised information
   (C) To list the steps required to change a password
   (D) To warn of the danger of suspicious inquiries

8. In the first e-mail, the word "conduct" in paragraph 2, line 3, is closest in meaning to
   (A) assist
   (B) continue
   (C) transmit
   (D) perform

9. What advice is given to customers?
 (A) Never send whole credit card numbers over the Internet
 (B) Wait for a confirmation e-mail before sending money
 (C) Carefully examine the "welcome" message
 (D) Make sure bank records for unexpected deductions

10. What did Mr. Hall neglect to do?
 (A) Send an e-mail to confirm his intent to pay
 (B) Check the shipped items against the printed invoice
 (C) Make his online payment under his new username
 (D) Confirm that he had accessed the correct Web site

11. What does Mr. Hall want to know?
 (A) Where the items he ordered are located now
 (B) Who to contact if his shipment does not arrive
 (C) Whether any of his information was compromised
 (D) How to set up a new account under a different name

Practiceの正解と解説

問題1-3は次のメールに関するものです。

送信者: Frederick Kenner <fkenner@netcoxnet.com> //
あて先: Marsha Root <marshar@grelandcom.com> // 件名：支払い送金 // 日付：6月12日 //
これは5月19日にいただいたお問い合わせへのお返事です / 4月28日付けの当社の542ドル98セントの送金に関する / オフィス設備の最後の支払いに充てるための / その前の月に御社のPalmdale支店から配達していただいた（オフィス設備の）。// 当方の記録によりますと / この金額は5月1日の合意期日までに御社に送金されていたのですが / 誤って別の口座に送金されていました / Firmington信託銀行の口座番号87387287、口座名「Greland社」に。// 私は6月10日に御社の本社経理部と話をしました / そしてGrelandオフィス用品の各支店は顧客からの支払いを受け取ると教えてもらいました / 各店それぞれの口座で。// 私たちが間違っていたのは送金すべきだったということです / Firmington信託銀行の口座番号13204800、口座名「Greland社Palmdale支店」へ。// 経理部で私が話した方は言いました / 翌日にそちらの口座に送金しておくと。// もしまだ受け取っていなければ / 直接彼女に連絡を取ってください。/ Kerrie Macy、Greland本社、内線4747です。// お手数をおかけして申し訳ありません。// よろしくお願いします。// Frederick Kenner

---

1. Frederick Kennerについて何が示されているか。
(A) 間違って別の銀行に支払った。
(B) オフィス家具を買って支払った。
(C) Firmington信託銀行に新しく口座を開くつもりだ。
(D) Greland社に払いすぎた分を払い戻してもらった。

解説 設問のキーワードはWhat、indicated、Frederick Kenner。漠然とした問いなので、2と3に解答してから答えると時間が節約できる。it was mistakenly transferred to the wrong account, No. 87387287 at Firmington Bank & Trust,、Our error was that we should have remitted the payment to Firmington Bank & Trust account No. 13204800から、間違えたのは銀行ではなく口座番号とわかるので(A)は不可。
解答 (B)

---

2. 商品がKenner氏の会社に配達されたのはいつか。
(A) 3月
(B) 4月
(C) 5月
(D) 6月

解説 キーワードはWhen、merchandise、delivered、Mr. Kenner's company。「時期」を問う個別情報タイプ。our remittance dated April 28 ... for office equipment delivered to us ... the previous monthから、4月の前の月に到着したとわかる。**解答** (A)

---

3. Kerrie Macyは何をするはずだったか。
(A) 1つの銀行口座から別の口座に送金する
(B) Marsha Rootあてに訂正した請求明細書を発行する
(C) 数日後にPalmdale支店を訪れる
(D) Kenner氏が支払ったか尋ねるため銀行に電話する

解説 「次の行動」を問う個別情報タイプ。文書の後半に注目。she would transfer the money to your account the following day. If you have not received it, please contact her directly: Kerrie Macyから、設問の主語であるKerrieの行動がわかる。**解答** (A)

問題4-6は次の記事に関するものです。
地元の小売コンサルタントがウェブに新たな仕事を見つける //
Steve Nelsonは父親が近所の食料品店を営むのを手伝いながら育った / ここRidgeborough地区で。// 彼自身は小売業に進むことはなかったが / 彼は常に、事業を効率化する独特の才能を持っていた。// 自身の経験に基づいて / 事業の成功はコストとスピードと商品の品質にかかっているのだと気づくようになった。// それ以来、起業家として / 彼は特に、顧客が商品を簡単に入手できるようにすることに焦点を当ててきた / そして最終的に独自の戦略を考案した / 注文と支払いのシステムの効率を上げるための / 手続きを簡略化させることで。// 現在彼はNelson & Sonsダイレクトマーケティング・コンサルタントを経営している / それは購買者の現象をどうやって減らすかに関して、インターネットのウェブサイトにアドバイスする / 彼ら（購買者）はネットワーク上のショッピングカートに品物を入れる / ただ、支払い手続きに至るとそれを放棄してしまうことになる。//「こうした見込み客の多くはやめてしまいます / 予想もしないほど高い送料に驚かされると / あるいは面倒な登録や支払いの手続きに（驚かされると）」と彼は言った / さらに彼は企業にウェブサイトのデザインの仕方をアドバイスできると付け加えた / 顧客を支払い手続きまで導くために / いら立ちやインターネット時代によくあるさまざまな気をそらす物事のために彼ら（顧客）を失うことなく。//

---

4. この記事の目的は何か。
 (A) ある企業の最新の販売業績を発表すること
 (B) ある就任演説の内容を読者に知らせること
 (C) ジョイント・ベンチャーの立ち上げ方に関する法的手続きを説明すること
 (D) ある企業幹部の人物像を紹介すること

解説 キーワードはWhat、purpose、article。「目的」を問う全体情報タイプ。タイトルと最初の1、2文がヒントとなる。ほかの設問に答えた後に解答すると、時間が節約できる。 **解答** (D)

---

5. 記事によると、Steve Nelsonは何者である可能性が最も高いか。
 (A) 繁盛している食料品店のオーナー
 (B) インターネット取り締まり当局のアドバイザー
 (C) 貨物運送会社の中級管理職
 (D) コンサルティング会社の最高経営責任者

解説 キーワードはwho、Steve Nelson。「職業」を問う個別情報タイプだ。中盤のNow he runs Nelson & Sons Direct Marketing Consultantsから正解がわかる。 **解答** (D)

---

6. Steve Nelsonの仕事の主な役目は何か。
 (A) 未払い請求の金額を減らすこと
 (B) 労使紛争の仲介をすること
 (C) 従業員の仕事ぶりを向上させること
 (D) 効率の悪さをなくすこと

解説 Steve Nelsonの「仕事の内容」を問う個別情報タイプ。as an entrepreneur ... he devised his own strategies for increasing the efficiency of ordering and payment systems by simplifying the proceduresの個所がヒント。 **解答** (D)

問題7-11は次のメールに関するものです。

文書1

送信者：cservice@shoppingxyz-amicom.com // あて先：Phillip Hall <phall@rcoxnet.com> //
件名：ShoppingXYZのお客様へ重要なお知らせ //（このメッセージには返信しないでください）//
すべてのお客様への重要なお知らせ // ShoppingXYZ.com //
皆様のオンラインショッピングモール //
ShoppingXYZ.comでは／皆様に絶対の安全と安心を提供することに尽力しています／究極のお買い得価格と品ぞろえに加えて。// だからこそ当社は皆様にお知らせすべきだと考えました／当社のセキュリティーチームが最近、一連の「フィッシング」の企てを発見したことを／（フィッシングとは）権限のない者が顧客の個人情報をだまし取る詐欺の企てです／ShoppingXYZ.comのような正規のウェブサイトを装うことによって。//
当社では現在のところ保証できます／当社の顧客のどなたの個人情報も漏えいしておりません。// しかしながら、ご注意されるよう申し上げたいと思います／当社のウェブサイトにアクセスしたり、オンラインで取引をなさる場合にはいつでも。// 特に、当社ではどのような状況であっても決して、情報をお尋ねすることはないのでご注意ください／住所、電話番号、社会保障番号、クレジットカード番号といった（情報を）／お客様がユーザー名とパスワードを使って正式にログインされる前には。// ログインする際には必ず、以下の簡単な手順に従ってください／ご自身のShoppingXYZ.comアカウントにアクセスするために：/

1)「www.shoppingxyz.com/login」というアドレスを確認してください／ウェブブラウザの一番上に出ます。//
2) ユーザー名とパスワード以外の情報を決して入力しないでください／ウェブサイトに最初にログインする際は。//
3)「ShoppingXYZ.comへようこそ、（お客様のお名前）様」というメッセージが現れることを確認してください／パスワードを入力した後、ウェルカム画面に。//

もし何かいつもと違うことがあれば／どんな情報も開示せずに／速やかに当社cservice@shoppingxyz-amicom.comまでご連絡ください。//

文書2

送信者：Phillip Hall <phall@rcoxnet.com> //
あて先：Customer Service <cservice@shoppingxyz-amicom.com> //
件名：「フィッシング」狙い //
カスタマーサービス御中 //
私は先日、インターネットで買い物をしていて、御社のウェブサイトにアクセスすることにしました。// 自分のShoppingXYZ.com用のパスワードとIDを入力し、商品をいくつか見ました／その後、コンピューターの電源を切り、用事を済ませに家を出なければいけませんでした。// これは御社の「フィッシング」狙いの警告を受け取る前のことです／ですから、正しいアドレスがウェブブラウザの一番上に出ていたかどうか気に留めませんでした／あるいは、正しい「ようこそ」のメッセージが出ていたかどうかも。// その後、私は御社の警告を読みました。// 念のため、自分のShoppingXYZ.comのアカウントを解約しました／そして別のユーザー名とパスワードで新しいアカウントを開きました。// 私の個人情報が何か漏えいしたかどうか、確認していただくことはできるでしょうか。// なるべく早くお知らせください。// よろしくお願いいたします。// Phillip Hall //

7. 最初のメールの主な目的は何か。
(A) 得意客に特別割引を提供すること
(B) 情報漏えいを謝罪すること
(C) パスワード変更に必要な手順を列挙すること
(D) 不審な問い合わせの危険を警告すること

解説 キーワードはWhat、main purpose、first e-mail。「目的」を問う全体情報タイプなので、最初のメールの件名、タイトルと最初の1、2文に注目する。すべての設問に答えた後に解答すると時間が節約できる。文中で何度も個人情報をうかつに開示しないよう警告しているので、それに最も近い選択肢を選ぼう。 **解答** (D)

---

8. 最初のメールの第2段落3行目の「conduct」に最も意味が近いのは
(A) assist（手助けする）
(B) continue（続ける）
(C) transmit（伝送する）
(D) perform（実行する）

解説 語彙問題。conductには① lead（〜を導く）、② carry out（〜を実行する、果たす）、③ behave（ふるまう）、④ transmit（〈熱・電気などを〉伝える）の意味があるが、文脈からここでは②の意味で使われているとわかる。 **解答** (D)

---

9. 顧客にはどんな忠告が与えられているか。
(A) インターネットを通じてクレジットカード番号全部を送らない
(B) 送金前に確認メールを待つ
(C)「ようこそ」のメッセージを注意深く調べる
(D) 予想外の引き落としがないか、銀行の記録を確かめる

解説 「アドバイスの内容」を問う個別情報タイプ。顧客への告知なので、最初のメールを参照する。3) のConfirm that the message "Welcome to ShoppingXYZ.com, (your username)" appears on the welcome pageがヒント。
解答 (C)

---

10. Hall氏は何をするのを怠ったか。
(A) 支払いの意思を確認するメールを送る
(B) 配送された品物を請求明細書と照らし合わせる
(C) オンラインでの支払いを新しいユーザー名で行う
(D) 正しいウェブサイトにアクセスしたことを確認する

解説 設問の主語のHall氏は2通目のメールの送信者。2通目の中からneglect to doに当たる表現を探す。中盤のI did not notice whether the correct address appeared ...で、正しいアドレスとメッセージが出たか確認しなかったと述べている。最初のメールでimpersonating legitimate Web sitesと、フィッシングの手口を説明しているので、この行為が正しいサイトにアクセスしたか確認する方法だとわかる。 **解答** (D)

11. Hall氏は何を知りたがっているか。
  (A) 自分の注文した品物が今どこにあるか
  (B) 配送品が到着しなかった場合、誰に連絡するか
  (C) 自分の情報が何か漏えいしたかどうか
  (D) どうやって別の名前で新しいアカウントを設定するか

解説 この設問の主語もHall氏なので、2通目のメールをチェックする。Will it be possible ... confirm whether any of my private information was compromised? から、漏えいの有無を知りたがっていることがわかる。

解答 (C)

いよいよ音読を開始しよう！

Task 1

それでは音読に挑戦する。まず、**1)** 英文をすべての区切り (/ と / と //) で区切って音読しよう**(短いチャンク)**。意味をつかみながら読めるようになったら、今度は**長いチャンク**に挑戦。**2)** 音声のポーズの部分でリピートしよう(音声は文書のみ)。**3)** プロソディーを意識しながら、スピーディーかつリズミカルにリピートできるようになったら、仕上げに**すべての英文を**長いチャンクで音読しよう。

1. What is indicated about Frederick Kenner? //
   (A) He accidentally made his payment to the wrong bank. //
   (B) He bought and paid for some office furniture. //
   (C) He plans to <u>open a new account</u> / at Firmington Bank & Trust. //
   (D) He <u>received a refund for overpayment</u> to Greland Co. //

2. When was the merchandise delivered to Mr. Kenner's company? //
   (A) March //
   (B) April //
   (C) May //
   (D) June //

3. What was Kerrie Macy expected to do? //
   (A) Transfer funds from one bank account to another //
   (B) <u>Issue a corrected invoice to</u> Marsha Root //
   (C) Visit the Palmdale Branch Office in a few days //
   (D) Call the bank to ask whether Mr. Kenner has paid //

From: Frederick Kenner <fkenner@netcoxnet.com> //
To: Marsha Root <marshar@grelandcom.com> //
Subject: Remittance of Payment //
Date: June 12 //
This is in response to your inquiry of May 19 /
regarding our remittance dated April 28 of $542.98 /
to cover the final payment for office equipment /
delivered to us from your Palmdale branch store the previous month. //
Our records show / that although this amount was remitted to your company /
by the agreed deadline of May 1, /
it was mistakenly transferred to the wrong account, /
No. 87387287 at Firmington Bank & Trust, /
under the account name "Greland Co., Inc." //
I spoke with the accounting department at your corporate headquarters /
on June 10, / and they informed me /
that each Greland Office Supply branch store receives payments from customers /
at its own separate bank account. //
Our error / was that we should have remitted the payment /
to Firmington Bank & Trust account No. 13204800 /
under the account name "Greland Co. Palmdale Branch Office." //
The person I spoke to in accounting said /
that she would transfer the money to your account the following day. //
If you have not received it, / please contact her directly: /
Kerrie Macy, Greland Main Office, extension 4747. //
I apologize for any inconvenience. //
Sincerely, //
Frederick Kenner //

要注意フレーズ！

TOEICに頻出の支払いや送金に関する表現が、選択肢・メールの両方に登場している。Part 5で一部が空所になって出題されてもわかるように、下線のフレーズをセットで覚えよう。

4. What is the purpose of the article? //
   (A) To announce the latest sales performance of an enterprise //
   (B) To notify readers of the content of an inaugural speech //
   (C) To describe legal procedures / regarding how to set up a joint venture //
   (D) To profile a corporate executive //

5. According to the article, / who most likely is Steve Nelson? //
   (A) The owner of a successful grocery store //
   (B) An advisor to Internet regulatory authorities //
   (C) A mid-level manager / at a cargo shipping company //
   (D) A CEO of a consulting firm //

6. What is the main function of Steve Nelson's work? //
   (A) To reduce the amount of unpaid bills //
   (B) To mediate labor-management disputes //
   (C) To increase employee performance //
   (D) To eliminate inefficiency //

CD 2-38

Local Retail Consultant Finds New Work on the Web //
Steve Nelson grew up / helping his father <u>run his neighborhood grocery store</u> /
here in the Ridgeborough area. //
Although he never <u>went into the retail business</u> himself, /
he always <u>had a particular talent for</u> making business more efficient. //
<u>On the basis of his experience</u>, /
he came to realize success in business depends on cost, speed, /
and quality of products. //
Since then, / <u>as an entrepreneur</u>, /
he <u>has been particularly focusing on</u> giving customers <u>easy access to products</u>, /
and eventually he <u>devised his own strategies</u> /
<u>for</u> increasing the efficiency of ordering and payment systems /
<u>by simplifying the procedures</u>. //
Now he runs Nelson & Sons Direct Marketing Consultants, /
which advises Internet Web sites /
on <u>how to cut down on</u> the phenomenon of shoppers /
who fill their virtual shopping carts, /
only to abandon them when they reach the check-out procedure. //
"Most of these potential customers give up /
when they are surprised by unexpectedly high shipping costs, /
or troublesome registration and payment procedures," he said, /
adding that he can advise companies / on how to design Web sites /
to <u>guide customers on</u> through the payment process /
without losing them to impatience /
or various common distractions of the Internet age. //

14日目

要注意フレーズ

そう長くない記事の中に、経営やビジネス戦略に関する書き言葉特有のフレーズが多数登場する。覚えておきたいものばかりなので、下線の部分を特に意識して、繰り返し音読しよう。

ダブルパッセージは英文が多いので、設問は割愛する。2つの文書をしっかりと読もう。

2-39

文書1

From: cservice@shoppingxyz-amicom.com //
To: Phillip Hall <phall@rcoxnet.com> //
Subject: Important Notice to ShoppingXYZ Customers //
 (Please do not reply to this message) //
AN IMPORTANT NOTICE FOR ALL OF OUR CUSTOMERS //
ShoppingXYZ.com // Your Online Shopping Mall //

At ShoppingXYZ.com, /
we are dedicated to providing you with absolute safety and security, /
in addition to the ultimate in bargains and variety. //
This is why we thought you should know /
that our security team has recently detected a series of attempts at "phishing" /
— fraudulent attempts by unauthorized parties /
to coax personal information from consumers /
by impersonating legitimate Web sites like ShoppingXYZ.com. //
We can assure you / that as of now, /
no personal information of any of our customers has been compromised. //
We would, however, / like to remind you to exercise caution /
whenever attempting to access our Web site / or conduct transactions online. //
In particular, / please be aware that we never, under any circumstances, ask you for information /
such as your address, phone number, social security number or credit card number /
before you have properly logged in / using your username and password. //
Please follow these simple steps whenever logging on /
to access your ShoppingXYZ.com account: /

1) Confirm that the address "www.shoppingxyz.com/login" /
   appears at the top of your Web browser. //
2) Never provide more information than your username and password /
   when initially logging on to the Web site. //
3) Confirm that the message "Welcome to ShoppingXYZ.com, (your username)" appears /
   on the welcome page / after you submit your password. //

If you experience any irregularities, / DO NOT disclose any information, /
and immediately contact us at cservice@shoppingxyz-amicom.com. //

文書2

From: Phillip Hall <phall@rcoxnet.com> //
To: Customer Service <cservice@shoppingxyz-amicom.com> //
Subject: "Phishing" Attempt //

Dear Customer Service, //
I was recently doing some Internet shopping, / when I decided to access your Web site. //
I entered my shoppingXYZ.com password and ID, / and looked at a few products /
before I had to turn off my computer and leave the house to run some errands. //
This was prior to receiving your warning of "phishing" attempts, /
and I did not notice whether the correct address appeared at the top of my Web browser, /
or whether the proper "welcome" message appeared. //
Since then, I have read your warning. //
Just to be safe, / I have canceled my account with shoppingXYZ.com, /
and opened a new one with a different username and password. //
Will it be possible for you to confirm /
whether any of my private information was compromised? //
Please advise at your earliest convenience. //
Many thanks, // Phillip Hall //

要注意フレーズ！

下線を引いた as of now、under any circumstances、at your earliest convenience といったビジネス文書のセットフレーズと、exercise caution、conduct transactions のような動詞と名詞の組み合わせに注意しながら音読しよう。

Task 2

CD 2-37~40

CDの音声を聞いて、ポーズの部分で**各チャンクの意味を頭に浮かべよう**（同時通訳の要領で声に出しても可）。ポーズの間にわからなければ、211～213ページの訳をチェックしよう。

Task 3

CD 2-37~40

CDの音声を聞いて、**スクリプトを見ないで**ポーズの部分でリピートしよう。

Task 4

CD 2-41~42 / 3-01~02

仕上げに216～221ページのスクリプトを見ながら、CD2のトラック41、42、CD3の01、02の音声に**オーバーラップさせて読んでみよう**。プロソディーを意識しながら繰り返して、ナチュラルスピードでの音読に慣れよう。

Task 5

CD 2-41~42 / 3-01~02

本日の学習を終えた後も、これらトラックをスクリプトを見ずに聞いて理解できるか、繰り返し確認するようにしよう。

学習エネルギーをチャージする今日の **格言**

> **Learning is not attained by chance, it must be sought for with ardor and attended to with diligence.**
>
> Abigail Adams
> (1744～1818：第2代アメリカ合衆国大統領ジョン・アダムズの妻)
>
> 学びとは偶然に得られるものではありません。
> 情熱と不断の努力をもって、自ら追い求めなければなりません。

Part 4 応用音読

今日は、Part 4の応用音読に挑戦する。本番より長めのトークが登場するので、最後まで集中力を持続させて聞き取ること。音読で内容をより深く理解しよう。

Practice

3-03〜05　▶解答：p.226〜

それでは練習問題に挑戦してみよう。CDの音声の冒頭に8秒のポーズを設けているので、この時間を利用して設問・選択肢を先読みしよう。

1. What is the report mainly about?
    (A) A trend in the fitness products industry
    (B) The popularity of environment-friendly goods
    (C) Changes in retail prices
    (D) The necessity of physical examinations　Ⓐ Ⓑ Ⓒ Ⓓ ☐

2. When would the report most likely be heard?
    (A) A fall evening
    (B) A winter morning
    (C) A spring night
    (D) A summer night　Ⓐ Ⓑ Ⓒ Ⓓ ☐

3. What is mentioned about the cause of the problem?
    (A) A lack of quality control
    (B) Too much investment in publicity
    (C) Breach of contracts by manufacturers
    (D) A sluggish economy　Ⓐ Ⓑ Ⓒ Ⓓ ☐

GO ON TO THE NEXT PAGE

4. Who most likely are the listeners?
   (A) Commuters driving a vehicle
   (B) Conductors working on the subway
   (C) An audience in a concert hall
   (D) Plumbers doing repairs

5. When will the streets in Pine Hills be blocked?
   (A) Wednesday
   (B) Thursday
   (C) Friday
   (D) Saturday

6. What will most likely be heard next?
   (A) Details on recommended detours
   (B) A music program
   (C) A schematic plan for the hall
   (D) Description of the marathon

7. What is the speaker doing?
   (A) Making recommendations on streamlining a publishing company
   (B) Giving a presentation on a research project
   (C) Conducting a tour of the company headquarters
   (D) Explaining a schedule for remodeling the office

8. What have the listeners seen most recently?
   (A) A publication department
   (B) An assembly plant
   (C) A general affairs office
   (D) A power plant

9. Why does the speaker mention the document processing room?
   (A) To show a successful example of streamlining
   (B) To introduce a new executive
   (C) To promote the new product
   (D) To demonstrate the latest computer software for designing

10. What can be inferred about Robin Computer Company?
   (A) It was established a decade ago.
   (B) It recently expanded internationally.
   (C) It will hire more than 100 new employees.
   (D) It specializes in industrial robots.

11. Where will the listeners go next?
   (A) A reception area for guests
   (B) A conference room for customers
   (C) The training center in the gym
   (D) The call center

Practiceの正解と解説

Questions 1-3 refer to the following excerpt from a news broadcast.

Good evening. This is Mary White with the 7 o'clock business news. Summer bathing suit season is only a few months away. And for manufacturers of exercise equipment, that means it's time to bring out new products for consumers eager to slim down and get into shape. One of the most heavily advertised exercise machines this year is the FitTest Cardio Super by Sport Fizz Incorporated. The FitTest Cardio Super is advertised as a single product that can improve all aspects of your physical fitness, good health, and even give you a slimmer body. Although it is the best selling of the more expensive exercise products this year, overall sales in the industry have been declining for two straight years. Analysts blame this on a worldwide economic slowdown that is now entering its third year.

問題1-3は次のニュース放送の抜粋に関するものです。

こんばんは。// Mary Whiteが7時のビジネスニュースをお送りします。// ほんの数カ月後には夏の水着シーズン。// そして、エクササイズ用品のメーカーにとって / それは顧客向けに新製品を売り出す時期ということになります / 彼らは体重を落として体を引き締めたがっています。// 今年最も宣伝に熱が入っているエクササイズ機器の1つは / Sport Fizz社のFitTest Cardio Superです。// FitTest Cardio Superは唯一の製品と銘打たれています / あらゆる面から体力、健康を増進させ / しかも、よりスリムな体形まで手に入ると。// 比較的高価なエクササイズ製品の中では、今年最も売れ行きがいいのですが / 業界全体の売上は2年連続で下降しています。// アナリストたちは、これを世界的な景気低迷のせいだとしています / それは現在3年目に入ったところです。//

1. この報道は主に何に関するものか。
   (A) フィットネス製品業界の動向
   (B) 環境に優しい製品の人気
   (C) 小売価格の変動
   (D) 健康診断の必要性

解説 設問のキーワードはWhat、report、about。「主題」を問う全体情報タイプ。個別情報タイプの設問に解答した後に解くといい。business news、for manufacturers of exercise equipmentなどからフィットネス業界の話題だとわかる。Although it is ... 以降で業界の動向が述べられている。

解答 (A)

2. この報道を聞く可能性が最も高いのはいつか。
   (A) 秋の夕方
   (B) 冬の朝
   (C) 春の夜
   (D) 夏の夜

解説 キーワードは When、report、heard。「季節と時間」を問う個別情報タイプ。放送番組の場合、時刻に関するヒントは冒頭に出る。Summer bathing suit season is only a few months awayから、季節が春であることもわかる。

解答 (C)

3. 問題の原因について何が言われているか。
   (A) 品質管理の欠如
   (B) 広告への過剰投資
   (C) 製造業者による契約不履行
   (D) 停滞気味の景気

解説　キーワードはWhat、mentioned、cause of the problem。「原因」を問う個別情報タイプ。トークの最後のAnalysts blame this on a worldwide economic slowdownから、A sluggish economyが正解となる。

解答　(D)

Questions 4-6 refer to the following excerpt from a radio broadcast.

This is Jill Farnsworth with your mid-day traffic report for Friday. Commuters northbound on Winston Avenue near Jackson Park can expect bumper-to-bumper traffic through the downtown area. A major road construction project is blocking all but one of the northbound lanes at Regent's Road, and is scheduled to continue through next Wednesday. So if you're planning on heading north through downtown, we'd recommend that you use Bay Avenue instead. Traffic on many of the major roads in the Pine Hills district will be blocked or restricted all day Saturday for the 36th annual Pine Hills International Marathon. And the local Park and Recreation Bureau has set up a toll-free number you can call for details on times, locations and recommended detours. That's 1-800-555-1234. Now back to Milt Hall and more music.

問題4-6は次のラジオ放送の抜粋に関するものです。

Jill Farnsworthが、金曜お昼の交通情報をお届けします。// Winston Avenueを北上してJackson Park付近にいる通勤者の方は / ダウンタウン地区を抜ける際、大渋滞が予想されます。// 大規模な道路工事プロジェクトのためRegent's Roadの北行き車線が、1本を残しすべて通行止めにされています / そして来週の水曜日まで続く予定です。// ですから、ダウンタウンを抜けて北に向かう予定がおありでしたら、/ 代わりにBay Avenueを利用することをお勧めします。// Pine Hills区域の主要道路の多くの交通は / 36回目となる毎年恒例のPine Hills国際マラソンのため、土曜日いっぱい通行止めまたは通行制限されるでしょう。// そこで、地元の公園・レクリエーション局では通話料無料の番号を開設しました / 時間や場所やお勧めの迂回路の詳細を電話でお問い合わせになれます。// それは1-800-555-1234です。// では、Milt Hallに戻しますので、さらに音楽をどうぞ。//

4. 聞き手が誰である可能性が最も高いか。
   (A) 車を運転している通勤者
   (B) 地下鉄で働いている車掌
   (C) コンサートホールの聴衆
   (D) 修理中の配管工

解説　設問のキーワードはWho、listeners。「聞き手」を問う個別情報タイプ。誰に向けた放送かは、たいてい冒頭でふれられる。traffic reportと告げた後に、Commuters northbound on Winston Avenue ...と続けているので正解は明らか。

解答　(A)

15日目

5. Pine Hillsの道路が通行止めになるの
はいつか。
(A) 水曜日
(B) 木曜日
(C) 金曜日
(D) 土曜日

解説 キーワードはWhen、streets、Pine Hills、blocked。「時」を問う個別情報タイプで、設問の主語のPine Hillsを待ち伏せる。Pine Hills district will be blocked ... all day Saturdayがヒント。
解答 (D)

6. 次に聞こえてくる可能性が最も高い
のは何か。
(A) お勧めの迂回路の詳細
(B) 音楽番組
(C) ホールの計画概要
(D) マラソンの説明

解説 キーワードはWhat、heard、next。「次のプログラム」を問う個別情報タイプ。トークの最後でふれられる。Now back to Milt Hall and more music. から次が音楽番組だとわかる。
解答 (B)

Questions 7-11 refer to the following talk.

All right, everyone. That just about concludes our tour today of the corporate headquarters here at Robin Computer Company. We've seen the assembly plant where we customize our personal computers before sending them out to the customer. And now I'd like to take a moment to draw your attention to this room here on the right. What do you see there? Three people, sitting at their desks. It's very quiet, isn't it? This is our document processing and publication department. And the reason I wanted to show it to you is that it's a model of efficiency. When our firm was established 10 years ago, this was a department with 15 employees, with an enormous budget, and taking up five times as much office space. Thanks to the cutting-edge technology, it's now much more streamlined. Next, we're going to see our call-center operation. The trend there has been the opposite of that in the document processing center — at least in terms of size. Initially, we didn't even have a call center. Now it's our most crucial interface with the customer. This is where any of our customers can call us for any reason, 24 hours a day. It has a large office-space of its own, a training center and a total staff of 125.

問題**7-11**は以下のトークに関するものです。
さて、皆さん。// これで本日のツアーはほぼ終わりです / ここ、Robin Computer社本社での。// 私たちはパーソナルコンピューターのカスタマイズを行っている組立工場を見ました / お客様に発送する前に。// そして今度はちょっと注目していただきたいと思います / 右側のこちらにあるこの部屋に。// そこに何が見えますか。// 3人がデスクに座っています。// とても静かですね？ // ここは、書類手続きと広報の部門です。// そして、ここを皆さんにお見せしたかった理由は / ここが効率化のモデルだからです。/ 弊社が10年前に設立された当時 / ここは社員15人を抱え、多額の予算を持つ部門でした / そして5倍のオフィススペースを占めていました。// 最新技術のおかげで、現在でははるかに合理化されています。// 次に、

コールセンター業務を見学します。// そこの傾向は書類手続き部門のそれとは正反対でした——/ 少なくとも規模に関しては。// 当初、弊社はコールセンターを持ってさえいませんでした。// 現在ではお客様との最も重要な接点です。// ここはお客様が誰でも、どんな理由でも、1日24時間いつでも電話をかけてこられる場所です。// そこは独立した広いオフィススペースを持っています / 訓練センターと計125人のスタッフも。//

7. 話者は何をしているか。
 (A) 出版社の合理化を推奨している
 (B) 調査プロジェクトのプレゼンテーションをしている
 (C) 企業本社のツアーを率いている
 (D) オフィス改装の日程を説明している

解説 トークの「主題」を問う全体情報タイプ。最後に答えると時間が節約できるが、冒頭のThat just about concludes our tour today of the corporate headquarters ... からも解答は可能。
解答 (C)

8. 聞き手はこの直前に何を見たか。
 (A) 広報部門
 (B) 組立工場
 (C) 総務オフィス
 (D) 発電所

解説 キーワードはWhat、listeners、seen、recently。「直前の行動」を問う個別情報タイプ。当然、ヒントは冒頭に登場すると考えられる。We've seen the assembly plant をチェック。
解答 (B)

9. 話者が書類手続きの部屋に言及したのはなぜか。
 (A) 合理化の成功例を見せるため
 (B) 新任の重役を紹介するため
 (C) 新製品の販売促進をするため
 (D) 最新のデザイン用コンピューターソフトの実演をするため

解説 「理由」を問う個別情報タイプ。document processing roomに当たる語句を待ち伏せる。the reason I wanted to show it ...以降で理由が述べられている。
解答 (A)

10. Robin Computer社について言えることは何か。
 (A) 10年前に設立された。
 (B) 最近、国際的な拡大をした。
 (C) 100人以上の新入社員を採用する予定だ。
 (D) 産業用ロボットを専門としている。

解説 キーワードはWhat、inferred、Robin Computer Company。漠然とした質問だが、選択肢に数字があるので先読みで頭に入れておく。When our firm was established 10 years ago がヒント。
解答 (A)

11. 聞き手は次にどこへ行くか。
 (A) ゲスト用応接エリア
 (B) 顧客用会議室
 (C) ジムの中のトレーニングセンター
 (D) コールセンター

解説 「次の行動」を問う個別情報タイプ。トークの後半に注意する。Next, we're going to see our call-center operation. から答えがわかる。
解答 (D)

いよいよ音読を開始しよう！

Task 1

それでは音読に挑戦する。まず、**1）** 英文をすべての区切り（/と/と//）で区切って音読しよう（**短いチャンク**）。意味をつかみながら読めるようになったら、今度は**長いチャンク**に挑戦。**2）** トラック06〜08の音声のポーズの部分でリピートしよう（音声はトークのみ）。**3）** プロソディーを意識して、スピーディーかつリズミカルにリピートできるようになったら、仕上げに**すべての英文を**長いチャンクで音読しよう。

1. What is the report mainly about? //
    (A) A trend in the fitness products industry //
    (B) The popularity of environment-friendly goods //
    (C) Changes in retail prices //
    (D) The necessity of physical examinations //

2. When would the report most likely be heard? //
    (A) A fall evening //
    (B) A winter morning //
    (C) A spring night //
    (D) A summer night //

3. What is mentioned about the cause of the problem? //
    (A) A lack of quality control //
    (B) Too much investment in publicity //
    (C) Breach of contracts by manufacturers //
    (D) A sluggish economy //

3-06

Good evening. //
This is Mary White with the 7 o'clock business news. //
Summer bathing suit season is only a few months away. //
And for manufacturers of exercise equipment, /
that means / it's time to bring out new products for consumers /
eager to slim down and get into shape. //
One of the most heavily advertised exercise machines this year /
is the FitTest Cardio Super / by Sport Fizz Incorporated. //
The FitTest Cardio Super is advertised as a single product /
that can improve all aspects of your physical fitness, / good health, /
and even give you a slimmer body. //
Although it is the best selling of the more expensive exercise products this year, /
overall sales in the industry have been declining for two straight years. //
Analysts blame this on a worldwide economic slowdown /
that is now entering its third year. //

要注意フレーズ！

トークに登場するフレーズよりも、選択肢の表現が高度になっている。下線の表現を中心に、意味を把握してから声に出して読もう。トークのほうでは、フィットネス関係の語彙に注目。

4. Who most likely are the listeners? //
   (A) Commuters driving a vehicle //
   (B) Conductors working on the subway //
   (C) An audience in a concert hall //
   (D) Plumbers doing repairs //

5. When will the streets in Pine Hills be blocked? //
   (A) Wednesday // (B) Thursday // (C) Friday // (D) Saturday //

6. What will most likely be heard next? //
   (A) Details on recommended detours //
   (B) A music program //
   (C) A schematic plan for the hall //
   (D) Description of the marathon //

CD 3-07

This is Jill Farnsworth / with your mid-day traffic report for Friday. //
Commuters northbound on Winston Avenue near Jackson Park /
can expect <u>bumper-to-bumper traffic</u> through the downtown area. //
A major road construction project /
is blocking all but one of the northbound lanes at Regent's Road, /
and <u>is scheduled to continue through</u> next Wednesday. //
So if you're planning on heading north through downtown, /
we'd recommend that you use Bay Avenue instead. //
Traffic on many of the major roads in the Pine Hills district /
will be blocked or restricted all day Saturday /
for the 36th annual Pine Hills International Marathon. //
And the local Park and Recreation Bureau has set up a toll-free number /
you <u>can call for details</u> on times, locations and recommended detours. //
That's 1-800-555-1234. // <u>Now back to</u> Milt Hall and more music. //

要注意フレーズ

交通情報らしいフレーズと、放送独特の表現、Now back to ～などに注目。下線部以外も、チャンクで意味をとらえながら音読しよう。

7. What is the speaker doing? //
   (A) Making recommendations / on streamlining a publishing company //
   (B) Giving a presentation on a research project //
   (C) Conducting a tour of the company headquarters //
   (D) Explaining a schedule for remodeling the office //

8. What have the listeners seen most recently? //
   (A) A publication department //
   (B) An assembly plant //
   (C) A general affairs office //
   (D) A power plant //

9. Why does the speaker mention the document processing room? //
   (A) To show a successful example of streamlining //
   (B) To introduce a new executive //
   (C) To promote the new product //
   (D) To demonstrate the latest computer software for designing /

10. What can be inferred about Robin Computer Company? //
   (A) It was established a decade ago. //
   (B) It recently expanded internationally. //
   (C) It will hire more than 100 new employees. //
   (D) It specializes in industrial robots. //

11. Where will the listeners go next? //
   (A) A reception area for guests //
   (B) A conference room for customers //
   (C) The training center in the gym //
   (D) The call center //

3-08

All right, everyone. //
That just about concludes our tour today /
of the corporate headquarters here at Robin Computer Company. //
We've seen the assembly plant / where we customize our personal computers /
before sending them out to the customer. //
And now I'd like to take a moment / to draw your attention /
to this room here on the right. //
What do you see there? //
Three people, sitting at their desks. //
It's very quiet, isn't it? //
This is our document processing and publication department. //
And the reason I wanted to show it to you / is that it's a model of efficiency. //
When our firm was established 10 years ago, /
this was a department with 15 employees, / with an enormous budget, /
and taking up five times as much office space. //
Thanks to the cutting-edge technology, / it's now much more streamlined. //
Next, we're going to see our call-center operation. //
The trend there /
has been the opposite of that in the document processing center — /
at least in terms of size. //
Initially, we didn't even have a call center. //
Now it's our most crucial interface with the customer. //
This is where any of our customers can call us / for any reason, 24 hours a day. //
It has a large office-space of its own, / a training center and a total staff of 125. //

要注意フレーズ！

That just about concludes、Thanks to、has been the opposite of など、聞けば意味がわかっても発信する際には使えない表現を、音読でしっかりと身に付けよう。

Task 2

CDの音声を聞いて、ポーズの部分で**各チャンクの意味を頭に浮かべよう**（同時通訳の要領で声に出しても可）。ポーズの間にわからなければ、226〜229ページの訳をチェックしよう。

Task 3

CDの音声を聞いて、**スクリプトを見ないで**ポーズの部分でリピートしよう。

Task 4

仕上げに231〜234ページのスクリプトを見ながら、トラック03〜05の音声に**オーバーラップさせて読んでみよう**。プロソディーを意識しながらリズミカルに繰り返して、ナチュラルスピードでの音読に慣れよう。

Task 5

本日の学習を終えた後も、このトラックをスクリプトを見ずに聞いて理解できるか、繰り返し確認するようにしよう。

学習エネルギーをチャージする今日の **格言**

The great pleasure in life is doing what people say you cannot do.
Walter Bagehot
（1826〜1877：イギリスの実業家・エッセイスト・ジャーナリスト・経済誌『エコノミスト』の編集長）

人生における大きな喜びは、
できるわけがないと人々が言っていることをやってのけることだ。

Part 6 応用音読

16日目 / 20

今日は、Part 6で最も難関となるDiscourse Marker（p.151参照）の問題を中心に取り上げる。Practice、音読と学習を進めよう。

Practice

▶解答：p.242〜

英文を読み、空所に入る語句として最も適切なものを1つずつ選ぼう。文書は全部で3つ、設問は14問となっている。全問の解答時間は**7分**。

Questions 1-4 refer to the following letter.

Dear Ms. Wilson,

Thank you for your letter dated April 16 ------- about individual orders of

1. (A) inquiring
   (B) inquired
   (C) being inquired
   (D) had inquired Ⓐ Ⓑ Ⓒ Ⓓ ☐

GoodWall interior wall covering materials. We appreciate your interest in our line of patented wall covering materials. -------, we cannot respond directly

2. (A) Relatively
   (B) Likely
   (C) Unfortunately
   (D) Seemingly Ⓐ Ⓑ Ⓒ Ⓓ ☐

to your request for individual orders, as we operate ------- as a wholesaler.

3. (A) strictly
   (B) lonely
   (C) exceedingly
   Ⓐ Ⓑ Ⓒ Ⓓ ☐ (D) fairly

Please allow us to direct you to the nearest approved GoodWall distributor in your area.
------- with this letter, please find brochures for our distributors Custom Interior

4. (A) Expected
   (B) Disclosed
   (C) Composed
   (D) Enclosed Ⓐ Ⓑ Ⓒ Ⓓ ☐

236

Accessories, Home Life Design Associates, and Architectural Ideas and More. All three of these local companies are approved GoodWall distributors, and will be able to advise you on the product type and color schemes to best complement your interior.

Sincerely,
Harry Masterson
Regional Manager
GoodWall Interior Wall Materials, Inc.

Questions 5-9 refer to the following article.

New York, September 25 — Software industry giant JayCo Computing Systems Corp. announced today that it plans to buy Keltingware Inc. for $1.2 billion. Keltingware began as a joint venture three years ago, partly ------- by JayCo

          5. (A) funded
              (B) promoted
              (C) processed
    Ⓐ Ⓑ Ⓒ Ⓓ ☐   (D) authorized

Computing, and provides software that helps Web site operators and advertisers ------- the effectiveness of their online advertisements and other

    6. (A) measure
        (B) withhold
        (C) moderate
        (D) fluctuate   Ⓐ Ⓑ Ⓒ Ⓓ ☐

announcements. JayCo Computing, ------- already owns 5 percent of

          7. (A) with which
              (B) which
              (C) what
              (D) that   Ⓐ Ⓑ Ⓒ Ⓓ ☐

Keltingware stock, ------- all remaining shares at a price 21 percent higher than

    8. (A) has purchased
        (B) purchased
        (C) will purchase
        (D) purchasing   Ⓐ Ⓑ Ⓒ Ⓓ ☐

the closing price on the Central Stock Exchange on October 1. On the same day, Keltingware's name will officially be changed to JayCo Keltingware Systems, Inc. Analysts say the purchase will help JayCo Computing round out ------- existing lineup of software products for corporate clients.

  9. (A) your
      (B) his
      (C) our
      (D) its   Ⓐ Ⓑ Ⓒ Ⓓ ☐

16
日目

Questions 10-14 refer to the following e-mail.

To: Renee Johnson <rjohnson@cxx.mlivmail.edu>
From: Thomas Rollins <trollins@acrosserv.com>
Sent: June 1
Subject: Invoice CORRECTION

A shipment of office supplies that you ordered from us ------- from our

    10. (A) was shipped
        (B) will be shipped
        (C) was supposed to be shipped
        (D) had been shipped

distribution center on May 31. It is scheduled to arrive at ------- office address

    11. (A) our
        (B) their
        (C) your
        (D) his

by Friday morning, as you requested.
Please note, -------, that we have discovered an error in our records indicating

    12. (A) although
        (B) however
        (C) despite
        (D) whereas

an inconsistency in the packing slip and invoice included with your shipment. Both were prepared for shipment on Tuesday morning, when the printer ink cartridges you ordered were not yet available. We had been planning to send these to you separately as soon as we received them. But they arrived before your package was shipped. One of our clerks added them to the shipment, revising the packing slip but NOT the invoice. -------, the invoice you will

    13. (A) Nevertheless
        (B) Therefore
        (C) Above all
        (D) In addition

receive is incorrect. Please ------- it and refer to the invoice we have just sent

    14. (A) summarize
        (B) preserve
        (C) reimburse
        (D) discard

to you by fax moments ago.
We apologize for the inconvenience.

T. Rollins
Customer Service

Practiceの正解と解説

英文の訳はチャンクで区切られているので、後で音読する際に参照しよう。

問題1-4は次の手紙に関するものです。
Wilson様 //
4月16日付のお手紙をありがとうございます / GoodWall内壁仕上げ材の個人注文についてお問い合わせいただきました。// 当社の特許取得済み壁仕上げ材に興味をお持ちくださいましたことに感謝申し上げます。// 残念ながら、個人注文のご要望に直接お応えすることはできません / 当社は、完全に卸売商として営業しているためです。// お住まいの地域にある、最寄りのGoodWall公認販売店をご紹介させてください。//
この手紙に同封します / 当社製品の販売店Custom Interior Accessoriesのパンフレットをご参照ください / Home Life Design Associates、Architectural Ideas and Moreのものも。// これら3つの現地企業は、どれもGoodWallの公認販売店ですので、/ 製品タイプや色について助言をしてくれるはずです / お客様のインテリアにぴったり合うように。// 敬具 /
Harry Masterson // 地域担当マネジャー // GoodWall Interior Wall Materials社 //

1. 訳は割愛

解説 空所の前のyour letterと、後のabout individual orders ...から、letter which inquires about ～(～を問い合わせる手紙)という**能動的な**つながりだとわかる。これを表すのは**現在分詞**inquiring。**解答** **(A)**

2. (A)【副詞】比較的
(B)【副詞】おそらく
(C)【副詞】残念ながら
(D)【副詞】見かけ上は

解説 前文のappreciate your interestと、空所を含む文のwe cannot respond directlyの**論理の流れに適している**のはUnfortunatelyだ。キーワード(下線部)と選択肢の＋(肯定的意味)、－(否定的意味)に注目すると判断しやすい。**解答** **(C)**

3. (A)【副詞】完全に
(B)【形容詞】孤独な
(C)【副詞】非常に
(D)【副詞】かなり

解説 空所の前後のcannot respond、individual ordersとoperate、as a wholesalerに注目して、論理の流れをチェックする。be strictly forbidden/prohibited/regulatedもよく使われる表現。**解答** **(A)**

4. (A)【他動詞】～だろうと予期する
(B)【他動詞】～を暴く
(C)【他動詞】～を構成する
(D)【他動詞】～を同封する

解説 空所の後のwith this letter, please find brochuresから、パンフレット類が同封されていると考えるのが自然。**解答** **(D)**

問題5-9は次の記事に関するものです。

ニューヨーク、9月25日 / ──ソフトウエア業界最大手JayCo Computing Systems社は / 同社がKeltingware社を買収する予定だと本日発表した / 12億ドルで。// Keltingwareは3年前にジョイント・ベンチャーとして創業したが、/ 資金の一部はJayCo Computingが拠出して、ソフトウエアを供給している / (このソフトは)ウェブサイトの運営者や広告主が、効果を測定するのを助ける / オンライン広告や告知の。// JayCo Computingは、すでにKeltingware社の株の5パーセントを保有しているが、/ 残りの株式を21パーセント増しの価格で購入する予定である / 10月1日の中央証券取引所の終値よりも。// 同日、Keltingwareの名称は正式にJayCo Keltingware Systems社に変更される。// アナリストによると今回の買収は、JayCo Computingが既存のラインアップを強化する助けになるだろうとのことだ / 法人顧客向けソフトウエア製品の。//

---

5. (A) 【他動詞】〜に資金を供給する
(B) 【他動詞】〜を促進する
(C) 【他動詞】〜を加工する
(D) 【他動詞】〜に権限を与える

解説 as a joint venture three years ago, partly ------- by JayCo Computing、と、ジョイント・ベンチャーであることが記されているので答えは明らか。**解答** (A)

---

6. (A) 【他動詞】〜を測定する
(B) 【他動詞】〜を控える
(C) 【他動詞】〜を和らげる
(D) 【他動詞】〜を変動させる

解説 helps Web site operators and advertisers ------- the effectivenessという文脈をつかみ、effectiveness と相性のいい動詞を選ぶ。measure the effectivenessはフレーズごと覚えよう。**解答** (A)

---

7. 訳は割愛。

解説 関係代名詞を問う設問。① 何の名詞を指しているか、② どんな働きか(主格／所有格／目的格)、③ 前置詞の有無をチェックする。Jayco Computingは会社で、主語の働きをしているのでwhichが正解。**解答** (B)

---

8. 訳は割愛。

解説 時制を問う設問。文中の日付や時間を示す表現に注意する。記事は9月25日付けで、購入が行われる10月1日は未来。冒頭のSoftware industry giant ... plans to buy Keltingware Inc.からも、購入が計画段階だとわかる。**解答** (C)

---

9. (A) あなた(たち)の
(B) 彼の
(C) 私たちの
(D) その

解説 文脈から「JayCoのlineupをround outする」という意味だとわかる。会社であるJayCoの代名詞はitなので、その所有格が正解。**解答** (D)

問題10-14は次のメールに関するものです。
あて先：Renee Johnson <rjohnson@cxx.mlivmail.edu> //
送信者：Thomas Rollins<trollins@acrosserv.com> //
日付：6月1日 //
件名：請求明細書の訂正 //

お客様が弊社に注文された事務用品のお荷物は、/ 弊社の流通センターから5月31日に出荷されました。// お客様のオフィスの住所に到着するのは、ご依頼どおり金曜朝の予定です。//
ただ、こちらの記録に誤りを発見いたしましたのでご注意ください / お客様のお荷物に同梱されている荷造伝票と請求明細書の内容が一致していないのです。// 両方とも火曜朝の出荷に合わせて用意されましたが、/ そのときにはまだ、ご注文いただいたプリンターインクカートリッジが入荷していませんでした。// それらは入荷次第、別便でお送りする予定でした。// しかし、お客様のお荷物が出荷される前に到着しました。// 弊社の事務員の1人がそれらをお荷物に加え、/ 荷造伝票を訂正したのですが、請求明細書については失念しました。// そのため、お客様がお受け取りになる請求明細書は間違っています。// どうぞ廃棄し、/ つい先ほどファクスでお送りした請求明細書をご参照ください。//
ご迷惑をおかけして申し訳ございません。//
T. Rollins //
お客様相談窓口 //

---

10. 訳は割愛。

解説 時制を問う設問。メールの送信日は6月1日なので、5月31日は過去になる。さらに次の文を読むと、It is scheduled to arrive とあるので、実際に出荷されたことがわかる。 **解答** (A)

---

11. (A) 私たちの
(B) 彼（それ）らの
(C) あなた（たち）の
(D) 彼の

解説 空所を含む文の文末にあるas you requestedから、顧客が希望した場所に到着するとわかる。顧客を示すyouの所有格が正解になる。 **解答** (C)

---

12. (A)【接続詞】〜であるけれども
(B)【副詞】けれども
(C)【前置詞】〜にもかかわらず
(D)【接続詞】〜であるのに対して

解説 空所を含む文とその前文との論理展開をチェックする。It is scheduled to arriveとwe have discovered an errorは逆接の展開。語法から、挿入できるのは文頭でなくても使用できるhoweverだけだ。despite（前置詞）の後は名詞（句）、although（接続詞）の後は主語＋動詞の形でなくてはならない。 **解答** (B)

13. (A)【副詞】それにもかかわらず
    (B)【副詞】それゆえに
    (C) 何よりも
    (D) それに加えて

    解説 空所を含む文とその前文の論理関係をチェックする。キーワードを見つけて判断しよう。NOT the invoiceは否定の意味（－）で、incorrectも否定的な意味（－）。よって、意味的にThereforeが適している。ここでは原因→結果の流れになっていて、追加の論理展開ではないのでIn additionは不適当。 **解答** (B)

14. (A)【他動詞】〜を要約する
    (B)【他動詞】〜を保存する
    (C)【他動詞】〜を返済する
    (D)【他動詞】〜を捨てる

    解説 前文の文末のincorrectと、空所を含む文の ------- it and refer to the invoice we have just sentの論理展開を考えると、discard が適している。選択肢の単語はどれもTOEICに頻出なので、意味を確認しておこう。 **解答** (D)

いよいよ音読を開始しよう！

Task 1

それでは音読に挑戦する。まず、**1)** 英文をすべての区切り (/ と / と //) で区切って音読しよう (**短いチャンク**)。意味をつかみながら読めるようになったら、今度は**長いチャンク**に挑戦。**2)** トラック09〜11の音声のポーズの部分でリピートしよう。**3)** プロソディーを意識しながら、スピーディーかつリズミカルにリピートできるようになったら、**仕上げにもう一度**、長いチャンクで音読しよう。

3-09

Dear Ms. Wilson, //
Thank you for <u>your letter dated April 16</u> /
<u>inquiring about</u> individual orders / of GoodWall interior wall covering materials. //
We appreciate your interest / in our line of patented wall covering materials. //
Unfortunately, / we cannot respond directly to your request for individual orders, /
as we <u>operate strictly as a wholesaler</u>. //
Please allow us to direct you /
to the nearest approved GoodWall distributor in your area. //
<u>Enclosed with</u> this letter, /
please find brochures for our distributors / Custom Interior Accessories, /
Home Life Design Associates, / and Architectural Ideas and More. //
All three of these local companies / are approved GoodWall distributors, /
and will be able to advise you on the product type / and color schemes /
to best complement your interior. //
Sincerely, /
Harry Masterson //
Regional Manager //
GoodWall Interior Wall Materials, Inc. //

要注意フレーズ！

問い合わせに答える手紙文の典型なので、下線の部分以外にも We appreciate your interest in our line、Please allow us to direct you などが口からスラスラ出るようにしよう。

New York, September 25 /
— Software industry giant JayCo Computing Systems Corp. /
announced today that it plans to buy Keltingware Inc. / for $1.2 billion. //
Keltingware began as a joint venture three years ago, /
partly funded by JayCo Computing, / and provides software /
that helps Web site operators and advertisers / measure the effectiveness /
of their online advertisements and other announcements. //
JayCo Computing, which already owns 5 percent of Keltingware stock, /
will purchase all remaining shares / at a price 21 percent higher /
than the closing price on the Central Stock Exchange on October 1. //
On the same day, /
Keltingware's name will officially be changed to JayCo Keltingware Systems, Inc. //
Analysts say / the purchase will help JayCo Computing round out its existing lineup /
of software products / for corporate clients. //

要注意フレーズ

企業買収に関するトピックは、Part 4や7にも頻出する。下線部の表現に注意しながら、記事を丸ごと覚えるつもりで音読しよう。

To: Renee Johnson <rjohnson@cxx.mlivmail.edu> //
From: Thomas Rollins <trollins@acrosserv.com> //
Sent: June 1 //
Subject: Invoice CORRECTION //
A shipment of office supplies that you ordered from us /
was shipped from our distribution center on May 31. //
It is scheduled to arrive at your office address by Friday morning, /
as you requested. //
Please note, however, / that we have discovered an error in our records /
indicating an inconsistency in the packing slip and invoice /
included with your shipment. //
Both were prepared for shipment on Tuesday morning, /
when the printer ink cartridges you ordered were not yet available. //
We had been planning to send these to you separately /
as soon as we received them. //
But they arrived before your package was shipped. //
One of our clerks added them to the shipment, /
revising the packing slip / but NOT the invoice. //
Therefore, the invoice you will receive is incorrect. //
Please discard it /
and refer to the invoice / we have just sent to you by fax / moments ago. //
We apologize for the inconvenience. //
T. Rollins // Customer Service //

要注意フレーズ！

ビジネス文書では用件を簡潔に伝えるため、無生物主語や名詞の後置修飾などが多用される。下線部を中心に、独特の言い回しを習得しよう。

Task 2

CDの音声を聞いて、ポーズの部分で**各チャンクの意味を頭に浮かべよう**(同時通訳の要領で声に出しても可)。ポーズの間にわからなければ、242~244ページの訳をチェックしよう。

Task 3

CDの音声を聞いて、**スクリプトを見ないで**ポーズの部分でリピートしよう。

Task 4

仕上げに246~248ページのスクリプトを見ながら、トラック12~14の音声に**オーバーラップさせて英文を読んでみよう**。プロソディーを意識して、リズミカルに繰り返し、ナチュラルスピードでの音読に慣れよう。

Task 5

本日の学習を終えた後も、これらのトラックをスクリプトを見ずに聞いて理解できるか、繰り返し確認するようにしよう。

学習エネルギーをチャージする今日の **格言**

Leave nothing for tomorrow which can be done today.
Abraham Lincoln
(1809-1865:第16代アメリカ合衆国大統領)
今日できることを明日に残すな。

900点突破者たちの体験談(4)
テスト対策・時間管理・やる気維持の3本柱で

(A.K.さん 会社員 女性)

855点→920点

　先日受けたTOEICのスコアは、920点(L490、R430)でした。自分では、「800点超えるかな?」くらいの気持ちだったので、かなり驚きました。

　リスニングに関しては、Part 3、4は先に3問ずつ設問を読んで、聞かれる要点を事前に把握し、会話やトークを聞きながらわかり次第解答していきました。おかげで、解答の際のリズムはうまく維持できたと思います。

　リーディングは時間との勝負で、タイムマネジメントが重要です。文法問題に弱い私は、「Part 7を全問解くことがスコアアップのカギ」という言葉を思い出し、時間が足りなくなるのが嫌だったので、Part 7から解き始めました。制限時間ギリギリでしたが、何とか全問解くことができました。

　ほかに自分が行って役立ったこととしては、机に向かって真面目に勉強するのが苦手なので、英語の歌をカラオケで歌えるよう何度も練習したことが挙げられます。これだとまったく飽きずに、上手に歌えるようになるまで頑張るので、耳と口が鍛えられ、プラクティカルな音読練習にもつながりました。

　語彙力を強化するという点では、ニュージーランドに滞在していた時、よくゴシップ雑誌を購入しました。いわゆる芸能情報やダイエット記事など、興味のある分野だと知りたいという気持ちが働き、辞書を片手に読む気になります。興味のある分野の教材を使って英語学習を継続するのはmotivation維持に有効だと思います。carbohydrate(炭水化物)という語は、雑誌で覚えました。

　また、英語勉強法のような本を読むのが好きで、何冊か読みました。これもmotivationアップに効果的でした。

　自分ではそれ程勉強したとは思っていないのですが、『新TOEICテスト直前の技術』(アルク)をテキストに、各Partを効果的に解くテクニックを学んだことと、チャンクで聞き、読み、理解し、音読したことは大変役立ったと思っています。

　実は、点数だけが上がってしまって、それほど英語力は伸びていない気がしているので、本当に使える英語を習得するための日々の積み重ねが必要だと感じています。英語学習の指標として、成果がわかりやすく、やる気を高めてくれる、こういう試験を有効活用するのは良い方法だと思います。今後はコミュニケーション力を強化するため、スピーキング力をアップさせることが私のテーマになりそうです。

17日目 / 20 チャレンジLittening!

今日は、11日目とは逆に、普段読んで解答しているPart 7、6をリスニングしながら解くというトレーニングを行う。音声についていけば「後戻りせずに英語の語順で読む」訓練ができるので、積極的に挑戦しよう。

Task 1

CD 3-15〜18　▶解答：p.258〜

このTaskでは、Part 7のシングルパッセージを2つ、ダブルパッセージを1つ取り上げる。冒頭に「設問チェック時間」として**8秒のポーズ**があり、その後すぐに文書の音声が流れる。文字を目で追いながら聞き、解答しよう。その際のポイントは以下のとおり。
① 文書全体の中の重要情報が、通常は最初と最後に来ることを意識し
② 各パラグラフの1、2文目を重視
③ パラグラフの冒頭の接続語や、文頭の接続語に注意して論理展開を把握し
④ 各文のメインの主語と述語に意識を向ける
⑤ 繰り返し登場する語、肯定的な語、否定的な語に注意して
⑥ 語順に従って追加されていく情報をチャンク単位で次々とキャッチし
⑦ 設問の答えのヒントを示すキーワードを見つける

文書の音声の後、**8秒**たつとGO ON TO THE NEXT PAGEの指示が流れる。その後に、**先読み用のポーズが8秒**設けられているので、次の設問の先読みを行おう。

1. When was the e-mail most likely written?
   (A) Wednesday
   (B) Thursday
   (C) Friday
   (D) Saturday　　　Ⓐ Ⓑ Ⓒ Ⓓ ☐

2. According to the e-mail, why didn't meeting participants listen to Craig's presentation attentively?
   (A) They thought Craig's proposal had been practiced before.
   (B) Craig was not prepared well enough to give an effective presentation.
   (C) They were anxious about the CEO's latest decision.
   (D) Craig was not successful when he was working at an overseas branch.
   　　　Ⓐ Ⓑ Ⓒ Ⓓ ☐

3. Why has Craig been asked to contact Linda or Brian?
   (A) Brian assigned Linda and Craig to the Budget Task Force.
   (B) He understands the need to cut advertising costs.
   (C) Linda and Brian share some ideas with him.
   (D) The company is eager to expand overseas operations.   Ⓐ Ⓑ Ⓒ Ⓓ ☐

Questions 1-3 refer to the following e-mail.

From: Linda Gatling <lindag21@integate.com>
To: Craig Lipmann <clipmann@integate.com>
Subject: Your Presentation

Hello Craig,

I was among the mid-level managers at the presentation you made to our latest Tuesday afternoon Budget Task Force. As sometimes happens, they scheduled your presentation for the final 10 minutes of the meeting, and only really gave you two or three minutes of their undivided attention. Brian Eddys and I could tell that you didn't have time to fully present your ideas. Also, I think some of the Task Force members were right in noting that your idea on cutting advertising costs has already been tried in the past. When you led off your presentation with that idea, I think everyone simply stopped listening. So they didn't hear your truly intriguing idea about creating a new managerial talent pool from among local employees at some of our international affiliates and subsidiaries. Have you done some research in this area? You sure sounded confident about it at the Task Force meeting the day before yesterday. Brian and I have been thinking along the same lines ourselves, and we're eager to explore new ideas for future projects and proposals. Please contact either of us at your earliest convenience if you'd like to talk it over and pursue what we think is an area of enormous untapped potential of our firm.

Linda

GO ON TO THE NEXT PAGE

4. What is indicated about the Rock River County Farmers' Cooperative Association?
   (A) It was recently officially incorporated.
   (B) It is partially funded by the federal government.
   (C) It has been making investments in environment-friendly businesses.
   (D) It has been running two farmers' markets.   Ⓐ Ⓑ Ⓒ Ⓓ ☐

5. According to the article, why has the new North Rock River Farmers' Market been planned?
   (A) To carry out the business contract
   (B) To respond to the growing market
   (C) To accelerate the success of the advertising campaign
   (D) To participate in the county's regeneration plan   Ⓐ Ⓑ Ⓒ Ⓓ ☐

6. Who most likely is Patti Langston?
   (A) The founder of North City Mall
   (B) The head of the farmers' cooperative association
   (C) The chairperson of Tea Tree Stadium
   (D) The commissioner of the county   Ⓐ Ⓑ Ⓒ Ⓓ ☐

Questions 4-6 refer to the following business news article.

LOCAL SMALL-SCALE FARMERS OPEN NEW MARKET

Due to the overwhelming popularity of farmers' markets in recent years, the Rock River County Farmers' Cooperative Association plans to hold a new Agriculture & Produce Fair next month to kick off its new North Rock River Farmers' Market. The association already has two farmers' markets, one at Tea Tree Stadium in the downtown area and the other on Old South Road near the Highway 16 turnoff. But thanks to increased demand from the growing suburbs north of the city, the new location will open on October 15 in the parking lot of North City Mall. Like the other markets, it will open on the second and fourth weekends (Saturday and Sunday) of each month, excluding January and February. With just one month to go before the grand opening, the new farmer's market has already confirmed that 98 stalls will be open, with items ranging from wild honey to fresh vegetables to processed food. That will make it the largest farmer's market in the county. "We're really looking forward to providing another outlet for the fantastic produce the farmers of our county provide directly to our local shoppers," said association chair Patti Langston.

7. Where most likely is Ms. Schultz posted currently?
   (A) Shanghai
   (B) New York
   (C) Hong Kong
   (D) Los Angeles   Ⓐ Ⓑ Ⓒ Ⓓ ☐

8. What problem do they mainly discuss?
   (A) A defect of the newly installed machine
   (B) An uncooperative tech staff
   (C) A poor telecommunications link
   (D) Lack of participation by the London office   Ⓐ Ⓑ Ⓒ Ⓓ ☐

9. What does Mr. Mack say about the last conference?
   (A) Ms. Schultz didn't miss out on significant information.
   (B) He needs to know whether any decisions were made.
   (C) It was supposed to start punctually.
   (D) He was originally unavailable to address the meeting.   Ⓐ Ⓑ Ⓒ Ⓓ ☐

10. What is true about Ms. Schultz and Mr. Mack?
    (A) They work for the same company.
    (B) Ms. Schultz has supplied Mr. Mack's company with merchandise.
    (C) Their firms merged into one larger firm.
    (D) They have entered the staple market in America.   Ⓐ Ⓑ Ⓒ Ⓓ ☐

11. Who has Ms. Schultz talked to for the preparation of the meeting planned for July 16?
    (A) A staff member dealing with electronics issues
    (B) A marketing consultant sent to her office from Los Angeles
    (C) A local real estate agent
    (D) The stockbroker who works for Mr. Mack   Ⓐ Ⓑ Ⓒ Ⓓ ☐

Questions 7-11 refer to the following e-mails.

From: David Mack <davidmack@gastonworldwide.com>
To: Renee Schultz <rschultz@gastonworldwide.com>
Subject: Teleconference Scheduling

Dear Ms. Schultz,

We all appreciate your participation in the May 3 (May 4 for you) teleconference with our offices in Los Angeles and here in New York. As we all have recognized, we have to coordinate our company's global operations so that the advertising campaign for the new model targeting the Asian market, which you are in charge of, may give rise to the maximum results. Let us quickly work out an effective program.

On a related subject, I noticed that about mid-way through the virtual meeting, we began having trouble with your audio connection. And I think our link with you was entirely lost during the final 10 minutes. Yet, you didn't miss any major decisions or substantive content, except for the fact that our next teleconference will be scheduled for July 15, more or less the same time. We'll be in touch about the details.

David Mack

From: Renee Schultz <rschultz@gastonworldwide.com>
To: David Mack <davidmack@gastonworldwide.com>
Subject: Re: Teleconference Scheduling

David,

Thank for your comments on my talk. It seems we share the same ideas about how to make our firm successful.

As for the transmission, when you say the next teleconference is set for July 15, I take it to indicate your time zone in New York. So unless otherwise advised, I'll set aside time on the morning of July 16, my time, at the same hour we used this time. And I'll expect more detailed instructions from your meetings facilitator at least three days before the conference begins. That will help me arrange to be available, and to ensure that we have a good telecommunications link. My tech staff is currently looking into what happened the last time, and we have found no malfunction in the new equipment. Therefore, I'm promised that I'll have a reliable connection next time. By the way, I'll be away for a couple of days on a business trip to Shanghai, so as soon as I return, let me give you feedback on the agenda for the forthcoming conference.

R. Schultz

Task 1 の正解と解説

問題1-3は次のメールに関するものです。

送信者: Linda Gatling <lindag21@integate.com> //
あて先: Craig Lipmann <clipmann@integate.com> // 件名: あなたのプレゼンテーション //
こんにちは、Craig //
私はあなたがプレゼンテーションをしたとき、中級管理職の中にいました / 直近の火曜午後の予算特別委員会に対するプレゼンです。// 時々あることですが / あなたのプレゼンテーションは会議の最後の10分間に予定され / 気を散らさず注目された時間は、実際には2、3分しか与えられませんでした。// Brian Eddysと私には、あなたが自分のアイデアを全部説明する時間がなかったとわかりました。// また、広告費を削るというあなたのアイデアに対する一部の特別委員の指摘は正しかったとも思います / それは過去にすでに試されたという(指摘は)。// あなたがそのアイデアでプレゼンの口火を切ったとき / 皆はあっさり聞くのをやめてしまったのだと思います。// ですから、彼らはあなたの本当に興味深いアイデアを聞いていませんでした / 新しい管理職人材プールの創設に関する(アイデアを) / 一部の国外支社や子会社の現地従業員の中からの。// この分野で何かリサーチはしているのでしょうか。// あなたは確かに自信のある様子でした / 一昨日の特別委員会では。// Brianと私も同じ方針を独自に考えていました / そして、将来の企画や提案のために、新しいアイデアを研究したいと思っています。// あなたの都合がつき次第、私たちのどちらかに連絡をください / もし話し合って追究をしたければ / わが社で手付かずになっている大きな可能性を秘めた分野と思われるものを。// Linda //

---

1. このメールはいつ書かれた可能性が最も高いか。
   - (A) 水曜日
   - (B) 木曜日
   - (C) 金曜日
   - (D) 土曜日

解説 設問のキーワードはWhen、e-mail、written。「時」を問う個別情報タイプ。I was among the mid-level managers at the presentation you made to our latest Tuesday afternoon Budget Task Force、the Task Force meeting the day before yesterday の2カ所の情報を統合すると解答がわかる。 **解答** (B)

---

2. メールによると、会議の参加者がCraigのプレゼンを注意深く聞かなかったのはなぜか。
   - (A) 彼らはCraigの提案を、以前実行されたものだと思った。
   - (B) Craigは効果的なプレゼンをするための十分な準備をしなかった。
   - (C) 彼らはCEOの最新の決定を気にしていた。
   - (D) Craigは海外支店での勤務中、成功しなかった。

解説 キーワードはwhy、didn't、meeting participants、listen to、Craig's presentation attentively。「理由」を問う個別情報タイプ。設問の中で「注意深く聞かなかった」という事実が述べられているので、それに相当する表現を探す。your idea on cutting advertising costs has already been tried ... の後に、When you led off your presentation with that idea, I think everyone simply stopped listening. と述べている。理由が先に登場するので、内容を把握しながら聞かないと解けない。 **解答** (A)

3. CraigがLindaかBrianに連絡を取るよう頼まれたのはなぜか。
(A) Brianが、LindaとCraigを予算特別委員に任命した。
(B) 彼は広告費を削減する必要性を理解している。
(C) LindaとBrianは彼と同じ考えを持っている。
(D) 会社が海外事業の拡大に意欲的である。

解説 キーワードはWhy、Craig、asked、contact Linda or Brian。「理由」を問う個別情報タイプ。Brian and I have been thinking along the same lines ourselvesの個所がヒントになる。ここでも、このヒントの後にPlease contact either of usと連絡に関する表現が出てくるので、文脈の把握が必要。**解答** (C)

問題4-6は次のビジネスニュースの記事に関するものです。

地元小規模農家が新たなマーケットをオープン
近年の農産物直売マーケットの圧倒的な人気から / Rock River郡農業協同組合は来月、新たに農産物フェアを開催する予定だ / 新規にNorth Rock River農産物直売マーケットを立ち上げるために。// 組合はすでに2つの農産物直売マーケットを持っている / 1つはダウンタウン地区のTea Treeスタジアムに / そしてもう1つはOld South Road沿い、16号線出入り口近くだ。// しかし、成長著しい市の北部郊外からの需要増のおかげで / 新マーケットはNorth Cityショッピングセンターの駐車場に、10月15日にオープンする予定だ。// ほかのマーケット同様 / ここは毎月第2・第4の週末(土日)に営業することになる / 1月と2月を除いて。// 新規開業までわずか1カ月だが / 新しい直売所はすでに98の売店がオープンすることを確認している / 天然はちみつから新鮮野菜、加工食品まで幅広い品物をそろえて。// そのため、郡内最大の農産物直売マーケットとなる。//「私たちは直売店をもう1つ開くのをとても楽しみにしています / そこではわが郡の農家が地元の購買者に直接、素晴らしい農産物を提供できますから」/ と、組合会長のPatti Langstonは語った。//

4. Rock River郡農業協同組合に関して何が示されているか。
(A) 最近、正式に法人化された。
(B) 連邦政府が資金の一部を出している。
(C) 環境に優しい事業に投資してきた。
(D) 2カ所の農産物直売マーケットを運営してきた。

解説 設問のキーワードはWhat、indicated、Rock River County Farmers' Cooperative Association。漠然とした設問なので、ほかの設問の後に解答するほうが、時間が節約できる。The association already has two farmers' markets, の個所がヒント。**解答** (D)

5. 記事によると、新しいNorth Rock River農産物直売マーケットが計画されたのはなぜか。
(A) 事業契約を遂行するため
(B) 成長する市場に対応するため
(C) 広告キャンペーンの成功を促進するため
(D) 郡の再生計画に参加するため

解説 キーワードはwhy、new North Rock River Farmers' Market、planned。「理由」を問う個別情報タイプ。タイトルから新マーケットのオープンが記事の主題だとわかるので、理由を示す表現を探す。thanks to increased demand from the growing suburbsがヒント。
解答 (B)

6. Patti Langstonは誰だと思われるか。
  (A) North Cityショッピングセンターの創設者
  (B) 農業協同組合の責任者
  (C) Tea Treeスタジアムの会長
  (D) 郡政委員

解説 キーワードはWho、Patti Langston。「職業」を問う個別情報タイプ。記事の末尾でコメントの後に said association chair Patti Langston と発言者を紹介している。 **解答** (B)

問題7-11は次のメールに関するものです。

文書1 🍁

送信者：David Mack <davidmack@gastonworldwide.com> //
あて先：Renee Schultz <rschultz@gastonworldwide.com> //
件名：テレビ会議日程 //
Schultz様 //
5月3日（そちらの時間では5月4日）のテレビ会議に参加いただきましたことを、私たち一同、感謝しております / ロサンゼルスとここニューヨークの各オフィスとの。// 全員が認識したとおり、私たちは世界中の事業所を連係させる必要があります / アジア市場をターゲットとした新モデルの広告キャンペーンが / これはあなたのご担当ですが / 最大の結果を生むために。// 早急に効果的な計画を立てましょう。//
それに関連して / 私はバーチャル会議の中ほどで気づきました / そちらとの音声通信が不調になり始めたことに。// そして最後の10分間、あなたとの通信は完全に途絶えていたと思います。// それでもあなたは主要な決定事項や実質的な内容はどれも聞き逃していません / 次回のテレビ会議が7月15日に行われるということ以外は / おおよそ同時刻に。// 詳細は後ほどご連絡します。// David Mack //

文書2 🇺🇸

差出人：Renee Schultz <rschultz@gastonworldwide.com>
あて先：David Mack <davidmack@gastonworldwide.com>
件名：Re: テレビ会議日程 //
David様 //
私の話へのコメントをありがとうございました。// わが社を成功させる方策について、どうやら同じ意見を共有しているようですね。//
通信についてですが / 次のテレビ会議が7月15日に設定されているとおっしゃる場合 / そちらのニューヨークの時間帯を指すものと受け取ります。// ですから、そうではないと言われない限り / こちらの時間の7月16日の午前を空けておきます / 今回使ったのと同じ時間で。// それと、そちらの会議準備役からもっと詳しい指示をいただけるものと期待します / 会議開始の3日以上前に。// そうすれば準備をする手助けとなるでしょう / また、良好なテレビ通信回線を確保するためにも。// 今、こちらの技術スタッフが、前回何があったのかを調べています / そして新しい機材には不調がないことを確認しました。したがって、次回はしっかりと接続されるとお約束します。ところで、私は上海出張で2、3日不在になります。戻り次第、来たるべき会議の議題のフィードバックをさせてください。// R. Schultz //

7. Schultzさんは現在どこに配属されていると思われるか。
(A) 上海
(B) ニューヨーク
(C) 香港
(D) ロサンゼルス

解説 キーワードはWhere、Ms. Schultz、posted、currently。「場所」を問う個別情報タイプ。文書1のWe all appreciate your participation in the May 3 (May 4 for you) teleconference、targeting the Asian market, which you are in charge ofの個所と、文書2の on a business trip to Shanghai から、Ms. Schultzが上海以外のアジアにいると推測できる。 **解答** (C)

---

8. 彼らはどんな問題を主に話し合っているか。
(A) 新しく設置された機械の不具合
(B) 非協力的な技術スタッフ
(C) 接続の悪い通信回線
(D) ロンドンオフィスの不参加

解説 キーワードはWhat problem、discuss。「話題」を問う全体情報タイプ。ほかの設問の後に解答したほうがいい。文書1でI think our link with you was entirely lost、文書2でensure that we have a good telecommunications link、I'm promised that I'll have a reliable connection next time.とふれていることから、A poor telecommunications linkが話題の1つだとわかる。文書2にwe have found no malfunction in the new equipmentとあるので、(A)は不正解。 **解答** (C)

---

9. Mack氏は前回の会議について何と言っているか。
(A) Schultzさんは重要な情報を聞き逃さなかった。
(B) 何らかの決定がなされたかどうか知る必要がある。
(C) 定刻に開始されるはずだった。
(D) その会議ではもともと演説はできなかった。

解説 キーワードはWhat、Mr. Mack、say、last conference。「発言内容」を問う個別情報タイプ。Mackは文書1の送信者なので、文書1を参照。Yet, you didn't miss any major decisions or substantive contentの個所を言い換えているのがMs. Schultz didn't miss out on significant information.だ。 **解答** (A)

---

10. SchultzさんとMack氏に関して、正しいのはどれか。
(A) 彼らは同じ会社で働いている。
(B) SchultzさんはMack氏の会社に商品を納入した。
(C) 彼らの会社は合併して大きな1つの会社になった。
(D) 彼らはアメリカの主要市場に参入した。

解説 キーワードはWhat、true、Ms. Schultz and Mr. Mack。選択肢には、彼らの関係や業務の内容が並んでいる。メールアドレスの@以下が同じことに気づけばその時点で解答可能。文書1の冒頭でも、As we all have recognized, we have to coordinate our company's global operationsと、社内の課題が示されている。 **解答** (A)

11. Schultzさんは7月16日に予定されている会議の準備のために誰と話したか。
(A) 電子機器関連を扱うスタッフ
(B) ロサンゼルスから彼女のオフィスに派遣されたマーケティングのコンサルタント
(C) 地元の不動産業者
(D) Mack氏のところで働く株式仲買人

> **解説** キーワードは Who、Ms. Schultz、talked to、preparation、meeting。「職業・役職」を問う個別情報タイプ。設問の主語のSchultzは文書2の送信者なので、文面をチェックする。後半で My tech staff is currently looking into what happened the last time, and we have found no malfunction ... と述べているので、技術スタッフと話したことがわかる。tech staffの言い換え表現として最も適切なのはA staff member dealing with electronics issues。 **解答** (A)

Task 2

今度は Part 6 を聞きながら解いてみる。各空所につき **5秒間のポーズ**を設けているので、その間に選択肢から正解を選ぼう。
解答のポイントは、p.252の①〜⑦に以下の項目が加わる。
⑧空所部分に来たら、選択肢にさっと目を通して正しいものを選び、すぐに続きに意識を集中させる。以後の空所も同様に解く。
文書の内容の流れを語順どおりにキャッチしていくことが大切だ。

Questions 1-3 refer to the following information.

Product Coverage

A product will only be restored to normal operating condition after it -------

1. (A) failed
   (B) was failed
   (C) has failed
   (D) has been failed

during normal single-family residence use, excluding malfunctions due to power surges. The plan covers all labor and parts costs necessary to repair your product for problems due to functional part failures. If you have more than one product ------- of the same type (e.g. two refrigerators, three central

2. (A) installed
   (B) enhanced
   (C) acclaimed
   (D) attributed

air/heating units), administrator will cover the first product for which you file a claim, ------- you have coverage on all products of the same product type.

3. (A) if
   (B) even
   (C) while
   (D) unless

Task 2の正解と解説

問題1-3は次の情報に関するものです。

製品の補償範囲 //
製品は故障した場合、正常な動作状態に復旧されます / 通常の一世帯住宅でのご利用中（に限り）/ 電圧の急増による誤作動を除く。// 本プランは製品の修理に要する人件費と部品代の全額を補償します / 機能部品の不具合から生じる問題に対して。// 同一の種類の製品を複数設置している場合 /（2台の冷蔵庫、3つのセントラル冷暖房ユニットなど）/ 弊社は最初にご請求された製品について補償いたします。// 同種の全製品を補償範囲になさっている場合は、この限りではありません。//

---

1. 訳は割愛

解説 タイトルのProduct Coverageから、製品の補償範囲を述べている文書だとわかる。A product will only be <u>restored</u> to <u>normal operating condition</u> after it ------- during <u>normal</u> single-family residence <u>use</u>, <u>excluding malfunctions</u> due to power surges.（下線部はキーワード）の空所の前は「製品が…した後に、正常な動作状態に復旧されます」、後は「通常の一世帯住宅での利用中に」と述べているので、「製品が故障した場合」の意味と判断する。ここでのfailは自動詞で、「＜機械などが＞機能が止まる、作動しなくなる」の意。また、excluding malfunctions due to power surges のmalfunctionsもヒントになる。「電圧の急増による誤作動を除き」とあるので、malfunctionsと同様の意味の語が入ると判断できるからだ。after以下が時・条件を表す副詞節になっているので、現在完了形を使う。 **解答** (C)

---

2. (A)【他動詞】設置する
(B)【他動詞】高める
(C)【他動詞】賞賛する
(D)【他動詞】起因すると考える

解説 キーワードに注目して空所を含む文をチェックすると、If you have <u>more than one product</u> ------- of the <u>same type</u> (e.g. <u>two</u> refrigerators, <u>three</u> central air/heating units), と述べており、「同一の種類の製品を2台以上…の場合（例：2台の冷蔵庫、3つのセントラル冷暖房ユニットなど）」という意味になるので、空所に入る語はinstall（設置する）が適している。 **解答** (A)

3. (A)【接続詞】もし
   (B)【副詞】〜さえ
   (C)【接続詞】〜する間に
   (D)【接続詞】〜しない限り

解説 キーワードに注意して空所の前後の論理関係をチェックする。administrator will <u>cover the first product</u> for which you file a claim, ------- you have coverage on <u>all products</u> of the same product typeで、空所の前（主節）では「最初に請求された製品について（のみ）補償」、後では「同種の全製品を補償範囲にしている」と述べている。文脈から、主節の内容が成り立たない唯一の条件を導く接続詞、unlessが正解となる。

解答 (D)

Task 3

Task 1、2の英文を、訳を参考にチャンクで区切り、意味を把握しながら音読しよう。

Task 4

3-15〜18、20

トラック15〜18と20の音声にオーバーラップさせて英文を読んでみよう。プロソディーを意識してリズミカルに繰り返し、ナチュラルスピードの音読に慣れよう。

Task 5

3-15〜18、20

本日の学習を終えた後も、これらトラックを英文を見ずに聞いて理解できるか、繰り返し確認するようにしよう。聞き取れなかった個所は、再度英文を見て内容をチェック！

学習エネルギーをチャージする今日の **格言**

I am not discouraged, because every wrong attempt discarded is another step forward.

Thomas A. Edison
(1847-1951：アメリカの発明家)

私は落胆してはいない。なぜなら、失敗に終わった試みはすべて、
次への新たな一歩になるからだ。

Review & Part 5

18日目 / 20

通常の学習は本日で最後。明日の模試に挑む前に、今週学習した内容をしっかり復習しよう。また、今日取り上げる Part 5 の文法問題は、パターンをつかめば確実に得点源にできる。自分の解き方が正しいか確認するつもりで取り組もう。

Review: Task 1

13〜17日目に学習した会話・トーク・文書を聞き、下線の部分をディクテーションしてみよう。細かいポイントよりも、強調されているキーワード（内容語）の聞き取りに注力すること。

13日目

CD 2-32 ▶解答はp.194参照

M: In fact, _____
_____. I think _____
_____ of the company. It looks _____
_____ was really a worthwhile idea.

W: _____. Can you make sure _____
_____?

14日目

CD 3-01 ▶解答はp.208参照

We can assure you _____
_____.

We would, however, like to remind you _____
_____.

In particular, _____, under any circumstances,
_____, phone number, social security number or credit card number _____
_____.

15日目

3-04 ▶解答はp.227参照

A major road construction project _____
_____ at Regent's Road, _____
_____.

So _____, we'd
recommend that you use Bay Avenue instead.

16日目

3-14 ▶解答はp.240参照

A shipment of office supplies _____
_____ on May 31.
_____
_____, as you requested.
Please note, however, _____
_____
included with your shipment.

17日目

3-16 ▶解答はp.255参照

But thanks to _____,
_____ of North City
Mall. Like the other markets, _____
(Saturday and Sunday) of each month, _____.

Task 2

では次に、以下のトラックを聞いてシャドーイングに挑戦する。スクリプトを見なくても意味をとらえられ、プロソディーを意識しながらリズミカルかつスピーディーに再生できるか、確認しよう。

❶ 2-31 ▶解答はp.193参照 ❷ 3-05 ▶解答はp.228参照

Part 5 解答のポイント

短文を読み、4つの選択肢の中から空所に入る最も適切な語句を選ぶ。全40問を1問平均20秒で解いて、パート全体を14分以内に解答しよう。選択肢に並ぶ語句から、全文を読まなくてもいい問題か、全文を読む問題かを判断し、後者は文頭からチャンクで意味をとらえながら速読する。判断に迷ったら、文頭から読もう。

●品詞＜全文を読まなくてもいい問題＞
語幹が同じで品詞が異なる語が選択肢に3つ以上並んでいたら品詞の問題。空所の前後だけ見れば解答できるので、5秒で正解したい。重要なのは次のようなパターン（下線部が問われる）。
①現在完了＋副詞：have unanimously decided
②不定詞＋副詞：The purpose of the discussion is to seriously consider the plan.
③副詞＋副詞：extremely carefully
④所有格の代名詞＋形容詞＋名詞：your generous offer、our final decision
⑤名詞＋形容詞（後置修飾）：the tools available
⑥名詞＋名詞：application form

●前置詞（句）VS接続詞VS副詞＜必要に応じて全文を読む問題＞
同じような意味の前置詞（句）と接続詞、または異なる意味の接続詞、副詞、前置詞（句）が選択肢に並んでいる。空所の後の形（構造）をチェックして品詞を絞り、絞りきれなければ意味（文脈）から判断する。
前置詞：Despite his efforts、接続詞：Although he made efforts
　　　　　　名詞（句）　　　　　　　　　　　主語 述語

●小さい接続詞（相関接続詞）＜全文を読まなくてもいい問題＞
both A and B、either A or B、neither A nor B、not only A but (also) B、whether A or B、so ... that、such ... thatなどの下線部のどちらかが並んでいる問題。文中から組になる語を探せばすぐに解答できる。

●大きい接続詞＜全文を読む問題＞
文や語句をつなぐ機能を持つ接続詞や副詞、前置詞（句）が並んでいる。空所の後の形（構造）をチェックして品詞を絞り込み、さらに意味（文脈）から判断する。

●代名詞＜格が同じ：全文を読む問題、格が異なる：全文を読まなくてもいい問題＞
選択肢にthey、their、themなど、指すものが同じで格が異なる代名詞が並ぶ場合、空所の前後を見れば解ける。his、her、theirのように格は同じで指すものが

異なる場合は全文を読むこと。

●関係詞＜全文を読む問題＞
空所に入る関係詞を問う問題では、関係詞で結ばれる前の２つの文を考えてみる。関係代名詞はどの名詞（人・物・物事）を指すか、どんな働き（主格・所有格・目的格）かをチェック。前置詞＋関係代名詞＝関係副詞（例：in/at/on/to + which = where）もチェックする。

●動詞の形＜必要に応じて全文を読む問題＞
同じ動詞の異なる活用が並んでいる。問われるポイントは①時制、②動詞の語法（不定詞か動名詞か）、③態（能動態か受動態か）、④分詞の修飾（現在分詞か過去分詞か）、⑤分詞構文の用法（文頭に来る、現在分詞か過去分詞か）、⑥主語と述語の一致（単数か複数か）、⑦使役動詞（make、have、let、get）の原形か過去分詞形かto不定詞かなど。
形（構造）と意味（文脈）から判断しよう。時制問題は文中で時に関わる語句を探し、それに対応する時制を選ぶ。

●比較＜全文を読まなくてもいい問題＞
原級、比較級や最上級が並んでいる。各級と一緒に使われるキーワードを探す。as＋原級＋asの形があれば原級の同等比較、thanがあれば比較級、the+比較級があればthe+比較級、of all、in the company、in the history of the firm、have ever experiencedなどの空間的、時間的に限定された枠組みを表すキーワードがあれば最上級。

●前置詞＜全文を読まなくてもいい問題＞
異なる前置詞が並んでいる。空所の前後を見て、慣用表現か否かを判断。
　例：at/of/for/inが並ぶ。be capable ------- ならofに確定
慣用表現でなければ、空所前後の文脈から適するものを選ぶ。
　例：for/toが並ぶ。be eligible ------- membershipならfor、be eligible ------- vote at the annual meetingならtoが正解。
知らなければ解けないので、かけていい時間は5秒程度。

●語彙＜必要に応じて全文を読む問題＞
同じ品詞の語が並んでいたら語彙の問題。まずは空所前後の語句をチェックし、コロケーションを問う問題か否かを判断する。絞り込めなければキーワードに注意しながら全文を読み、文脈から適する語を選ぶ。解答時間は最大30秒。

Part 5: Practice

▶解答：p.273〜

空所に入る語句として、最も適切なものを1つ選ぼう。全15問の解答制限時間は5分。

1. NB Inc. plans to develop 30,000 square meters of space, building 3,000 homes and apartment units which will be ------- priced.
   (A) moderate
   (B) moderated
   (C) moderately
   (D) moderation

2. Please write your phone number here so that we can contact ------- when the luggage is found.
   (A) yours
   (B) you
   (C) your
   (D) yourself

3. Current law gives police 14 days to question suspects before they are ------- charged or released.
   (A) both
   (B) unless
   (C) either
   (D) without

4. Annual upgrades are not required, but be sure to upgrade at least every three years to take ------- of improvements to the system.
   (A) merit
   (B) service
   (C) advantage
   (D) renovation

5. For the customers' peace of mind, shipping insurance will be added to all orders ------- no extra cost.
(A) at
(B) by
(C) from
(D) over

6. Enclosed is the latest listing of ------- companies within this sector of the hospitality industry.
(A) distinguish
(B) distinguished
(C) distinguishing
(D) distinguishable

7. As ------- in our telephone conversation, Ms. Rodriguez and the committee members will arrive at the headquarters at 3 o'clock.
(A) discuss
(B) discussed
(C) discussing
(D) discussion

8. The business consultant stressed that ensuring the feasibility of a project is most important for ------- setting one up.
(A) theirs
(B) it
(C) anyone
(D) yourself

9. BMA corporation is considering implementing new standards ------- they assess their employees' performance.
(A) which
(B) what
(C) by which
(D) whose

10. The scale model city features a gorgeous array of the homes, shops and canals, accurate in ------- detail.
(A) any
(B) other
(C) every
(D) either

GO ON TO THE NEXT PAGE

11. Checking the records revealed that no ------- than 40 percent of last month's invoices were still unpaid.
    (A) sooner
    (B) longer
    (C) rather
    (D) less

12. According to the latest e-mail from our boss, the report for the new project is ------- on November 30.
    (A) due
    (B) valid
    (C) authentic
    (D) conclusive

13. The new game, which is expected to ------- baseball fans, will be unveiled to the public next month.
    (A) value
    (B) observe
    (C) attract
    (D) capture

14. At the end of March, MiniSoft Inc. CEO Ms. Donaldson ------- this small, efficient company for five years.
    (A) ran
    (B) will have run
    (C) has been running
    (D) will have been run

15. The revolutionary software is used ------- by the registered members of the popular Social Networking Service.
    (A) vaguely
    (B) exclusively
    (C) generously
    (D) impulsively

Practiceの正解と解説

3-21

1. NB Inc. plans to develop 30,000 square meters of space, building 3,000 homes and apartment units which will be ------- priced.
(A) moderate
(B) moderated
(C) moderately
(D) moderation

NB社は、3万平方メートルの土地を開発し、手ごろな価格の3000戸の戸建て住宅と集合住宅を建設する予定だ。
(A) 形 適度な
(B) 過去形 抑えた
　　過去分詞形 抑えられた
(C) 副 適度に
(D) 名 適度

解説 語幹が同じで品詞が異なる語が並んでいるので品詞問題。空所前後の数語をチェックし、5秒で解く。受動態の動詞を修飾できるのは副詞。副詞の頻出パターンはp.268「品詞」の項の、①〜③を参照しよう。**解答** (C)

---

2. Please write your phone number here so that we can contact ------- when the luggage is found.
(A) yours
(B) you
(C) your
(D) yourself

お手荷物が見つかった際にご連絡できるよう、こちらに電話番号をお書きください。
(A) 代 あなたのもの
(B) 代 あなた
(C) 代 あなたの
(D) 代 あなた自身

解説 異なる格の代名詞が並んでいるので、全文を読まなくてもいい問題。空所の前後をチェックすると、動詞contactの目的語が入るとわかる。(D)の再帰代名詞は、①主語と動詞の対象が同じ: Mr. Benson praised himself.(自分自身を)、②動作主を強調: The lecturer fixed the projector himself.(自ら)、③慣用表現: beside himself (われを忘れて)でのみ使われる。
解答 (B)

---

3. Current law gives police 14 days to question suspects before they are ------- charged or released.
(A) both
(B) unless
(C) either
(D) without

現行法では、起訴または釈放されるまでに警察が容疑者を尋問できるのは、14日間だ。
(A) 副 両方の
(B) 接 〜でなければ
(C) 副 いずれかの
(D) 前 〜なしで

解説 小さい接続詞（相関接続詞）の問題。空所の後に接続詞のorがあるので、ペアとなるeitherが正解となる。**解答** (C)

4. Annual upgrades are not required, but be sure to upgrade at least every three years to take ------- of improvements to the system.
(A) merit
(B) service
(C) advantage
(D) renovation

毎年アップグレードする必要はありませんが、システムの改良をご利用になれるよう、最低でも3年に1度は必ずアップグレードしてください。
(A) 名 利点
(B) 名 サービス
(C) 名 有利
(D) 名 修繕

解説 同じ品詞の語が並んでいる語彙問題。文全体を読んで文脈を理解し、解答する。take advantage of 〜（＜機会など＞を利用する）が意味として適している。この表現には、ほかに「（人・人の申し出・親切など）に甘える；（親切・無知など）に乗じる」の意味もある。 **解答** (C)

---

5. For the customers' peace of mind, shipping insurance will be added to all orders ------- no extra cost.
(A) at
(B) by
(C) from
(D) over

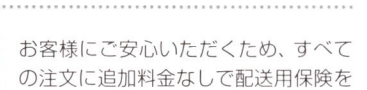

お客様にご安心いただくため、すべての注文に追加料金なしで配送用保険を掛けています。
(A) 前 〜で
(B) 前 〜によって
(C) 前 〜から
(D) 前 〜を超えて

解説 前置詞の問題は全文を読まなくてもいい。will be added to all orders ------- no extra costから「追加費用なしで」の意のat no extra costと判断しよう。costを含む重要表現にはat all cost(s)（ぜひとも）、at any cost（どんな犠牲を払っても）、at the cost of 〜（＜結果として＞〜を犠牲にして）などがある。 **解答** (A)

3-22

6. Enclosed is the latest listing of ------- companies within this sector of the hospitality industry.
(A) distinguish
(B) distinguished
(C) distinguishing
(D) distinguishable

サービス業の分野における優良企業の最新リストを同封しております。
(A) 他 〜を区別する
(B) 形 優れた
(C) 現在分詞 際立っている
　　動名詞 区別すること
(D) 形 区別できる

解説 品詞と動詞の形、分詞の複合問題。動詞の原形、形容詞／過去形／過去分詞、現在分詞／動名詞、形容詞のいずれが空所に入るか問われている。前置詞の後には名詞か動名詞が続くが、その間に入るのは、名詞を修飾する形容詞か冠詞のみ。意味的に(B)が適切だ。 **解答** (B)

7. As ------- in our telephone conversation, Ms. Rodriguez and the committee members will arrive at the headquarters at 3 o'clock.
(A) discuss
(B) discussed
(C) discussing
(D) discussion

電話で話したように、Rodriguezさんと委員会のメンバーは3時に本社に到着します。
(A) 他 〜を話し合う
(B) 過去形 話し合った
　　過去分詞 話し合われた
(C) 現在分詞 話し合っている
　　動名詞 話し合うこと
(D) 名 話し合い

解説 品詞と動詞の形、分詞の複合問題。As ------- in our telephone conversation から、「電話で〜したように」という文脈だとわかる。As was discussedと考えればいい。as (is) stated[remarked] above（上記[上述]のように）もよく使われる表現だ。 **解答** (B)

---

8. The business consultant stressed that ensuring the feasibility of a project is most important for ------- setting one up.
(A) theirs
(B) it
(C) anyone
(D) yourself

プロジェクトを計画する人にとっては、その実現可能性を確保することが最も重要だ、とそのビジネスコンサルタントは強調した。
(A) 代 彼らのもの、それらのもの
(B) 代 それ
(C) 代 誰でも
(D) 代 あなた自身

解説 代名詞問題。①どの名詞を指しているか、②単数か複数か、③どんな働きか、をチェックして選ぼう。ここでは「プロジェクトを計画する人なら誰でも」という意味になるanyoneが最適だ。 **解答** (C)

---

9. BMA corporation is considering implementing new standards ------- they assess their employees' performance.
(A) which
(B) what
(C) by which
(D) whose

BMA社は自社の従業員の業績を評価するための新基準の施行を検討中だ。

解説 関係詞の問題。2文に分けるとBMA corporation is considering implementing new standards. と ------- they assess their employees' performance. なので、空所に入る言葉を考える。「新基準で業績を評価する」のだから、by new standardsが入るはず。共通部分のnew standardsを関係代名詞whichに置き換えると正解がわかる。 **解答** (C)

10. The scale model city features a gorgeous array of the homes, shops and canals, accurate in ------- detail.
(A) any
(B) other
(C) every
(D) either

その縮尺模型の街には、あらゆる細部が正確な家や店、運河が豪華にずらりと並んでいる。
(A) 形 どの
(B) 形 ほかの
(C) 形 あらゆる
(D) 形 どちらかの

解説 同じ品詞の語が並んでいる語彙問題。「あらゆる細部において」という意味の成句、in every detail が正解となる。in great detail（こと細かに）、for further[full] detail（さらなる詳細については）、go[enter] into detail(s)（くどくどと言う）、in complete detail（もれなく詳細に）なども覚えておこう。 **解答** (C)

---

11. Checking the records revealed that no ------- than 40 percent of last month's invoices were still unpaid.
(A) sooner
(B) longer
(C) rather
(D) less

記録を調べたところ、先月の請求書のうち40パーセントもが未払いであることが発覚した。
(A) 形 より早い
(B) 形 より長い
(C) 副 いくぶん、むしろ
(D) 形 より少ない

解説 同じ品詞（形容詞）の語が選択肢に3つある語彙問題。no less than ～は「～ほども（多く）の」（= as many[much] as ～）と、数・量が多いことを強調する表現で、この文脈に合致している。no sooner ... than ～（…するとすぐに～する）、no longer ～（もはや～ない）、rather A than B、A rather than B（BよりもむしろA）もそれぞれ重要な表現。 **解答** (D)

---

12. According to the latest e-mail from our boss, the report for the new project is ------- on November 30.
(A) due
(B) valid
(C) authentic
(D) conclusive

上司からの最近のメールによれば、新規プロジェクトの報告書の提出期限は11月30日だ。
(A) 形 支払い[提出]期限の来た
(B) 形 有効な
(C) 形 本物の
(D) 形 最終の[断固とした]

解説 同じ品詞の語が並んでいる語彙問題。文脈から、レポートの提出期限のことを述べていると考えられる。due には、①支払い[提出]期限の来た：It is due at the end of the month.（それは月末に払うことになっている）に加え、②(人・乗り物が)[場所に/時間に]到着予定で：The train is due to arrive in London at 5:30.（その列車は5時30分ロンドン着の予定だ）という用法もある。 **解答** (A)

13. The new game, which is expected to ------- baseball fans, will be unveiled to the public next month.
(A) value
(B) observe
(C) attract
(D) capture

その新しいゲームは、野球の愛好者を引き付けると期待されており、来月、一般に公開される。
(A) 他 〜を評価する
(B) 他 〜を観察する
(C) 他 〜を引き付ける
(D) 他 〜を捕らえる

解説 他動詞が並んでいる語彙問題。(A)、(B)は文脈から不適当。(D)のcaptureは力・計略などで捕らえるというニュアンスなので、やはり不適当。 **解答** (C)

---

14. At the end of March, MiniSoft Inc. CEO Ms. Donaldson ------- this small, efficient company for five years.
(A) ran
(B) will have run
(C) has been running
(D) will have been run

3月末には、MiniSoft社の最高経営責任者であるDonaldsonさんが、この能率のよい小さな会社を経営して5年になる。

解説 動詞の形の問題。ここでは時制が問われているので、時に関する語句をまず探す。at the end of Marchが未来の1点を指し、for five yearsが期間を示している。未来完了（will have + 過去分詞）は未来のある時点までの動作の完了・結果・経験・継続を表すことから、正解は明らか。 **解答** (B)

---

15. The revolutionary software is used ------- by the registered members of the popular Social Networking Service.
(A) vaguely
(B) exclusively
(C) generously
(D) impulsively

その画期的なソフトウエアは、人気のソーシャルネットワーキングサービスの登録会員が独占的に利用している。
(A) 副 ぼんやりと
(B) 副 独占的に
(C) 副 寛大に
(D) 副 衝動的に

解説 同じ品詞が並んでいる語彙問題。文脈から最適なものを判断する。知らない語の意味は考えても時間の無駄なので、わからなければどれかにマークして次に進もう。考える時間は30秒を超えないように。 **解答** (B)

Task 3

1〜15の英文の空所に正解を入れて、チャンクで区切って音読しよう。その際、**英文の意味を把握しながら読む**こと。

Task 4

CD
3-21〜23

仕上げに英文を見ながら、トラック21〜23の音声に**オーバーラップさせて英文を読んでみよう**。プロソディーを意識して、リズミカルに読み上げ、ナチュラルスピードでの音読に慣れよう。

Task 5

CD
3-21〜23

本日の学習を終えた後もこれらのトラックを聞いて、チャンクに基づいて語順通りに理解できるか、繰り返し確認するようにしよう。

学習エネルギーをチャージする今日の **格言**

We are what we repeatedly do.
Excellence, then, is not an act, but a habit.

Aristotle
(384-322 B.C.：古代ギリシアの哲学者)
人は繰り返し行うことの集大成である。
ゆえに優秀さとは、一度の行いではなく習慣なのだ。

Part 3, 4, 6, 7 模擬試験

TOEIC®テスト 難関パート

19日目 / 20

- それでは本書の学習の仕上げとして、900点突破のカギとなるPart 3、4、6、7のみの模試を受験する。巻末のマークシートを切り取るか、コピーして使おう。
- Part 3から始まるので、心の準備をしておくこと。今日は、受験と答えあわせだけにして、内容の確認と音読は明日行う。

▶解答一覧：p. 300

LISTENING SECTION

Part 3　会話：5　設問：15
Part 4　トーク：5　設問：15

各パートの冒頭には、**先読みのためのポーズが8秒ずつある**。CDの指示に従って解答しよう。

READING SECTION

Part 6　英文：2　設問：6
Part 7　シングルパッセージ：5　設問：15
　　　　ダブルパッセージ：2　設問：10

Reading Sectionの**解答時間は30分**。必ず時間を計りながら受験すること。できればListening Sectionに続いて受けるようにしよう。

LISTENING SECTION

CD
3-24~33

Part 3

1. What are the speakers mainly discussing?
    (A) Permission to enter the office
    (B) Where to show an I.D.
    (C) Issuing admission tickets
    (D) Seating arrangements for the presentation

2. Why does the woman ask the man to go through the procedure?
    (A) A design of the company's logo has been renewed.
    (B) The new security regulation has been implemented.
    (C) Advance notice is required for entry.
    (D) The man has to pick up goods at an office.

3. What will the man most likely do next?
    (A) Call his business associates
    (B) Notify the woman when he comes back
    (C) Get in touch with his boss
    (D) Contact the reception desk

4. What is most likely the man's job?
    (A) A real estate agent
    (B) A cabin attendant
    (C) A hotel manager
    (D) A travel agent

5. What is the woman concerned about?
    (A) She has to transit in Mexico.
    (B) She is unable to travel this year.
    (C) She has only 14 days off.
    (D) Her budget is limited.

6. What will the man do next?
    (A) He will issue a shipping invoice.
    (B) He will recommend using a public transportation.
    (C) He will offer a small reduction in price.
    (D) He will quote the cost of the tour.

7. Where does the conversation most likely take place?

(A) At a pharmacy
(B) At a veterinary hospital
(C) At a cosmetics counter
(D) At a dentist's office

8. What does the woman indicate?

(A) The man should take medication.
(B) She will give an injection to the man.
(C) The man's treatment is over now.
(D) She was fined two days ago.

9. What does the man most likely intend to do?

(A) Come back later in the week
(B) Contact his insurance company
(C) Reschedule his appointment for an operation
(D) Get a prescription for his chronic headache

10. What has the woman heard?

(A) The renovation of the office building will be launched soon.
(B) New equipment will be installed in her workplace.
(C) The firm may relocate soon.
(D) A new call center is opening downtown.

11. What is the woman looking forward to next month?

(A) An official announcement
(B) A transfer to the overseas branch
(C) An industry conference in the downtown area
(D) An award ceremony

12. How long has the man been working at the company?

(A) Two years
(B) Five years
(C) Ten years
(D) Twenty years

GO ON TO THE NEXT PAGE

13. What are the speakers mainly discussing?
   (A) How to finalize the new contracts
   (B) How to maintain the company's workforce
   (C) When to let employees have vacations
   (D) Where to relocate the company

14. When does the conversation most likely take place?
   (A) January
   (B) July
   (C) September
   (D) December

15. What does the man imply?
   (A) They will be able to manage the situation.
   (B) The office equipment needs to be replaced.
   (C) They are required to update the data.
   (D) The woman's forecast is too optimistic.

Part 4

16. Who most likely are the listeners?

(A) Shoppers looking for furniture
(B) People who need groceries
(C) Plant managers
(D) People searching for used goods

17. According to the announcement, what does the speaker care about?

(A) Environmental issues
(B) An extended warranty
(C) Security systems
(D) A fast delivery

18. What is mentioned as an incentive?

(A) The price of some fruits are more than 30 percent off.
(B) Free samples of new stationery are offered.
(C) Confectionery is sold at half-price.
(D) All dairy products are discounted by 20 percent.

19. Where does the talk probably take place?

(A) In a university classroom
(B) At a sports stadium
(C) On a car radio
(D) In an office building

20. What does the speaker imply about the drill?

(A) The building must be evacuated.
(B) It is a safety exercise.
(C) The instruction manual has to be read carefully.
(D) Manufacturing procedures have to be followed.

21. What does the speaker say will happen next?

(A) Attendance records will be disclosed.
(B) The test signals will be heard.
(C) The school excursion will begin.
(D) Mechanical engineers will adjust a heating system.

GO ON TO THE NEXT PAGE

22. Who most likely is the speaker addressing?
(A) Floor managers
(B) Local dairy farmers
(C) Newly trained mechanics
(D) Plant supervisors

23. Where will the participants spend the afternoon?
(A) The package section
(B) The distribution division
(C) The new product development division
(D) The reception room for the guests

24. What does the speaker say not to do?
(A) Take photos in the plants
(B) Eat or drink in the laboratory
(C) Visit the construction site
(D) Touch the machine in the show room

....

25. What is the news mainly about?
(A) Today's weather forecast
(B) Problems with the helicopter service
(C) An accident involving a vehicle
(D) Delays in public transportation

26. What does the speaker imply?
(A) Commuters have to evacuate immediately.
(B) An electric problem will be fixed soon.
(C) The Newbury exit is closed temporarily.
(D) A thunderstorm warning has been issued.

27. When can the next report be expected?
(A) 3:40 P.M.
(B) 4:00 P.M.
(C) 4:30 P.M.
(D) 5:00 P.M.

28. According to the report, what will be accepted from now on?
   (A) Different modes of payment to the government
   (B) Submission of bidding over the Internet
   (C) Donations to the municipal council
   (D) The civic right to participate in the budget committee

29. Who is most likely Mr. Mike Freeson?
   (A) A bank manager
   (B) A government officer
   (C) A financial consultant
   (D) A principal

30. According to the report, what is expected on the basis of the decision?
   (A) The unemployment rate will decrease.
   (B) Residents in the district will be required to pay less tax.
   (C) The incumbent governor will resign soon.
   (D) The local government will have smaller debts.

This is the end of the Listening test. Turn to Part 6 in your test book.

Part 6

Questions 31-33 refer to the following memo.

Intraoffice Memorandum

ATTN: All employees,
Our company's fire and earthquake safety procedures are being changed in keeping with recent changes in local ordinances. -------, some new rules and
                        31. (A) Accordingly
                              (B) Notwithstanding
                              (C) Otherwise
                              (D) Still

changes in existing rules will affect numerous details of our work environment. -------, some of the changes will affect the location and installation of fire
32. (A) On the contrary
     (B) For instance
     (C) By the way
     (D) Ever since

extinguishers, the areas designated as smoking sections within the office complex, the methods for storing flammable liquids such as certain cleaning fluids, alcohol for disinfectant, heating oil, and numerous other items.

All employees are responsible for reading and understanding the new regulations, which will be published in this week's edition of the in-house newsletter. All supervisors of employees whose job descriptions involve the handling of designated flammable materials must ensure that the rules are prominently ------- in affected work areas.
     33. (A) prevented
          (B) impaired
          (C) posted
          (D) generated

The management

Questions 34-36 refer to the following letter.

Dear Ms. Graves,

Our records show that your last regular dental cleaning and check-up was on January 20 of this year. To help you ------- optimum dental health, we

    34. (A) maintain
        (B) allocate
        (C) cure
        (D) substitute

recommend regular cleanings and examinations every six months. Please take a moment to fill in the form on the enclosed postage-paid postcard indicating your date and time -------, and drop it in a mailbox at your convenience.

    35. (A) preferences
        (B) references
        (C) expectations
        (D) guidelines

Our reception staff will contact you to confirm an appointment.
-------, please be sure to write down any changes in your address or

36. (A) In contrast
    (B) Also
    (C) In brief
    (D) Conversely

telephone number in the contact information portion of the form.

We look forward to helping you brighten your smile!

Sincerely,

Robert Cushing, DDS
Cushing Dental Offices

Part 7

Questions 37-38 refer to the following e-mail.

From: Cindy Brock <cbrock@mgmt-argylistinc.com>
To: Customer Service <cserv-help@foroffice.com>
Subject: Order Received

Thank you for the latest shipment of office supplies. All of the items have been received on time and in good condition. We should note, however, that although our original order and payment (as well as the packing list and invoice) all specify 144 reams of standard white inkjet printer paper, we received the same amount of high-quality bond paper. Although we are perfectly satisfied with the high-quality paper, we felt you should know about the error. Please feel free to have the paper picked up and replaced with standard white stock if you wish. We will keep it unused in inventory for three weeks, and begin using it after that if we do not hear from you.

Sincerely,

Cindy Brock

37. What is the main purpose of the e-mail?
(A) To notify the supplier of a misdelivery of goods
(B) To complain about an error regarding the amount in the invoice
(C) To offer a partial refund for the damaged products
(D) To request an immediate exchange of merchandise

38. What does the e-mail imply?
(A) Only three weeks remain before the expiration date on the package.
(B) They have received defective products before.
(C) The office supply company has signed a long-term supply contract.
(D) Ms. Brock's company does not intend to pay extra.

Questions 39-41 refer to the following article.

New Startup Promises Better Mobility

A new business venture located in the Henderson Bay district is offering innovative designs that could make conventional wheelchairs and scooters a thing of the past. GF Enterprises Inc. was formed two years ago by Wendy Trilling and business partner Sandra Evans, who at the time were postgraduate students at a university laboratory. Both now hold a PhD in mechanical engineering and have been recently awarded a prize for being the most promising young researchers. "We were both dissatisfied with the wheelchair and electric scooter options available in the market, and decided to design something better," said Trilling. The result was the SpeedyHelper, a computerized electric device that provides more power, speed and mobility. Some models of the new device have been so successful that cargo transport companies have purchased them to help employees in their busy warehouse operations reduce footwork and on-the-job fatigue. As for the prospects for further developments, according to Mr. John Kent, the company's director of public relations, several philanthropists have recently expressed their intention to financially support GF Enterprises' on-going research projects.

39. What is indicated about Ms. Evans?
(A) She is a co-founder of the firm.
(B) She is a recipient of the best scientist award.
(C) She is a former professor.
(D) She used to be an industrial designer.

40. What advantage does the new product provide?
(A) Better mobility
(B) A lower price
(C) Longer battery life
(D) Easier operation

41. What does Mr. Kent mention?
(A) The board members unanimously approved the budget for research projects.
(B) He will be in charge of the finance department.
(C) Benefactors will provide funds for research.
(D) The department of public relations will advertise its services.

GO ON TO THE NEXT PAGE

Questions 42-44 refer to the following memo.

ATTN: All Management Personnel

Sign Up for the Denby Ace Manufacturing Fresh Ideas Summit!

We remind you that this year's Fresh Ideas Summit is approaching, and your participation is strongly urged. Instituted in 1972 by the founder of Denby Ace Manufacturing Co., FIS has developed into an annual two-day training session and award banquet that provides our younger employees and senior management with opportunities to communicate and learn from each other. The event begins with presentations by employees hired within the past five years, demonstrating their ideas for innovative products, organizational reforms, evaluation programs or any other "Fresh Ideas" that could help make Denby Ace Manufacturing a better company. Presentations are followed by sessions with senior managers that include follow-up questions, critiques and collaborative refinement of the presented ideas. A final round of the top five presentations on the second day of the event is followed by an award ceremony in which the best idea is selected for subsequent presentation before the board of directors. Past FIS events have resulted in innovations integral to the success and expansion of Denby Ace Manufacturing, and the development of some of our most outstanding administrative talent. If you have not done so, we strongly urge you to sign up for participation in this year's event. Contact Marcia Trent, General Affairs Div. (ext. 7274).

42. What is the main purpose of the notice?
 (A) To encourage managers to sign up for the FIS event
 (B) To solicit fresh ideas on how to improve the company
 (C) To remind all employees that FIS participation is mandatory
 (D) To institute a new annual awards banquet

43. Where would the notice most likely be seen?
 (A) On a bulletin board in a hotel lobby
 (B) In a restaurant near the office
 (C) In a lounge for executives
 (D) In the company parking garage

44. What is mentioned about the event?
 (A) The founder of the corporation will present the award directly.
 (B) There will be a banquet for special guests.
 (C) Awards will be given to the top three finalists.
 (D) It has been helpful in terms of staff progress.

Questions 45-47 refer to the following advertisement.

Sales Help Wanted
Milton Home Furnishings

You have a special appreciation for fine home furnishings, and you love working with people. If this description fits you, we would like to talk about a uniquely rewarding career opportunity. We are Milton Home Furnishings, a leading nationwide furniture and interior design accessory retailer with a 75-year history of growth and success. We are looking for highly motivated people to join us in making our brand-new store in the Arista Plaza Shopping Center a success. In exchange for your effort and talent, we offer the best compensation package in the industry, including unbeatable salary levels, full medical and dental insurance coverage, generous paid vacation and a great optional stock investment plan. For more information on this great opportunity, please fax your résumé to Louise at 555-123-4567, or send it by e-mail to newjobapplications@ miltonhomefurnishings.com. Or you can stop by our exciting new showroom at the south end of the main arcade at Arista Plaza Shopping Center. We look forward to exploring the possibilities with you.

45. What is indicated about Milton Home Furnishings?
  (A) It is a well-established real estate agency.
  (B) It is located at the north end of the main arcade.
  (C) It has been operating plants in multiple places.
  (D) It was founded more than seven decades ago.

46. What is NOT a requirement of the position?
  (A) The ability to recognize high quality
  (B) Eagerness to work hard
  (C) Previous work experience
  (D) A social attitude

47. What has to be sent to the company when applying for the job?
  (A) A copy of the applicant's work history
  (B) A cover letter
  (C) A duplicate of the certificate
  (D) A letter of recommendation

Questions 48-51 refer to the following letter.

RFGS
Promoting understanding through interaction

November 12

Wayne Peters, PhD
505 University Circle
Arling CA, 92481

Dear Prof. Peters,

Thank you for your inquiry regarding opportunities for speaking engagements through RFGS. The first step toward the potential formation of a permanent speaking relationship with RFGS is to participate as a volunteer presenter in one of our three annual conferences: The Global Forum for Intercultural Relationships, Technical Innovations for Environment-friendly Development, and Science Education for Young Generations. You may apply to become a speaker at one of these conferences by submitting the application form found at our Web site, together with a 150-word summary of your presentation. Speakers at these events do not receive compensation, and are not reimbursed for travel expenses. In addition, a registration fee is required.

Two outstanding volunteer speakers from each of these conferences will be chosen by membership vote and/or approved by our panel of directors for invitation to speak at our Annual Global Trends Seminar. These six speakers will be reimbursed for travel and related expenses, and receive invitations to RFGS membership. Occasionally, some are nominated for long-term sponsored speaking engagements, typically on a three-year contractual basis. Payment and other compensation is to be negotiated on an ad hoc basis.

Thus, the next step for you at this stage would be to visit our Web site and complete the initial application process mentioned above. Thank you again for your inquiry. Should you have further questions, please do not hesitate to contact me by e-mail at: laineanderson-publicrel@RFGS.org

Sincerely,

Laine Anderson
Laine Anderson
Director of Public Outreach
The Rogers Foundation for Global Studies

48. What is the purpose of the letter?
   (A) To finalize the on-going negotiation for a merger
   (B) To ask for a book on the latest technical innovations
   (C) To request the issuance of a letter of recommendation
   (D) To explain a process of registration

49. What is mentioned in the letter?
   (A) The RFGS is a university-affiliated organization.
   (B) The RFGS only accepts six job applications each year.
   (C) Prof. Peters made an inquiry about becoming an RFGS speaker.
   (D) Prof. Peters has dealt with the RFGS European headquarters.

50. What presentation subjects are most likely to be heard at the RFGS annual conferences?
   (A) Fashion trends among the youth
   (B) Facilities utilizing solar and wind energies
   (C) Financial schemes for international banking systems
   (D) Life-long education for the aged

51. Which of the following is true?
   (A) Expenses are paid only for speakers invited to the annual seminar.
   (B) Prof. Peters has prepared more than one summary of his presentations.
   (C) The Global Forum for Intercultural Relationships event was canceled last year.
   (D) Invitations to speak at this year's annual seminar have already been sent.

Questions 52-56 refer to the following letter and e-mail.

Grace Rhodes
3428 Richmond St., Apt. 210
Gabriel TX   77332

Dear Ms. Rhodes,

I was informed by Ms. Martha Reynolds in our market research department that she occasionally hires you to provide us with business reports and industry analyses on an outsourced basis. In relation to this work I would be grateful if you'd complete the following forms.
Enclosed please find two copies of our non-disclosure agreement (NDA). This is a standard contractual agreement stipulating that all information that you provide to us on assignment becomes our property when we receive it. Please read through the contract carefully. Write your initials in the areas specified in the text (I have marked these with pink stickers), and put your signature in the space provided at the end of the agreements.
There are two copies, one of which you should keep for your records after signing, and the other of which you must return to us in the envelope provided. Thank you in advance for your understanding and prompt cooperation.

Sincerely,

Stanley Fitzgerald
Stanley Fitzgerald
Staff Council, Legal Affairs Div.
Tidewater Consulting Co., Inc.

From: Grace Rhodes <grhodes@opinnets.com>
To: Stan Fitzgerald <stanfitz@tdwatercons.com>
Subject: NDA

Dear Mr. Fitzgerald:
Thank you for your letter. I've been enjoying working with Ms. Reynolds and her team members to promote your firm's services. Today I sent the signed NDA to you by registered mail. I'm told that you should receive it within two working days. Please note that I received and signed only one copy of the document. I have scanned a digital image of the signed agreement, and this is sufficient for my record-keeping purposes. You do not need to send me an

additional original of the NDA in the future unless you prefer to do so. Thank you very much for your continued support.

Grace Rhodes

52. What does Mr. Fitzgerald ask Ms. Rhodes to do?
 (A) Return a copy of the document by registered mail
 (B) Create a digital copy of the contract right away
 (C) Make sure her company's board members approve collaboration
 (D) Formally agree to keep some information secret

53. In the letter, the word "stipulating" in paragraph 2, line 2, is the closest in meaning to
 (A) summarizing
 (B) replacing
 (C) stating
 (D) customizing

54. What most likely is Ms. Rhodes' occupation?
 (A) A security officer
 (B) A marketing consultant
 (C) A photographer
 (D) A legal advisor

55. What does Mr. Fitzgerald recommend?
 (A) Increasing the company's capital
 (B) Reading the NDA attentively
 (C) Hiring a new consultant
 (D) Reassessing the current compensation package

56. What mistake did Mr. Fitzgerald make?
 (A) He neglected to attach the file to the e-mail.
 (B) He marked the wrong parts of the text with stickers.
 (C) He only sent one copy of the NDA.
 (D) He dispatched the contract without informing Ms. Reynolds.

GO ON TO THE NEXT PAGE

Questions 57-61 refer to the following letter and e-mail.

Amy Butler
President, Weller Historical Society
9011 Spruce Ave.
Weller WA 98031

Dear Amy,

I hope you're doing well. During my weekly round on the golf course recently, I met a man who is on the board of directors at Mason Steel Co. We got to talking, and he mentioned in passing that his company owns the old Johnston Metalworks Plant on Hemingway Avenue in your town. He mentioned that his company plans to completely renovate the factory, which means they will be discarding all of their old machinery. When I worked there as a boy, I remember that it was a treasure house of old equipment, much of it handmade, and some of it dating back to the 1920s. I am sure that you would be interested in obtaining any items of interest for the local history museum you've been planning. Enclosed with this letter, you'll find my friend's business card. Please contact him if you're attracted by my suggestion and let him know about your activities. I'm sure he'll be receptive.
Sincerely,
Dan Kruger
Dan Kruger
122 Southearl Dr., Apt. 505
Newton WA 98128

From: Amy Butler <amybutler@anglecoms.com>
To: Dan Kruger <dkruger@localnets.com>
Subject: Johnston Metalworks

Hi Dan,
I just received your letter last week, and I can't thank you enough. Actually, we at the historical society have known about the Johnston Metalworks Plant for years now. I'd been in touch with some lower-level public relations people at the parent company, but they hadn't given me any good information on the plant.
On your advice, I contacted Mr. Graves. He was very friendly and helpful. He

is a great lover of antiques himself, and has promised to donate several very important collectible antiques to our project.

Thank you so much for your help. When our museum opens next year, it's going to be better than ever!

Sincerely,

Amy

57. What most likely is Ms. Butler's main interest?

(A) Artifacts in her town
(B) The economic revitalization of the foundation
(C) Community health and welfare
(D) Investment in municipal bonds

58. What can be inferred about Mr. Kruger?

(A) He exercises regularly.
(B) He holds a weekly meeting with Mr. Graves.
(C) He has a large collection of antiques.
(D) He owns a metalworks plant.

59. What do we know about Ms. Butler?

(A) She visited Johnston Metalworks to ask for donations.
(B) She once worked at the Johnston Metalworks Plant.
(C) She had contacted Mason Steel company previously.
(D) She manages an antique shop in her neighborhood.

60. In the e-mail, the word "donate" in paragraph 2, line 2, is the closest in meaning to

(A) assess
(B) deposit
(C) scrutinize
(D) contribute

61. What can be expected to happen next year?

(A) The charity auction will be held.
(B) The renovation project of the school will be launched.
(C) The institution will be partially funded by a municipal government.
(D) The new museum will be inaugurated.

Stop! This is the end of the test. If you finish before time is over, you may go back to Part 6 and 7 and check your work.

解答一覧

#	Ans	#	Ans	#	Ans	#	Ans
1	(A)	17	(A)	33	(C)	49	(C)
2	(B)	18	(A)	34	(A)	50	(B)
3	(D)	19	(D)	35	(A)	51	(A)
4	(D)	20	(B)	36	(B)	52	(D)
5	(C)	21	(B)	37	(A)	53	(C)
6	(D)	22	(D)	38	(D)	54	(B)
7	(D)	23	(C)	39	(A)	55	(B)
8	(C)	24	(C)	40	(A)	56	(C)
9	(A)	25	(C)	41	(C)	57	(A)
10	(C)	26	(C)	42	(A)	58	(A)
11	(A)	27	(C)	43	(C)	59	(C)
12	(D)	28	(A)	44	(D)	60	(D)
13	(B)	29	(B)	45	(D)	61	(D)
14	(B)	30	(D)	46	(C)		
15	(A)	31	(A)	47	(A)		
16	(B)	32	(B)	48	(D)		

学習エネルギーをチャージする今日の **格言**

Wisdom is the power to put our time and our knowledge to the proper use.

Thomas J. Watson
(1874〜1956：「世界一のセールスマン」と呼ばれたIBM社の社長)

知恵とは、われわれの時間と知識を適切に用いるための力だ。

20日目

答えあわせと音読

最終日の今日は、昨日の模試の詳細な答えあわせと、問題文の音読を行う。問題文は量が多いので、不正解が多かったり、苦手と感じた英文を中心に音読しよう。
プロソディーを意識しリズミカルかつスピーディーに読む。チャンクで意味を把握しながら発言者になりきろう。

LISTENING SECTION

Part 3

1-3　CD 3-24　W:🇦🇺　M:🇺🇸

W: Hello, sir. May I see your pass, please?
M: Do I need an I.D.? Perhaps there's been a misunderstanding. I'm not an employee here. My name is Bill Wallace. I come here once a month to advise the board of directors on legal matters.
W: I apologize for any inconvenience, sir. But Design26 Incorporated has just established a new office building security policy. I must say I am not authorized to allow anyone to enter without an I.D. Would you please go to the reception desk to get your temporary identification badge issued so that you can get in?
M: Thank you. I'll follow your advice.

W: こんにちは。通行証を拝見できますか。
M: 私も身分証明書が必要ですか？ どうやら誤解があるようですね。私はこちらの従業員ではありません。Bill Wallaceと申します。1カ月に1度、取締役会に法律関係の助言をするため、伺っているんですよ。
W: ご面倒をお掛けして申し訳ありません。しかしながらDesign26社では、最近新たに、オフィスビルのセキュリティポリシーを定めたんです。私の一存では、身分証明書のない方の入館を許可することはできません。受付カウンターで、臨時身分証明バッジを受け取ってからご入館いただけますか。
M: わかりました。ご忠告に従います。

1. 話者たちは主に何について話しているか。
　(A) オフィスに入る許可
　(B) どこで身分証明書を見せるか
　(C) 入場券の発行
　(D) プレゼンテーション時の席順

解説　設問のキーワードはWhat、speakers、discussing。「主題」を問う全体情報タイプ。冒頭の身分証明書に関する会話や、I am not authorized to allow anyone ...以降からわかる。
解答 (A)

301

2. 女性が男性に手続きを踏むよう頼んでいるのはなぜか。
  (A) 会社のロゴが新しくなった。
  (B) 新しい保安規則が施行されている。
  (C) 入館には事前通知が必要。
  (D) 男性はオフィスで品物を受け取らなければならない。

解説 キーワードはWhy、woman、ask、man、go through the procedureで、「理由」を問う個別情報タイプ。設問の主語である女性の発言に注意する。Design26 Incorporated has just established ... 以降がヒント。
解答 (B)

3. 男性は次に何をすると思われるか。
  (A) 仕事関係者に電話をする
  (B) いつ戻るかを女性に知らせる
  (C) 上司と連絡を取る
  (D) 受付デスクと連絡を取る

解説 キーワードはWhat、man、do、next。「次の行動」を問う個別情報タイプ。会話の後半にヒントがある。please go to the reception desk ...という依頼にI'll follow your advice.と応じている。**解答** (D)

4-6 CD 3-25 M: 🇬🇧 W: 🇨🇦

M: How are you going to spend your holiday this summer, Ms. Dobbs?
W: Well, we originally thought we'd have about six weeks of vacation time on one of those luxury cruise ships that go all over the world. But our plans have changed. Unfortunately, we won't be able to take more than two weeks off.
M: Here's an idea. I can set you up on a one-way cruise to a port that's about a week away– in Mexico, or Canada perhaps. Then you could spend a week at a resort before flying home. Shall I see what's available?
W: Oh, yes. That sounds wonderful. We'll have the best of both worlds– a cruise and a stay at a tropical beach resort. How much does it cost?

M: 今年の夏の休暇は、どのように過ごされる予定ですか、Dobbsさん。
W: そうですね、もともとは、6週間くらい休暇を取って、世界中を巡る豪華客船で過ごすつもりでいたんです。でも、計画が変わりました。残念ながら、2週間以上の休暇は取れないようなので。
M: こうしてはいかがでしょう。1週間くらいで行ける港まで、片道のクルーズをご用意できますよ。メキシコとか、カナダの港になるでしょうかね。そうすれば、1週間ほどリゾートで過ごしてから、空路で帰国できます。どんなものがあるか、調べてみましょうか。
W: まあ、ぜひ。とても良さそうですね。クルージングと南国ビーチリゾートへの滞在なんて、2つのいいとこ取りですもの。料金はどのくらいですか。

4. 男性の職業は何だと思われるか。
  (A) 不動産業者
  (B) 客室乗務員
  (C) ホテルの支配人
  (D) 旅行代理店の社員

解説 キーワードはWhat、man's job。「職業」を問う全体情報タイプ。夏休みの予定を聞いて、I can set you up on a one-way cruise to a portと提案していることから正解がわかる。
解答 (D)

5. 女性は何を心配しているのか。
  (A) メキシコを経由しなければならない。
  (B) 今年は旅行できない。
  (C) 14日間しか休暇を取れない。
  (D) 予算が限られている。

解説 女性の「懸念」を問う個別情報タイプ。女性の発言内の心配や不安を示す表現を待ち伏せる。Unfortunatelyの後のwe won't be able to take more than two weeks offがヒント。
解答 (C)

---

6. 男性は次に何をすると思われるか。
  (A) 輸送明細書を発行する。
  (B) 公共交通機関の利用を勧める。
  (C) 料金をわずかに割引する。
  (D) ツアー料金の見積もりを出す。

解説 「次の行動」を問う個別情報タイプ。会話の後半に注意。Shall I see what's available? How much does it cost? というやり取りがある。
解答 (D)

7-9 CD 3-26 W: 🇨🇦 M: 🇺🇸

W: Well, Mr. Wells, we're finished with your treatment for today. I've repaired the damage to that chipped tooth of yours.
M: Thanks. It feels much better now. I really appreciate the fact that you made time for me on an emergency basis.
W: It's no problem. Now, I've treated your mouth with a painkiller. When the effect of the drug wears off in a few hours, you might feel a minor ache. But it should feel fine in a day or two.
M: OK. I'll certainly let you know if it starts hurting again. And I think I'll see your receptionist about scheduling a cleaning for later this week. I haven't had that done in about a year.

W: はい、Wellsさん、本日の治療はこれで終了です。欠けてしまった歯を修復しましたよ。
M: ありがとうございます。ずいぶん良くなりました。緊急にお時間を作っていただき、本当に感謝しています。
W: いいんですよ。ところで、お口に痛み止めを打ちました。数時間後、薬の効果が切れると、少し痛むかもしれません。でも、1日か2日で良くなるはずです。
M: わかりました。また痛くなってきたら、必ずご連絡します。それと、これから受付の方にお話をして、今週中にクリーニングの予約を入れるつもりです。もう1年ほど、クリーニングをしていないので。

7. この会話はどこで行われている可能性が高いか。
  (A) 薬局で
  (B) 動物病院で
  (C) 化粧品カウンターで
  (D) 歯科医院で

解説 キーワードはWhere、conversation、take place。「場所」を問う全体情報タイプ。your treatment、damage to that chipped tooth、treated your mouthなどから歯科医院だとわかる。 **解答** (D)

8. 女性は何を示唆しているか。
(A) 男性は薬を服用すべきだ。
(B) 彼女はこれから男性に注射する。
(C) 男性の治療はもう終わった。
(D) 彼女は2日前に罰金を科された。

解説 キーワードはWhat、woman、indicate。「示唆」を問う個別情報タイプ。女性の発言に注目する。冒頭のwe're finished with your treatment for todayを聞き逃さないよう注意。 **解答** (C)

---

9. 男性は何をするつもりだと思われるか。
(A) 今週中にまた来る
(B) 保険会社に連絡する
(C) 手術の予約を変更する
(D) 慢性頭痛の処方を書いてもらう

解説 キーワードはWhat、man、intend to do。「次の行動」を問う個別情報タイプだ。会話の後半に注意しよう。see your receptionist about scheduling a cleaning for later this weekがヒント。 **解答** (A)

10-12 CD 3-27   W: 🇦🇺 M: 🇬🇧

W: Have you heard the latest rumor about relocating the company's offices?
M: No. We certainly could use some extra office space. But I usually don't pay much attention to news from unreliable sources. What have you heard?
W: Well, it seems that senior management is seriously considering moving our offices to the Galaxy Executive Tower downtown. An announcement by our CEO could come as soon as next month!
M: Let me tell you something. When I first started working here, one of the first things my coworkers said was that we'd soon have spacious new offices downtown. That was two decades ago, and this piece of gossip seems to come up every year. So I would take it with a grain of salt if I were you.

W: 会社のオフィス移転について、最新のうわさは聞いた?
M: いいや。確かに、もっとオフィスのスペースは欲しいところだけれどね。でも僕は普段、信頼できない出所からの情報にはあまり耳を貸さないんだ。どんなうわさなの?
W: それがね、上層部が真剣に、中心街のGalaxy Executive Towerへの移転を考えているらしい、って。来月にもCEOが発表するかもしれないんですって!
M: ひとつ言っておこう。僕がここで働き始めたとき、まず最初に同僚たちから聞かされた話のひとつが、もうすぐ中心街に新しく広いオフィスができるというものだった。それはもう20年も前のことだ。それに、この手のゴシップは、毎年流れているようだよ。だから、もし僕が君の立場だったら、その情報をうのみにはしないな。

10. 女性は何を耳にしたのか。
(A) オフィスビルの改築が間もなく始まる。
(B) 職場に新しい機器が設置される。
(C) 事務所が間もなく移転する。
(D) 中心街に新しいコールセンターが開設される。

解説 「女性が聞いたこと」を問う個別情報タイプ。女性の発言に注意する。冒頭のHave you heard ...を聞くだけでも解答可能。後半のsenior management is ...で繰り返されている。 **解答** (C)

11. 女性は来月何を期待しているか。
(A) 正式な発表
(B) 海外支店への転勤
(C) 中心街での業界の会議
(D) 授賞式

解説 「来月に期待していること」を問う個別情報タイプ。設問の主語である女性の発言に注目。「来月」という具体的な時の表現を待ち構えて聞こう。An announcement by our CEO ...がヒント。
解答 (A)

12. 男性はどのくらいこの会社で働いているか。
(A) 2年間　(B) 5年間
(C) 10年間　(D) 20年間

解説 「勤続年数」を問う個別情報タイプ。設問の主語である男性の発言に注目。When I first started working here ... That was two decades agoから答えがわかる。
解答 (D)

13-15 W: 🇨🇦 M: 🇺🇸

W: The last item on the meeting agenda today is the most difficult. It's our summer schedule.

M: You're right. We've just taken on two major new contracts. The next two months will be the busiest period our company has ever been through in spite of the fact that we're right in the middle of summer vacation season.

W: Well, I've spoken to all of the staff supervisors. We think we can maintain a staff strength of 90 percent in all departments from now until September.

M: Good. I've been in touch with our three main temporary employment agencies. It's not an ideal situation. But with their help, I'm pretty sure we'll be able to make it to the end of vacation season without serious trouble.

W: 本日の議題の最後の項目は、一番の難問ですね。わが社の夏のスケジュールについてです。

M: おっしゃるとおりですね。私たちは最近、新たに大きな契約を2つ取り付けました。これからの2カ月間は、これまで経験したことがないほど忙しくなるでしょう。しかし現在は、夏の休暇シーズンのまっただ中です。

W: ええ、役職者全員に話を聞いてみました。これから9月まで、全部署、90パーセントの労働力を維持できそうです。

M: それはよかった。私は、主要な人材派遣会社3社と連絡を取りあっています。理想的な状況とは言えません。しかし、派遣会社の助けを借りれば、大きな問題もなく、休暇シーズンの終わりまで乗り切ることができると確信しています。

13. 話者たちは主に何を話しているか。
(A) 新しい契約をどうまとめるか
(B) 会社の労働力をどう維持するか
(C) いつ従業員に休暇を取らせるか
(D) 会社をどこに移転するか

解説 「主題」を問う全体情報タイプ。14、15に解答してから解くと効率的だ。The next two months will be the busiest period、we can maintain a staff strengthなどから絞り込める。
解答 (B)

14. この会話はいつ行われている可能性が高いか。
(A) 1月
(B) 7月
(C) 9月
(D) 12月

解説　「時」を問う個別情報タイプ。選択肢に並ぶ「月」に関する情報を待つ。we're right in the middle of summer vacation season、from now until Septemberから絞り込もう。
解答　(B)

---

15. 男性は何を示唆しているか。
(A) 彼らは状況に対処できるだろう。
(B) オフィスの機器を取り替える必要がある。
(C) データをアップデートする必要がある。
(D) 女性の予測が楽観的すぎる。

解説　男性が「示唆すること」を問う個別情報タイプ。男性の後半の発言に注意。with their help, I'm pretty sure ...以降がヒントとなる。
解答　(A)

Part 4

16-18　CD 3-29

Questions 16-18 refer to the following announcement.
Welcome to YouFoods grocery store. This is Kyle, your store manager, here to remind you about some of our special discounts and everyday low prices. We have fresh fruits and vegetables today, including grapes, watermelons, and tomatoes, all at one-third off our regular low prices. Alto Farms premium dairy products, including whole milk, low-fat milk and cream cheese, are on sale at 20 percent off our regular low price. Don't miss our fresh deli counter, where you can have sandwiches and salads made to order. And remember, a donation of 1 percent of all purchase proceeds this week will be given to the local Environmental Help Foundation. It's our way of saying, we care. Thank you for shopping at YouFoods.

問題16-18は次のアナウンスに関するものです。
YouFoods食料品店へようこそ。// 私は店長のKyleです / 特売品と毎日のお値打ち商品をいくつかご案内いたします。// 本日は新鮮な果物と野菜をご用意しています / ぶどう、スイカ、トマトなど / 全品が当店の通常お手ごろ価格から3分の1のお値引きです。// Alto Farmsの特選乳製品は / 全乳、低脂肪乳、クリームチーズなど / 当店の通常お手ごろ価格から20パーセント割引です。// 作りたてデリのカウンターもお見逃しなく / そこではご注文を受けてから作るサンドイッチやサラダがお求めになれます。// さらに、お忘れなく / 今週、全売上の1パーセント分の寄付が / 地元の環境保護基金に贈られます。// 「関心を持っている」という私たちなりの表明です。// YouFoodsでのお買い物ありがとうございます。//

16. 聞き手は誰である可能性が最も高いか。
(A) 家具を探している買い物客
(B) 食料雑貨を必要とする人々
(C) 工場長
(D) 中古品を探している人々

解説 キーワードはWho、listeners。「聞き手」を問う全体情報タイプ。Welcome to YouFoods grocery store.、We have fresh fruits and vegetables today、Thank you for shopping at YouFoods.などから推測可能。
解答 (B)

---

17. アナウンスによると、話者は何に関心を持っているか。
(A) 環境問題
(B) 保証の延長
(C) 警備システム
(D) 迅速な配送

解説 キーワードはwhat、speaker、care about。話者の「関心」を問う個別情報タイプ。a donation of ... 以降で、売り上げの一部を環境保護団体に寄付すると述べている。It's our way of saying, we care.の意味を取り違えないよう注意。
解答 (A)

---

18. インセンティブとして何が言及されているか。
(A) 一部の果物の値段が30パーセント以上割引になる。
(B) 文房具の新製品の無料サンプルが提供される。
(C) 菓子類が半額で販売される。
(D) 乳製品がすべて20パーセント割引になる。

解説 インセンティブとは、購買を促すための特典・プレゼントなどのこと。We have fresh fruits and vegetables today ... all at one-third off our regular low pricesがヒントとなるが、他の選択肢が間違いであることも確認しなければならないので、設問の先読みが必須だ。トークを最後までしっかり聞いてから解答しよう。
解答 (A)

19-21

Questions 19-21 refer to the following announcement.

Attention all employees. We are conducting a regular test of the emergency public address system for the Winston & Morris Office Tower Complex. This is a routine procedure required by local disaster management and safety laws. Following this announcement, you will hear a series of test signals broadcast over the speakers in your office for a duration of approximately 30 seconds. This is not an emergency alarm. The signal will enable our engineers to adjust sound levels and confirm the condition of public address system equipment. In the event of a real emergency, you would be given instructions for safety and or evacuation procedures. This is only a sound test. The test begins in five seconds.

問題19-21は次のアナウンスに関するものです。

全従業員にお知らせします。// 緊急全館放送システムの定期検査を行っています / Winston & Morris オフィスタワー複合施設の。// これは通常の手続きです / 当地の災害管理及び安全関係の法律によって定められているものです。// このアナウンスに引き続き / 一続きの試験信号が聞こえてきます / 皆さんのオフィスのスピーカーを通じて放送されます / およそ30秒の間。// これは緊急警報ではありません。// この信号によって技師はできるのです / 音響レベルの調整 / と全館放送システム設備の状態の確認が。// 実際の緊急事態の際には / 指示が出されます / 安全と避難手順に関して。// これは単なる音響テストです。// テストは5秒後に始まります。//

19. このトークはどこで行われていると思われるか。
(A) 大学の教室
(B) スポーツのスタジアム
(C) 車のラジオ
(D) オフィスビルの中

解説「場所」を問う全体情報タイプ。We are conducting ... for the Winston & Morris Office Tower Complex、broadcast over the speakers in your office、などからわかる。
解答 (D)

20. 話者は訓練に関して何を示唆しているか。
(A) ビルから避難しなければならない。
(B) これは安全訓練である。
(C) 取扱説明書はよく読む必要がある。
(D) 製造手順に従わなければならない。

解説 drillは訓練。「示唆」を問う全体情報タイプ。This is not an emergency alarmで、本当の緊急事態には避難の指示が出ると言っているので、(A)は不適当。 **解答** (B)

21. 話者は次に何が起きると言っているか。
(A) 出勤簿が公開される。
(B) 試験信号が聞こえる。
(C) 学校の遠足が始まる。
(D) 機械技師が暖房装置を調整する。

解説「次の出来事」を問う個別情報タイプ。中盤でFollowing this announcement, you will hear a series of test signalsと告げ、最後にThis is only a ...と繰り返している。 **解答** (B)

22-24

Questions 22-24 refer to the following talk. Welcome to the Huntington Mash Beverage plant. Since all of you work for firms from different sectors, we've prepared a special tour for you today. We'll begin in just a moment with a look at our front-office operation. This includes departments such as general affairs, public relations, accounting, human resources, etc. Following that, we'll have a look at the distribution end of the operation, where we bottle, package and ship our products. Then, after a break for complimentary lunch, we'll move on to what I'm sure is the main attraction for most of you as plant managers – our new product development division. This is where we experiment with new styles of soft drinks, and the process involves lots of sampling and tasting. We've set aside the whole afternoon for that part of the tour. One thing I should remind you is that you are required not to enter the restricted area under construction. If you have any questions, feel free to ask.

問題22-24は次のトークに関するものです。

Huntington Mash Beverageの工場へようこそ。// 皆さんは全員会社の異なる部門で働いていらっしゃるので / 本日は皆さんのために特別なツアーをご用意いたしました。// 間もなく、本社業務の見学から始めます。// これに含まれる部門は / 総務、広報、経理、人事などです。// それに引き続き / 社の流通部門を見学します / そこでは製品の瓶詰め、箱詰め、出荷を行っています。// それから、休憩して無料の昼食を取った後 / 進む先は / 工場長である皆さんの多くにとって最大の関心事に違いないもの―― / 新商品開発部です。// ここは新しいスタイルのソフトドリンクの実験をする場所です / そして、その過程で多くの試飲が行われます。// 午後は丸々確保しました / ツアーのこの部分のために。// 1つだけご注意が必要なのは / 工事中の立ち入り禁止区域に入らないでいただきたいということです。// もし何かご質問がありましたら / ご遠慮なくお尋ねください。//

22. 話者は誰に向かって話している可能性が最も高いか。
(A) 売り場責任者
(B) 地元の酪農家
(C) 新人の整備士
(D) 工場の責任者

解説「聞き手」を問う個別情報タイプ。聞き手と話し手の情報は冒頭に出てくる。all of you work for firms from different sectorsがそれ。さらに、most of you as plant managersで答えがわかる。**解答** (D)

23. 参加者は午後をどこで過ごすか。
  (A) 箱詰め部門
  (B) 流通部
  (C) 新商品開発部
  (D) 来客用の応接間

解説 「場所」を問う個別情報タイプの問題。afternoonの予定であることに注意しよう。after a break for complimentary lunch, の後、our new product development division と、部署を告げている。 **解答** (C)

---

24. 話者は何をするなと言っているか。
  (A) 工場内で写真を撮ること
  (B) 研究所内で飲食すること
  (C) 工事現場に入ること
  (D) ショールームの機械に触ること

解説 「禁止事項」を問う個別情報タイプ。禁止に関する表現に注意する。you are required not to enter the restricted area under construction から正解は明らか。 **解答** (C)

25-27

Questions 25-27 refer to the following news broadcast.

This is J.C. Gibbs reporting from the Super News Station Eye-in-the-Sky Traffic Helicopter. This is a special alert. We're flying over the Newbury exit on northbound Interstate Highway 15, where a truck carrying a load of paint overturned at 4 P.M. That was 20 minutes ago, and emergency workers are on the scene trying to clear the exit. The scene looks quite colorful from up here. Fortunately, no injuries were reported. The Highway Traffic Management Office is warning that the exit could remain closed for at least an hour. So if you're heading north on Highway 15 with plans to use the Newbury exit, you're going to want to take the Ingraham exit to the south of Newbury and use Wilson Avenue to get into the Newbury area. I'll be back with regular traffic reports on the half-hour.

問題25-27は次のニュース放送に関するものです。

こちらはJ.C. Gibbsです / Super News Stationの上空中継交通ヘリコプターからお伝えしています。// これは臨時警報です。// われわれは、州間道15号線北行きのNewbury出口上空を飛んでいます / ここでは積荷のペンキを運んでいたトラックが / 午後4時に横転しました。// それは20分前のことでした / そして（現在は）緊急作業員たちが現場に到着して / 出口を片付けようとしています。// 現場は、ここ上空からとてもカラフルに見えます。// 幸い、けが人の報告はありませんでした。// 自動車道交通管理局は注意を呼び掛けています / この出口が少なくとも1時間は閉鎖される可能性があると。// ですから、もし15号線を北上していて / Newbury出口を使う予定でしたら / Newburyの南のIngraham出口を使わなければならなくなるでしょう / そしてWilson通りを使ってNewbury地区に入ります。// 通常の毎正時30分の交通情報でまたお会いしましょう。//

25. ニュースは主に何に関するものか。
(A) 今日の天気予報
(B) ヘリコプターサービスの問題
(C) 車両の関係した事故
(D) 公共交通の遅れ

解説「主題」を問う全体情報タイプ。ただしニュースの場合は、主題が冒頭で告げられるので、最初だけ聞けば解答できることが多い。a truck carrying a load of paint overturned at 4 P.M. がわかれば解答可能。**解答** (C)

26. 話者は何を示唆しているか。
(A) 通勤者はただちに避難する必要がある。
(B) 電気系統の問題は間もなく修復される。
(C) Newbury出口は一時的に閉鎖されている。
(D) 雷雨警報が発令された。

解説「示唆」を問う個別情報タイプ。交通情報の場合は、事故の影響やそれによる混雑を避ける方法などが予想される。the exit could remain closed for at least an hourがヒント。迂回路も示されているが、選択肢にない。
解答 (C)

27. 次のリポートはいつだと予想されるか。
(A) 午後3時40分
(B) 午後4時
(C) 午後4時30分
(D) 午後5時

解説「時」を問う個別情報タイプ。時間に関する表現を聞き逃さないこと。a truck carrying a load of paint overturned at 4 P.M. That was 20 minutes ago、I'll be back with regular traffic reports on the half-hourの3カ所の情報を統合すると解答できる。**解答** (C)

28-30

Questions 28-30 refer to the following news bulletin.

Now it's time for our business news. The local government of Sheppard County plans to begin accepting local tax, fines and municipal fee payments by credit card and over the Internet this year. The City Council gave final approval on Tuesday to a plan to accept new payment methods, including electronic money. The decision is aimed at making it more convenient for local residents to pay their taxes, utility bills, traffic violation penalties and other public fees. Up to now, the town government has only accepted payments made by check, money order or cash, according to Municipal Finance Director Mike Freeson. But he says that many people simply don't pay, and that the town doesn't have the manpower to follow up and collect unpaid debts. Freeson added that making payment more convenient is expected to cut the percentage of uncollected municipal debts nearly in half, from the current 13 percent to 6 percent.

問題28-30は次のニュース速報に関するものです。

今度はビジネスニュースの時間です。// Sheppard郡の地方当局は / 地方税、罰金、自治体の手数料の支払い受け付けを開始する予定です / 今年からクレジットカードやインターネットで。// 市議会は火曜日に最終承認をしました / 新しい支払い方式を認める計画を / 電子マネーも含む。// この決定は、地元住民にとって、もっと便利にすることが目的です / 税金や公共料金や交通違反の罰金などの公の支払いを。// これまで / この自治体では小切手か郵便為替か現金による支払いのみ受け付けていました / Mike Freeson郡経理部長によると。// しかし彼が言うには / とにかく支払いをしない人が多く / 当局には未払い債務を追跡徴収する人員がいません。// Freeson氏がさらに言うには / 支払いをもっと便利にすることで / 当局の未回収債務の割合を約半分に減らせると期待されています / 現在の13パーセントから6パーセントへと。//

28. この報道によると、今後何の受け付けがされるようになるか。
(A) 当局へのさまざまな支払い方法
(B) インターネット経由の入札手続き
(C) 地方議会への寄付
(D) 予算委員会に参加する市民としての権利

解説 キーワードはwhat、accepted、from now on。「主題」を問う全体情報タイプと考える。ニュースなので冒頭のplans to begin accepting local tax ... by credit card and over the Internet this yearが聞き取れれば解答できる。
解答 (A)

29. Mike Freeson氏は誰である可能性が最も高いか。
(A) 銀行の支店長
(B) 政府(自治体)職員
(C) 会計コンサルタント
(D) 校長

解説 「職業」を問う個別情報タイプ。名前の前に肩書きが登場することが多いので注意しよう。Municipal Finance Director Mike Freesonから正解がわかる。**解答** (B)

30. この報道によると、この決定によって何が期待されているか。
(A) 失業率が減少する。
(B) 地域住民に課せられる税が減る。
(C) 現職の知事が間もなく辞職する。
(D) この地方自治体の債務が減る。

解説 設問のキーワードはwhat、expected、on the basis of the decision。「これから起きること」を問う個別情報タイプ。making payment more convenient is expected to cut the percentage of uncollected municipal debts nearly in halfがヒント。 **解答** (D)

READING SECTION

Part 6

31-33 CD 3-34

問題31-33は次のメモに関するものです。
社内回覧 // 全従業員あて //
わが社の火災と地震の安全手順が、変更されます / 最近の地方条例の改正に合わせてのことです。 // その結果、いくつかの新規則や、現行規則の変更が、われわれの職場環境の細かい点に、多くの影響を与えます。 // 例として挙げると、規則の変更によって影響を受けるのは、/ 消化器の場所や設置方法、/ オフィスビル内の喫煙場所、/ 可燃性液体の保存方法などです / (可燃性液体というのは) たとえば、特定の洗剤、消毒用アルコール、暖房用の灯油、その他多くのものです。
すべての従業員は、新しい法律をよく読み、理解しなければなりません / 新しい法律は、今週の社内報に掲載されます。 // 指定された可燃性物質の取り扱いが職務説明書に含まれている従業員の上司は、/ 影響のある作業区域の目立つ場所に規則が張り出されるよう、確実に手配してください。 // 経営管理者

31.
(A) 副 それに応じて
(B) 副 それでも
(C) 副 さもなければ
(D) 副 それにも関わらず

解説 品詞の同じ語（副詞）が並ぶ語彙の問題。文頭の語句なので、空所の前後の文を見て論理展開をチェックし、適する語句を選ぶ。論理の流れは原因→結果で、「したがって」、「それに応じて」などの意味の語が入る。 **解答** (A)

32.
(A) それどころか
(B) たとえば
(C) ところで
(D) それ以来ずっと

解説 大きい接続詞の問題。こちらも文頭の語句なので、空所の前後の文を見て論理展開をチェックする。ここでの論理の流れは一般論→具体例となっている。 **解答** (B)

33.
(A) 動 ～を妨げる
(B) 動 ～を損なう
(C) 動 ～を掲示する
(D) 動 ～を生み出す

解説 品詞の同じ語（動詞）が並ぶ語彙の問題。前文も参照し、空所が前文の語句の言い換えになっていないか、慣用表現、決まり文句ではないかもチェックする。文脈から「～を提示する」が適している。 **解答** (C)

34-36

問題34-36は次の手紙に関するものです。

Graves様 //
私たちの記録によると、前回あなたが定期的な歯のクリーニングと検診を受けたのは、今年の1月20日です。 // 最適な歯の健康状態を保つためには、/ 定期的なクリーニングと検査を、6カ月ごとに受けることをお勧めします。 // お手数ですが、/ 同封の郵便料金支払い済みはがきのフォームに、ご希望の日時を記入して、/ ご都合のよろしいときにポストにご投函ください。//
こちらの受付スタッフより、予約を確認するためにご連絡いたします。 //
また、ご住所やお電話番号の変更があれば、フォームの連絡先の部分に必ず書き込んでください。 //
あなたの笑顔を輝かせるお手伝いができますようお待ち申し上げます！ //
敬具 // Robert Cushing、歯科医 // Cushing歯科医院 //

34.
(A) 動 〜を維持する
(B) 動 〜を配分する
(C) 動 〜を治療する
(D) 動 〜を代わりにする

解説 品詞の同じ語（動詞）が並ぶ語彙の問題。空所の前後の文脈から適切な語を判断する。前回の検診時期を知らせ、6カ月ごとのクリーニングを勧める文脈から、空所には「維持する」という意味の語が入る。 **解答** (A)

35.
(A) 名 好み
(B) 名 出典
(C) 名 予想
(D) 名 指針

解説 こちらも品詞の同じ語（名詞）が並ぶ語彙の問題だ。fill in the form、indicating your date and time、Our reception staff will contact ...という文脈から、日時の希望を示すよう指示しているとわかる。 **解答** (A)

36.
(A) 対照的に
(B) 副 それから
(C) 手短に
(D) 副 逆に

解説 大きい接続詞の問題。文頭の語句なので、空所の前後の文を見る。前文までの伝達事項に「追加」して住所変更の情報を求めているので、Also以外は不適当。 **解答** (B)

Part 7

37-38

問題37-38は次のメールに関するものです。
送信者：Cindy Brock <cbrock@mgmt-argylistinc.com> //
あて先：顧客サービス <cserv-help@foroffice.com> //
件名：受け取った注文品

先日のオフィス用品のご発送、ありがとうございました。// すべての品物が届きました / 予定通り、かつ良好な状態で。// しかしながら、私たちは指摘しなくてはなりません / 当方の本来の注文と支払いが（さらには納品書と請求明細書も）/ すべて普通紙の白色インクジェットプリンター用紙144連と指定しているのですが / 私たちが受け取ったのは同じ分量の上質ボンド紙でした。// 当方は上質紙でも申し分なく満足ですが、/ この間違いについてはお知らせすべきだと思ったものですから。// どうぞご遠慮なく / この紙を回収して普通の白色紙と交換してください / もしお望みでしたら。// 3週間の間は使わずに取っておきます / そしてそれ以降は使い始めます / もしそちらからご連絡がなければ。//

敬具 // Cindy Brock //

37. このメールの主な目的は何か。
(A) 納入業者に品物の誤配を知らせること
(B) 請求明細書の数量の誤りについて苦情を言うこと
(C) 破損した商品の一部返金を申し出ること
(D) 商品の速やかな交換を求めること

解説「目的」を問う全体情報タイプ。**冒頭近くに記される**ことが多い。注文品の到着を知らせた後、We should note, however, と、問題があったことを切り出している。although ... all specify .... standard white inkjet printer paper, we received ... high-quality bond paper. がヒント。
解答 (A)

38. メールは何を示唆しているか。
(A) パッケージにある商品の使用期限まであと3週間しかない。
(B) 彼らは以前、不良品を受け取ったことがある。
(C) このオフィス用品の納入業者は長期の納入契約を結んでいる。
(D) Brockさんの会社は追加費用を払うつもりはない。

解説「示唆すること」を問う個別情報タイプ。**文書をじっくり読む前に、選択肢の要点に目を通したほうが解答時間を節約できる。**(A)～(C)の事項は本文に登場しない。請求明細書の訂正を求める表現はなく、Please feel free to have the paper picked up and replaced、We will keep it unused ... and begin using と言っているので、取り替えないのなら普通紙の値段のままで上質紙を使うと考えられる。**解答** (D)

39-41

問題39-41は次の記事に関するものです。
新規参入事業がより優れた機動性を約束 //
Henderson Bay地区にある新しいビジネス・ベンチャーが / 画期的なデザインを提案している / それは従来の車いすやスクーターを過去のものにするかもしれない。// GF Enterprises社は2年前に設立された / Wendy Trillingと共同経営者Sandra Evansによって / その当時、大学院生だった / 大学の研究所で。// 2人とも現在は機械工学の博士号を持っている / そして最近、賞を授与された / 最も有望な若手研究者であるとして。//「私たちは2人とも不満でした / 市場で手に入る車いすや電気スクーターの選択肢に / そこで、もっといいものを設計しようと決めました」と Trillingは語った。// その結果が「SpeedyHelper」、/ コンピューター制御の電動装置だ / それは、さらなる力とスピードと機動性を発揮する。// この新装置の幾つかのモデルは非常に好評で / 貨物輸送会社がそれらを購入したほどだ / 多忙な倉庫作業に携わる従業員を助けて / 徒歩移動と作業の疲労を軽減するために。// さらなる開発の見通しに関しては / 同社の広報部長であるJohn Kent氏によると / 複数の慈善家が最近、意向を表明した / GF Enterprisesの進行中の研究プロジェクトに資金援助をすると。//

39. Evansさんについて何が示されているか。
(A) 彼女は会社の共同設立者だ。
(B) 彼女は最優秀科学者賞の受賞者だ。
(C) 彼女は元教授だ。
(D) 彼女はかつて工業デザイナーだった。

解説　「職業／立場」を問う個別情報タイプ。Evansさんの肩書きや背景を文書中から探す。まずは名前を見つけ出そう。GF Enterprises Inc. was formed two years ago by Wendy Trilling and business partner Sandra Evansから正解がわかる。**解答** (A)

40. 新製品はどのような利点を発揮するか。
(A) より優れた機動性
(B) より安い価格
(C) より長持ちするバッテリー寿命
(D) より簡単な操作性

解説　「利点」を問う個別情報タイプ。文書自体のタイトルにもヒントがある。The result was the SpeedyHelper ... that provides more power, speed and mobility.とあるので「機動性」が答え。**解答** (A)

41. Kent氏は何と言っているか。
(A) 取締役会は全会一致で研究プロジェクトの予算を承認した。
(B) 彼は経理部の責任者になるだろう。
(C) 慈善事業家たちが研究の資金を提供してくれるだろう。
(D) 広報部はサービスの宣伝をするだろう。

解説　Kent氏の「言及内容」を問う個別情報タイプ。Kent氏が登場する個所をチェックする。several philanthropists have recently expressed their intention to financially supportは、Benefactors will provide fundsと同じ意味。**解答** (C)

42-44 CD 3-38

問題42-44は次の社内メモに関するものです。
あて先：管理職各位 // Denby Ace Manufacturingの新発想サミットにご参加を！//
あらためてお知らせします / 本年度の新発想サミットが近付いています / 皆さんぜひともご参加ください。// 1972年にDenby Ace Manufacturing社の創業者によって設けられて / FISは毎年恒例の2日間の講習会と授賞パーティーへと進化しました / それは若手従業員と上級管理職に機会を提供します / 言葉を交わし、お互いから学ぶための。// このイベントはプレゼンテーションから始まります / 入社5年以内の従業員による / アイデアを披露します / 画期的な商品、組織改革、評価プログラムのための / あるいはそれ以外のいかなる「新鮮な発想」でも / それがDenby Ace Manufacturingをより良い企業にする助けとなり得るのなら。// プレゼンテーションの後には上級管理職のセッションが続きます / それには、プレゼンテーションされたアイデアへの関連質問、批評、協力的な手直しが含まれます。// 上位5つのプレゼンテーションによる最終ラウンドは / イベント2日目にあり / 授賞式へと続きます / そこでは最優秀のアイデアが選ばれます / その後の取締役会を前にしたプレゼンテーションのためにです。// 過去のFISイベントは革新につながりました / Denby Ace Manufacturingの成功と拡大に欠かせない（革新に）/ さらには、わが社でも特に傑出した管理職人材の育成に。// まだお済みでないなら / 今年のイベントへの参加申し込みを強くお願いします。// 総務部のMarcia Trent（内線7274）までご連絡ください。//

42. この通知の主な目的は何か。
(A) 管理職社員にFISのイベントに申し込むよう促すこと
(B) 会社を改善する方法について斬新なアイデアを求めること
(C) 全従業員にFISへの参加は義務だとあらためて知らせること
(D) 新たに年に1度の授賞パーティーを実施すること

解説　「目的」を問う全体情報タイプ。とはいえ、あて先とタイトルから解答が可能だ。冒頭のyour participation is strongly urgedと、最後のwe strongly urge you to sign up for participationなどからも、目的は明らか。
解答 (A)

43. この通知を目にする可能性が最も高いのはどこか。
(A) ホテルのロビー内の掲示板
(B) オフィス近くのレストラン内
(C) 重役用ラウンジの中
(D) 社用駐車場の中

解説　「場所」を問う個別情報タイプ。これもあて先と末尾の発信者から社内文書だとわかるので、(A)と(B)は不適当。our younger employees and senior management with opportunities to communicate and learn from each otherとあるので、executivesも告知対象だとわかる。
解答 (C)

44. イベントに関して何が言われているか。
(A) 会社の設立者が直接賞を授与する。
(B) 特別ゲストのための晩さん会が開かれる。
(C) 上位3名に賞が与えられる。
(D) スタッフの向上に役立ってきた。

解説　イベントに関する漠然とした質問なので、選択肢の要点にさっと目を通してから本文を読む。the development of some of our most outstanding administrative talentの言い換えがhelpful in terms of staff progressに当たる。
解答 (D)

45-47

問題45-47は次の広告に関するものです。

販売要員を募集 //
Milton Home Furnishings //
高級家庭用家具に対する並外れた鑑賞眼がある / そして、ほかの人たちと一緒に働くのが大好きだ。// もしこの記述があなたに当てはまるなら / 独特のやりがいのある就業機会についてお話をさせてください。// 当社はMilton Home Furnishingsです / 大手の全国展開をしている家具およびインテリアデザイン小物の小売業者で / 75年におよぶ成長と成功の歴史を有します。// 当社では、一緒に働ける意欲の高い人々を求めています / Arista Plaza Shopping Centerの新店舗を成功させるために。// あなたの努力や才能と引き換えに / 当社は業界最高の待遇を提示します / 含まれるのは、ずば抜けた給与水準 / 完全保障型の医療および歯科保険 / たっぷりの有給休暇 / それに、素晴らしい、任意で選択できる株式投資プランです。// この素晴らしいチャンスの詳細は / 555-123-4567のLouiseまで履歴書をファクスしてください / または、newjobapplications@miltonhomefurnishings.comまでメールで送ってください。// あるいは、当社の刺激的な新しいショールームに立ち寄っていただいても結構です / Arista Plaza Shopping Centerのメインアーケードの南端の。// あなたと一緒に可能性を探るのを楽しみにしています。//

45. Milton Home Furnishingsについて何が示されているか。
(A) 老舗の不動産会社である。
(B) メインアーケードの北の端に位置している。
(C) 複数の場所で工場を稼動させてきた。
(D) 70年以上前に設立された。

解説　「広告主である会社に関すること」を問う個別情報タイプ。正解に結びつくヒントは1カ所だが、各選択肢の内容の真偽を確認するには全体を読む必要がある。retailer with a 75-year history of growth and successから解答可能。
解答 (D)

46. この職の条件でないものは何か。
(A) 品質の高さがわかる力
(B) 一生懸命働く熱意
(C) 過去の実務経験
(D) 社会性のある態度

解説　「応募の必要条件」を問う個別情報タイプ。NOT問題なので、記事中の条件に関する部分をしっかりと読む。(A)はspecial appreciation、(B)はhighly motivated people、(D)はlove working with peopleを指す。**解答** (C)

47. この職に応募する際、会社に何を送る必要があるか。
(A) 応募者の職歴書を1部
(B) 添え状
(C) 証明書のコピー
(D) 推薦状

解説　設問のキーワードはWhat、to be sent、the company、when applying。「応募時に送る物」を問う個別情報タイプ。please fax your résuméのrésuméの言い換えに当たるのは、applicant's work history。**解答** (A)

48-51

問題48-51は次の手紙に関するものです。

RFGS // 相互交流を通じて理解を深める // 11月12日
Wayne Peters, PhD // 505 University Circle // Arling CA, 92481 //
Peters教授 //
お問い合わせありがとうございました / RFGSを通じた講演活動の機会に関して。// 最初のステップは / RFGSと正規の講演関係を形成する可能性のために / ボランティアのプレゼンターとして参加することです / 当団体の3つの年次会議のうちの1つに / 「異文化間関係のための世界フォーラム」「環境に優しい開発のための技術革新」 / そして、「若い世代のための科学教育」です。// これらの会議のいずれかの講演者になる申し込みができます / 私どものウェブサイトにある申し込みフォームを提出することによって / 150語にまとめたプレゼンテーションの概要とともに。// これらのイベントの講演者に報酬はありません / また、交通費も支払われません。// さらに、登録料が必要です。//
これらの会議から各2名の傑出したボランティア講演者が / 会員投票によって選ばれます / また、場合によっては理事会の承認を受けます / 当団体の年次「世界動向セミナー」での講演に招待するため。// これら6人の講演者には交通費および関係諸費用が支払われます / そしてRFGS会員に招かれます。// 時には / 長期の資金援助付き講演契約の候補者となる人もいます / 通例、3年契約の条件で。// 報酬その他の待遇は / 個別に交渉することになります。//
したがって、現段階でのあなたの次なるステップは / 当団体のウェブサイトを訪問することになります / そして上記の新規申し込み手続きを完了することです。// お問い合わせいただいたことに、重ねてお礼を申し上げます。// もし、さらにご質問がありましたら / ご遠慮なく以下へメールでご連絡ください：/ laineanderson-publicrel@RFGS.org //
敬具 / Laine Anderson / 広報部長 // 国際研究のためのRogers基金 //

48. この手紙の目的は何か。
(A) 進行中の合併交渉を最終決定すること
(B) 最新の技術革新に関する本を所望すること
(C) 推薦状の発行を依頼すること
(D) 登録手続きを説明すること

解説　「目的」を問う全体情報タイプ。冒頭に opportunities for speaking engagements through RFGSとあり、続いてThe first step toward the potential formation、最後の段階でthe next step for you at this stage would be …と述べ、順を追って説明しているので、explain a processが適当。**解答** (D)

49. 手紙の中で何が言われているか。
(A) RFGSは大学の付属団体である。
(B) RFGSは毎年6通の求職応募しか受け付けない。
(C) Peters教授はRFGSの講演者になる件で問い合わせをした。
(D) Peters教授はRFGSのヨーロッパ本部と取引をしたことがある。

解説　手紙の内容について問う個別情報タイプ。選択肢の内容を、本文と照合していく。the potential formation of a permanent speaking relationship with RFGSがbecoming an RFGS speakerを指している。**解答** (C)

50. RFGS年次会議で聞くと思われるプレゼンテーションの話題は何か。
(A) 若者のファッションの流行傾向
(B) 太陽エネルギーと風力エネルギーを活用した施設
(C) 国際金融機関の財政計画
(D) 高齢者のための生涯教育

解説 設問のキーワードはWhat presentation subjects、to be heard、RFGS annual conferences。「プレゼンのテーマ」を問う個別情報タイプ。3つの年次会議のテーマを見れば、解答を絞り込むことができる。 **解答** (B)

---

51. 次のうち正しいものはどれか。
(A) 諸費用は年次セミナーに招待された講演者にだけ支払われる。
(B) Peters教授はプレゼンテーションのための概要を複数用意してある。
(C) 「異文化間関係のための世界フォーラム」は去年中止になった。
(D) 今年の年次セミナーでの講演依頼はすでに発送された。

解説 「正しい選択肢」を問う個別情報タイプ。漠然とした設問なので、先に選択肢を読んでから本文の内容と照合する。These six speakers will be reimbursed for travel and related expenses, and receive invitations to RFGS membership. がヒント。 **解答** (A)

52-56　CD 3-41、42　文書1: 🇨🇦　文書2: 🇺🇸

問題52-56は次の手紙とメールに関するものです。

【文書1】
Grace Rhodes様 // 3428 Richmond St., Apt. 210 // Gabriel TX　77332 //
Rhodes様 //
当社マーケットリサーチ部のMartha Reynoldsから聞きました / 彼女があなたを時々雇っていると / 業績リポートと業界分析をしてもらうために / 外部委託の形で。// この仕事に関しては / 以下の書類に記入していただけますようお願い申し上げます。//
同封の守秘契約書（NDA）2部をご確認ください。// これは標準的な契約上の取り決めで、明記するものです / 依頼によってあなたが提供した情報はすべて / 当社が受け取った時点で当社の所有になると。//
契約書をよくお読みください。// 文中の指定個所にイニシャルを記入してください /（ピンクの付箋で印を付けてあります）/ そして署名をしてください / 契約書の最後に用意されたスペースに。//
コピーは2部あります / そのうちの1部は署名後、そちらの控えとして保管してください / そしてもう1部は用意した封筒に入れて当社に返送してください。// ご理解と速やかなご協力のほどよろしくお願いします。// 敬具 / Stanley Fitzgerald / 法務部スタッフ評議会 // Tidewater Consulting株式会社 //

【文書2】
送信者：Grace Rhodes <grhodes@opinnets.com> //
あて先：Stan Fitzgerald <stanfitz@tdwatercons.com> //
件名：NDA // Fitzgerald様 //
お手紙をありがとうございます。// ReynoldsさんやチームのメンバーのかたがたとはVIと楽しく仕事をしています / 御社のサービスを推進するため。// 本日、署名済みのNDAをお送りしました / 書留で。// 私は言われています / そちらには2営業日以内に届くはずだと。// ご承知おきください / 私が受け取って署名した書類は1部だけでした。// 署名済みの書類のデジタル画像をスキャンしました / ですから記録保存の目的にはこれで十分です。// 追加でNDAの原本を送っていただく必要はありません / そちらがそう希望されない限り。// 今後ともよろしくお願いいたします。// Grace Rhodes //

52. FitzgeraldさんはRhodesさんに何をするよう頼んでいるか。
(A) 書類を1部、書留で返送する
(B) 契約書のデジタルコピーをすぐに作る
(C) 彼女の会社の取締役たちに確実に提携を承認してもらう
(D) 情報を秘密にすることに正式に同意する

> **解説**　「依頼内容」を問う個別情報タイプ。Mr. Fitzgeraldは手紙の差出人なので、手紙を参照する。Please read through the contract ...以降に具体的な行動の指示があるが、contractの内容については、その前にour non-disclosure agreement (NDA)、all information that you provide to us on assignment becomes our property when we receive itと書かれている。「書留で」という指示はないので(A)は不可。　**解答**　(D)

---

53. 手紙の中の第2段落2行目にある「stipulating」に最も近い意味は
(A) 〜を要約する
(B) 〜と置き換える
(C) 明確に示す
(D) 〜を注文に応じて作る

> **解説**　語彙の問題。文脈から推測するようにしよう。agreementの説明として、守秘義務が示されており、stipuleteは「〜を規定する、明記する」という意味で使われているので、「規定する、明確に示す」という意味のstateが正解となる。　**解答**　(C)

---

54. Rhodesさんはどんな仕事をしている可能性が最も高いか。
(A) 警備員
(B) マーケティングのコンサルタント
(C) 写真家
(D) 法律顧問

> **解説**　「職業」を問う個別情報タイプ。手紙の冒頭　にhires you to provide us with business reports and industry analyses on an outsourced basisとあるので、最も可能性が高い選択肢を選ぶ。　**解答**　(B)

---

55. Fitzgeraldさんは何を勧めているか。
(A) 会社の増資をすること
(B) NDAを注意深く読むこと
(C) 新しいコンサルタントを雇うこと
(D) 現在の給与体系を見直すこと

> **解説**　「提案の内容」を問う個別情報タイプ。これも設問の主語がMr. Fitzgeraldなので手紙を見る。行動の指示に関してなので、設問52と同じ部分を参照しよう。　**解答**　(B)

---

56. Fitzgeraldさんがしてしまったミスは何か。
(A) メールにファイルを添付し忘れた。
(B) 文中の間違った個所に付箋で印を付けた。
(C) NDAを1部しか送らなかった。
(D) Reynoldsさんに知らせずに契約書を発送した。

> **解説**　「ミスの内容」を問う個別情報タイプ。ミスを指摘するとしたらMs. Rhodesが出したメールのほうなので、内容に目を通す。Please note that ...以下で、契約書が1部しか入っていなかったとわかる。手紙のほうにはThere are two copies ...とあるので、ミスの内容は契約書を1部しか入れなかったことだとわかる。　**解答**　(C)

57-61 　CD 3-43、44　　文書1: 🇺🇸　文書2: 🇨🇦

問題57-61は次の手紙とメールに関するものです。

【文書1】
Amy Butler様 // Weller歴史協会　会長 // 9011 Spruce Ave. // Weller WA　98031 //
Amyへ //
お元気ですか。// 先日、毎週恒例のゴルフに出掛けた時に / ある男性に会いました / その人はMason Steel社の取締役です。// われわれは話し始めました / すると、ふと彼の話に出ました / 彼の会社が古いJohnston Metalworks Plantを所有していると / あなたの町のHemingway Avenueにある。// 彼は言いました / 彼の会社はその工場を全面改装する計画だと / それはつまり、古い機械をすべて廃棄するということです。// 私が少年時代にあそこで働いていた時に / そこが古い設備の宝庫だったことを覚えています / その多くが手作りで / 中には1920年代までさかのぼるものもありました。// 私は確信しています / あなたが気になる品々を手に入れたいだろうと / あなたが計画してきた地元の歴史館のために。// この手紙に同封します / 友人の名刺があるでしょう。// どうぞ彼に連絡してください / もし私の提案に魅力を感じたら / そして彼にあなたの活動を知らせるのです。// 彼なら理解してくれるでしょう。//
敬具 / Dan Kruger // 122 Southearl Dr., Apt. 505 // Newton WA　98128 /

【文書2】
送信者：Amy Butler <amybutler@anglecoms.com> //
あて先：Dan Kruger <dkruger@localnets.com> //
件名：Johnston Metalworks //
こんにちは、Dan /
先週のあなたの手紙をさっき受け取りました / そして、感謝してもしきれません。// 実は / 私たち歴史協会の者は / もう何年も前からJohnston Metalworks Plantのことを知っていました。// 私は親会社の下位レベルの広報関係者に連絡を取ってきました / しかし、彼らは工場に関するいい情報を何もくれませんでした。//
あなたの助言どおり / Gravesさんに連絡してみました。// 彼はとても親切で頼りになりました。// 彼自身、アンティークの大の愛好家で / 約束してくれました / いくつかのとても重要な収集価値のあるアンティーク品を私たちのプロジェクトに寄付してくれると。//
ご協力に心から感謝します。// 歴史館が来年オープンしたあかつきには、/ 今までにない素晴らしいものになるでしょう！/ 敬具 / Amy //

57. Butlerさんの主要な関心はどれである可能性が最も高いか。

(A) 自分の町の工芸品
(B) 財団の経済再生
(C) 地域の保健福祉
(D) 地方債への投資

【解説】「主な関心」を問う個別情報タイプ。手紙の中でMs. Butlerのinterestにふれているのは I am sure that you would be ... 以降。歴史館の収蔵物を求めているとわかる。【解答】(A)

58. Krugerさんについて何が言えるか。

(A) 彼は定期的に運動している。
(B) 彼はGravesさんと毎週打ち合わせをしている。
(C) 彼はアンティークの一大コレクションを所有している。
(D) 彼は金属加工工場を所有している。

【解説】Krugerさんに関する漠然とした設問なので、選択肢を読んでから手紙をチェックする。冒頭のDuring my weekly round on the golf course recentlyがヒント。【解答】(A)

322

59. Butlerさんについてわかっていることは何か。
(A) 彼女は寄付を頼むためJohnston Metalworks社を訪ねた。
(B) 彼女はかつてJohnston Metalworks Plantで働いていた。
(C) 彼女は以前Mason Steel社に連絡を取ったことがあった。
(D) 彼女は近所でアンティーク店を経営している。

解説 Butlerさんに関するこれも漠然とした設問。選択肢を読むと、Johnston Metalworks社とMason Steelに関する内容だとわかる。手紙にMason SteelがJohnston Metalworksを所有している、とあり、メールでI'd been in touch with some lower-level public relations people at the parent companyと書いているので、Butlerさんが親会社のMason Steelに連絡したことがわかる。 **解答** (C)

60. メールの中の第2段落2行目にある「donate」に最も近い意味は
(A) 評価する
(B) 預け入れる
(C) 吟味する
(D) 寄付する

解説 donateは「寄付する、贈与する」の意。選択肢の中で同様の意味になるのはcontributeだ。 **解答** (D)

61. 来年何が起こると予想されるか。
(A) チャリティーオークションが開催される。
(B) 学校の改修プロジェクトが着工される。
(C) この施設が地方政府から一部出資を受ける。
(D) 新しい博物館が開館する。

解説 「来年の予定」について問う個別情報タイプ。「来年」を示す語句を文書から探す。メールの最後にWhen our museum opens next yearとあるのがヒント。 **解答** (D)

Task

模試の問題についても、1) 自分でチャンクで区切って音読、2) 音声にオーバーラップさせてスクリプトを読む、3) スクリプトを見ずに音声を聞いて理解できるかチェックする、といったタスクを実行しよう。

学習エネルギーをチャージする今日の 格言

**Don't judge each day by the harvest you reap,
but by the seeds you plant.**

Robert Louis Stevenson
(1850〜94：イギリスの作家)
毎日を収穫高で判断するのではなく、どれだけ種をまいたかで判断しなさい。

TOEIC®テスト 難関パート
模擬試験用マークシート

LISTENING SECTION

	PART 3				PART 4			
	NO.	ANSWER A B C D 勘	NO.	ANSWER A B C D 勘	NO.	ANSWER A B C D 勘	NO.	ANSWER A B C D 勘
	1	ABCD☐	11	ABCD☐	16	ABCD☐	26	ABCD☐
	2	ABCD☐	12	ABCD☐	17	ABCD☐	27	ABCD☐
	3	ABCD☐	13	ABCD☐	18	ABCD☐	28	ABCD☐
	4	ABCD☐	14	ABCD☐	19	ABCD☐	29	ABCD☐
	5	ABCD☐	15	ABCD☐	20	ABCD☐	30	ABCD☐
	6	ABCD☐			21	ABCD☐		
	7	ABCD☐			22	ABCD☐		
	8	ABCD☐			23	ABCD☐		
	9	ABCD☐			24	ABCD☐		
	10	ABCD☐			25	ABCD☐		

READING SECTION

	PART 6		PART 7					
	NO.	ANSWER A B C D 勘	NO.	ANSWER A B C D 勘	NO.	ANSWER A B C D 勘	NO.	ANSWER A B C D 勘
	31	ABCD☐	37	ABCD☐	47	ABCD☐	57	ABCD☐
	32	ABCD☐	38	ABCD☐	48	ABCD☐	58	ABCD☐
	33	ABCD☐	39	ABCD☐	49	ABCD☐	59	ABCD☐
	34	ABCD☐	40	ABCD☐	50	ABCD☐	60	ABCD☐
	35	ABCD☐	41	ABCD☐	51	ABCD☐	61	ABCD☐
	36	ABCD☐	42	ABCD☐	52	ABCD☐		
			43	ABCD☐	53	ABCD☐		
			44	ABCD☐	54	ABCD☐		
			45	ABCD☐	55	ABCD☐		
			46	ABCD☐	56	ABCD☐		

※マークシートは、コピーして使おう。

ハイスコアを目指すために
～900点突破のために贈る言葉と行動指針～

　お疲れさまでした。本書の学習は以上で終わりです。20日間で学んだ英文を繰り返し聞いて、語順に従ってチャンク単位で理解し、登場人物になりきってリズミカルかつスピーディーに音読する練習を今後も続けましょう。

　最後に、英語力向上とハイスコア獲得を目指している皆さんに、私自身が力を与えてもらった言葉をお贈りします。

　また、TOEIC990点並びに英検1級を獲得するまでのさまざまな試行錯誤の過程で体得し、役に立った「英語力アップのための25カ条の指針」も紹介します。壁にぶつかった時など、何らかのヒントになれば幸いです。読者の皆さんの夢の実現を心から願っています。

小山克明

Never, never, never quit.
Sir Winston Leonard Spencer-Churchill
（1874～1965：イギリスの首相）
決して、決して、決してやめてしまうな。

＊

You must be the change you want to see in the world.
Mahatma Gandhi
（1869～1948：インド独立の父）
あなた自身が、この世で見たいと思う変化とならなければならない。

＊

Hitch your wagon to a star!
Ralph Waldo Emerson
（1803～1882：アメリカの評論家、哲学者、詩人）
汝の車を星につなげ。

英語力アップのための25カ条の指針

1	志を立てる	◆将来の大きな夢を描く ◆目標スコアと達成時期を具体的に決める
2	正しい情報を得る	◆インターネット、スクール、セミナー、対策本などからTOEIC情報を入手する
3	必要な力を知る	力の内訳：①リスニング力、②リーディング力（速読力含む）、③語彙力、④文法力、⑤各partのパターン別解答力、⑥集中力、⑦タイムマネジメント力、⑧受験力、⑨スピーキング力、⑩ライティング力、⑪総合力
4	現状分析をし、弱点を補強	◆誤答分析から弱点、不得意分野を知り、改善する
5	学習内容・計画を決定し、ルーティーンを確立する	◆ライフスタイルに合わせた無理のない計画を作成する
6	適切な教材を選ぶ	◆本試験の内容に沿った教材を使用する ◆990点獲得、またはTOEIC受験が豊富な著者の教材を選ぶ（1. 戦略本、2. ボキャブラリー集、3. TOEIC公式問題集、4. 文法問題集、5. 文法参考書）
7	自分に合った学習法を確立し、習慣化する	◆効果的、効率的、実践的、本質的な、自分に適した方法を採用する
8	毎日継続する	◆短時間でも時間を確保し、学習する
9	達成度の記録を付け、分析する	◆進歩・達成度の記録を付ける
10	モチベーションのアップと維持をする	◆ロールモデルを見つけてまねる ◆スコアアップした人の体験談を読む ◆指導が上手な、相性のいい教師を見つける ◆学習法の本を読む ◆仲間作りをする ◆好きな分野を通して英語を学ぶ ◆感動的な内容を英語で学ぶ

11	インプット量を増やす	◆多読・多聴を実践し、英語漬けの日を設ける ◆語彙はセット表現で覚える ◆英語で特定分野を学ぶ
12	アウトプット量を増やす	◆音読を実践する ◆実際に使う機会を増やす（話す、書く）
13	受験術をマスターし、シミュレーションを行う	◆書籍、スクール、セミナー、インターネットを活用する ◆模試練習（公式問題集などで）を行う
14	現状打破をする	◆常に勉強法を工夫する ◆刺激を受け、マンネリを打破する ◆思い切って学習法、参考書を変える
15	集中力を養う	◆タイムマネジメントを実践する
16	常にポジティブに考える	◆ネガティブにとらえず、前向きに、柔軟に考える 例：勉強してもスコアが伸び悩んだり、ダウン ➡ トンネル内でははっきり感じられないが、目的地に向かって前進している
17	完ぺき主義から脱却する	◆早急な100パーセントの成果を求めない
18	気分転換を図る	◆自分なりのスランプ対処法を見つける
19	体調を管理する	◆休息、睡眠、栄養にも留意する
20	連続受験をする	◆強化ポイントを決めて受験する
21	学びを楽しむ	◆自分を高めるための幸運な機会ととらえる ◆感情を込めたなりきり音読で役を演じる
22	自分を褒める	◆頑張ったら何か「ごほうび」をあげる
23	簡単にあきらめない	◆後悔しないよう最善の努力をする
24	体質を変える	◆長時間英語を聞いても、読んでも、話しても、書いても疲れない自分に変える
25	達成感を得る	◆各段階の目標を小刻みに作り、達成感を得る

著者プロフィール

小山克明（おやま　かつあき）
東京都市大学環境情報学部・関東学院大学人間環境学部・日本大学商学部非常勤講師。財団法人国際教育振興会TOEIC講座講師。ペンシルベニア州立テンプル大学大学院教育学修士課程修了（TESOL：英語教授法専攻）。早稲田大学卒。新TOEIC990点満点・英検1級取得。企業、大学、語学教育機関にてTOEIC、Cultural Comparisons、Modern Society等の講座を担当。TOEIC満点や900点突破をはじめ200点以上アップの受講生を輩出。共著に『3週間で攻略 新TOEIC®テスト730点！』、大学向けテキスト『TOEIC®テストステップ式徹底演習上級編』（以上アルク）、『新TOEIC®Test レベル判定模試』（Z会）、執筆協力に『新TOEIC®テスト直前模試3回分』（アルク）などがある。モットーは、英語が好きになり、楽しめる授業を実現すること。

新TOEIC®テスト　900点突破　20日間特訓プログラム

2010年4月14日　初版発行

著者：小山克明

英文作成協力：Braven Smillie
英文校正：Peter Branscombe / Owen Shaefer / Joel Weinberg
AD：伊東岳美
ナレーター：Howard Colefield / Soness Stevens / Chris Koprowski / Julia Yermakov / Andree Duffleit / Iain Gibb / Jeffrey Rowe / Marcus Pittman / Emma Howard / Sorcha Chisholm / Sarah Greaves / Stuart O / 島ゆうこ
CD編集：有限会社ログスタジオ
CDプレス：株式会社学研教育出版
DTP：朝日メディアインターナショナル株式会社
印刷・製本：図書印刷株式会社

発行人：平本照麿
発行所：株式会社アルク
　〒168-8611 東京都杉並区永福2-54-12
　TEL 03-3327-1101（カスタマーサービス部）
　TEL 03-3323-2444（英語出版編集部）
アルクの出版情報：http://www.alc.co.jp/publication
編集部e-mail：shuppan@alc.co.jp

© Katsuaki Oyama 2010 Printed in Japan
PC: 7009177

落丁本、乱丁本、CDに不具合が発生した場合は、弊社にてお取替えいたしております。
弊社カスタマーサービス部（電話：03-3323-1101、受付時間：平日9時～17時）までご相談ください。
定価はカバーに表示してあります。

アルクのキャラクターです　WOWI（ウォーウィ）
WOWIは、WORLDWIDEから生まれたアルクのシンボルキャラクターです。温かなふれあいを求める人間の心を象徴する、言わば、地球人のシンボルです。
http://alcom.alc.co.jp/
学んで教える人材育成コミュニティ・サイト